THE QUOTABLE
CHESTERTON

THE QUOTABLE
CHESTERTON

Selected and edited

by KEVIN BELMONTE

THOMAS NELSON
Since 1798

NASHVILLE DALLAS MEXICO CITY RIO DE JANEIRO

Published in Nashville, Tennessee, by Thomas Nelson. Thomas Nelson is a trademark of Thomas Nelson, Inc.

Thomas Nelson, Inc., titles may be purchased in bulk for educational, business, fund-raising, or sales promotional use. For information, please e-mail SpecialMarkets@ ThomasNelson.com.

A search was completed to determine whether previously published material included in this book required permission to reprint. If there has been an error, a correction will be made on subsequent editions.

Library of Congress Cataloging-in-Publication Data

Chesterton, G. K. (Gilbert Keith), 1874–1936.
  The quotable Chesterton / selected and edited by Kevin Belmonte.
    p. cm.
  ISBN 978-1-59555-205-1
  1. Chesterton, G. K. (Gilbert Keith), 1874–1936—Quotations. 2. Faith—Quotations, maxims, etc. 3. Christianity—Quotations, maxims, etc. 4. Authorship—Quotations, maxims, etc. 5. Wisdom—Quotations, maxims, etc. 6. Quotations, English. I. Belmonte, Kevin Charles. II. Title.
PR4453.C4A6 2010
828'.91209—dc22
2010011624

Printed in the United States of America

11 12 13 14 15 RRD 6 5 4 3 2 1

Over the whole landscape lay a luminous and unnatural discoloration, as of that disastrous twilight which Milton spoke of as shed by the sun in eclipse; so that Syme fell easily into his first thought, that he was actually on some other and emptier planet, which circled round some sadder star. But the more he felt this glittering desolation in the moonlit land, the more his own chivalric folly glowed in the night like a great fire.[1]

—

No man knows how much he is an optimist, even when he calls himself a pessimist, because he has not really measured the depths of his debt to whatever created him and enabled him to call himself anything. At the back of our brains, so to speak, there was a forgotten blaze or burst of astonishment at our own existence. The object of the artistic and spiritual life was to dig for this submerged sunrise of wonder; so that a man sitting in a chair might suddenly understand that he was actually alive, and be happy.[2]

Contents

EDITOR'S NOTE

All but twenty-five of the quotations in this collection are taken from works in the public domain—largely writings published between 1900 and 1914, the years when scholars generally agree that Chesterton was at the height of his powers.

Those familiar with Chesterton have long known what an important writer and thinker he was. For a good many years, there has been a need for a standard collection of his best thoughts, arranged alphabetically by topic, with complete original source documentation.

Such is *The Quotable Chesterton*, replete with chapter identification for each of the original sources cited. Editions of Chesterton's works are legion, and differ widely in terms of pagination. This anthology will allow readers to know which chapters of various works have been consulted, regardless of the edition they have at hand. For consistency, British spellings have been used even when citing American editions.

It is hoped this book (containing some 870 quotations) will serve as both an introduction and a long-overdue anthology. Chesterton is too little read today—which is a great pity. Few men have written more widely, more ably, or more presciently. He has much to say to us still.

KEVIN BELMONTE
Woodholme
February 2010

A Fixture of the Times
An Introduction to G. K. Chesterton

When the *New York Times* first took note of G. K. Chesterton—in an article entitled "Boston Notes," published in the *Saturday Review of Books and Art* on Wednesday, August 31, 1901—the man the world would one day know as GKC was just twenty-seven years old. The *Times* went on taking note of Chesterton for the rest of his life, quoting him, referencing him, or reviewing his books some 556 times in all—an astonishing number. When he died on June 14, 1936, the *Times* obituary for him was page 1 news—sent by wireless from the United Kingdom. The article described him as a "brilliant English essayist," "a master of paradox," and "for more than a generation the most exuberant personality in English literature."[1] All this before the close of the first paragraph.

But it was not in words alone that the *Times* conveyed a sense of Chesterton's standing in the world of literature. It used visual images as well, as in a 1916 review of three books profiling George Bernard Shaw, Rudyard Kipling, and Chesterton, entitled "Three Literary Giants of Today." Inset were three artist renderings of the writers so arranged as to form a kind of triptych. The implication was clear: these three writers were leading literary lights, and they all belonged in the same conversation.[2]

George Bernard Shaw called his great friend Chesterton a "colossal genius"[3]—and it is beyond question that Chesterton was a writer of extraordinary gifts. During a five-year period, 1903–8, he published six books, many of which are now widely acknowledged as classics: two acclaimed literary studies, *Robert Browning* and *Charles Dickens*; a novel, *The Napoleon of Notting Hill*; a suspense thriller, *The Man Who Was Thursday*; and two works of apologetics, *Heretics* and *Orthodoxy*. In fact, 1908 proved his *annus mirabilis*. For in that year, he published both *The Man Who Was Thursday* and *Orthodoxy*. By this time, he was a preeminent man of letters. His writings from this period sparkle with creativity, originality, and a wisdom far beyond the age of a man who had only just entered his midthirties by the time the last two works above were published. It was as the *Times* had stated in its review of *Robert Browning*: here was "a fresh and original mind."[4]

Within a few years, literary references to Chesterton started cropping up in books by other authors—and not just any authors. F. Scott Fitzgerald referred to *The Man Who Was Thursday* in the pages of his first great novel, *This Side of Paradise*.[5] Not to be outdone, Fitzgerald's great literary rival Ernest Hemingway wrote Chesterton into "The Three-Day Blow," a story in one of his early and best works, *In Our Time*—published during his expatriate years in Paris in 1924:

"I'd like to meet Chesterton," Bill said.

"I wish he was here now," Nick said. "We'd take him fishing to the 'Voix tomorrow."

"I wonder if he'd like to go fishing," Bill said.

"Sure," said Nick. "He must be about the best guy there is. Do you remember 'Flying Inn'?"

> If an angel out of heaven
> Gives you something else to drink,
> Thank him for his kind intentions;
> Go and pour them down the sink.

"That's right," said Nick. "I guess he's a better guy than Walpole."

"Oh, he's a better guy, all right," Bill said.

"But Walpole's a better writer."

"I don't know," Nick said. "Chesterton's a classic."

"Walpole's a classic, too," Bill insisted.

"I wish we had them both here," Nick said. "We'd take them both fishing to the 'Voix tomorrow."[6]

Chesterton achieved success in every form of writing he turned his hand to. Chesterton was also a highly visible public personality, and he took the stage in a variety of roles—epic debates with George Bernard Shaw and H. G. Wells,[7] frequent stints as a presenter on the BBC (his resonant and expressive voice making him popular), and as a lecturer whose services were much in demand.

Chesterton was a man of ample girth—six feet four inches tall and tipping the scales at three hundred pounds. His great size, tradition holds, led to a famous exchange during World War I. At this time, a lady in London is said to have asked why he wasn't "out at the Front." His reply: "If you go round to the side, you will see that I am."[8]

Yet at the back of it all—that is to say, at the heart of the matter—was Chesterton's faith. No one has ever talked about God as he did, mingling laughter, creativity, intellectual acumen, eloquence, imagery, and power. Chesterton's vibrant curiosity seemingly encompassed every conceivable subject, and on whatever subject he chose to write about, God was there.

Doubtless, Chesterton was a great apologist for the faith, but the ways in which he gave voice to that faith extended far beyond specific books on apologetics. It touched, infused, and enriched everything he wrote. Words he once wrote of Robert Browning apply no less justly to him:

What [Browning] really was was a romantic. He offered the cosmos as an adventure rather than a scheme. He did not explain evil, far less explain it away: he enjoyed defying it. He was a troubadour even in theology and metaphysics: like the *Jongleurs de Dieu* of St. Francis.[9]

The Pulitzer Prize–winning author Garry Wills has famously observed that Chesterton was a jester.[10] It was in this role as jester that André Maurois discerned Chesterton's enduring importance:

> Without his paradoxes, without his jokes, without his rhetorical switchbacks, Chesterton might perhaps be a cleverer philosopher. But he would not be Chesterton. It has been supposed that he is not serious, because he is funny; actually he is funny because he serious. Confident in his truth, he can afford to joke. . . . During an age of morbid rationalism, Chesterton reminded men that reason is indeed a wonderful tool, but a tool that needs material to work on, and produces nothing if it does not take the existing world as its object. . . . To Chesterton as to Browning, the universe stands constant, solid—wondrous, under all the theories built up by intelligence, each as different from the others as were the reports of the blind men on the elephant. In that universe, with Chesterton's help we can grow deep spreading roots, and the shifting winds of the mind cannot drag us out of the soil for those brief and glorious flights that can only end in a quick fall.[11]

But then it needs to be said as well that Chesterton was a jester who felt he had been given the answer to the greatest riddle of all: the riddle of the cosmos. The answer was Christianity—"the philosophy," he wrote, "in which I have come to believe. I will not call it my philosophy, for I did not make it. God and humanity made it; and it made me."[12]

Some initially found all this talk about God off-putting, C. S. Lewis famously writing that prior to his conversion he found "Chesterton had more sense than all the other moderns put together; bating, of course, his Christianity."[13] But then, Chesterton's writings would eventually prove a powerful catalyst in the process of Lewis's embrace of Christianity. "In reading Chesterton, as in reading [George] MacDonald, I did not know what I was letting myself in for. A young man who wishes to remain a sound Atheist cannot be too careful of his reading. There are traps everywhere—'Bibles laid open, *millions of surprises*,' as [George] Herbert says, 'fine nets and stratagems.' God is, if I may say it, very unscrupulous."[14] Lewis would later remember:

> I read Chesterton's *Everlasting Man* and for the first time saw the whole Christian outline of history set out in a form that seemed to me to make sense. Somehow I contrived not to be too badly shaken. You will remember that I already thought Chesterton the most sensible man alive "apart from his Christianity." Now, I veritably believe, I thought—I didn't of course *say*; words would have revealed the nonsense—that Christianity itself was very sensible.[15]

Perhaps, in the end, it is best to let the *New York Times* have the last word as to how Chesterton's faith infused his writing, and why this is of central significance to understanding his literary legacy. "Mr. Chesterton talks about God," a *Times* review stated in May 1916, "because God is the most interesting subject for conversation that there is."[16]

A

Academia

THOUGH THE ACADEMIC authorities are actually proud of conducting everything by means of Examinations, they seldom indulge in what religious people used to describe as Self-Examination. The consequence is that the modern State has educated its citizens in a series of ephemeral fads.[1]

Accommodation

WHEN MODERN SOCIOLOGISTS talk of the necessity of accommodating oneself to the trend of the time, they forget that the trend of the time at its best consists entirely of people who will not accommodate themselves to anything. At its worst it consists of many millions of frightened creatures all accommodating themselves to a trend that is not there.[2]

Accountability

BOTH MEN AND women ought to face more fully the things they do or cause to be done; face them or leave off doing them.[3]

Adventure

THE LIFE OF man is a story; an adventure story; and in our vision the same is true even of the story of God.[4]

Adventures

ADVENTURES HAPPEN ON dull days, and not on sunny ones. When the chord of monotony is stretched most tight, then it breaks with a sound like song.[5]

THE PERFECT HAPPINESS of men on the earth (if it ever comes) will not be a flat and solid thing, like the satisfaction of animals. It will be an exact and perilous balance; like that of a desperate romance. Man must have just enough faith in himself to have adventures, and just enough doubt of himself to enjoy them.[6]

Agnosticism

COMPLETE AGNOSTICISM IS the obvious attitude for man. We are all Agnostics until we discover that Agnosticism will not work.[7]

BUT NOW THE last gleam of red dies in the grey ashes: and leaves English men in that ancient twilight of agnosticism, which is so natural to men and so depressing to them. The echo of the last oracle still lingers in my ears. For though I am neither a Protestant nor a Pagan, I cannot see without sadness the flame of vesta extinguished, nor the fires of the Fifth of November: I cannot but be touched a little to see Paganism merely a cold altar and Protestantism only a damp squib.[8]

I HAVE DEALT at length with such typical triads of doubt in order to convey the main contention that my own case for Christianity is rational; but it is not simple. It is an accumulation of varied facts, like the attitude of the ordinary agnostic. But the ordinary agnostic has got his facts all wrong. He is a non-believer for a multitude of reasons, but they are untrue reasons. He doubts because the Middle Ages were barbaric, but they weren't; because Darwinism is demonstrated, but it isn't; because miracles do not happen, but they do; because monks were lazy, but they were very industrious; because nuns are unhappy, but they are particularly cheerful; because Christian art was sad and pale, but it was picked out in peculiarly bright colours and gay with gold; because modern science is moving away from the supernatural, but it isn't, it is moving towards the supernatural with the rapidity of a railway train.[9]

AMERICA

WHEN I WENT wandering about the States disguised as a lecturer, I was well aware that I was not sufficiently well disguised to be a spy. I was even in the worst possible position to be a sight-seer. A lecturer to American audiences can hardly be in the holiday mood of a sight-seer. It is rather the audience that is sight-seeing; even if it is seeing a rather melancholy sight.[10]

PERHAPS THERE ARE other examples of old types and patterns, lost in the old oligarchy and saved in the new democracies. I am haunted with a hint that the new structures [of New York City] are not so very new: and that they remind me of something very old. As I look from the balcony floors the crowds seem to float away and the colours to soften and grow pale, and I know I am in one of the simplest and most ancestral of human habitations. I am looking down from the old wooden gallery upon the courtyard of an inn. This new architectural model, which I have described, is after all one of the oldest European models, now neglected in Europe and especially in England, it was the theatre in which were enchanted innumerable picaresque comedies and romantic plays, with figures ranging from Sancho Panza to Sam Weller.[11]

SHALL I BLASPHEME crimson stars any more than crimson sunsets, or deny that those moons are golden any more than that this grass is green? If a child saw these coloured lights, he would dance with as much delight as at any other coloured toys; and it is the duty of every poet, and even of every critic, to dance in respectful imitation of the child. Indeed I am in a mood of so much sympathy with the fairy lights of this pantomime city, that I should be almost sorry to see social sanity and a sense of proportion return to extinguish them. I fear the day is breaking, and the broad daylight of tradition and ancient truth is coming to end all this delightful nightmare of New York at night.[12]

THEN, AS IT chanced, I looked across at the statue of Liberty, and saw that the great bronze was gleaming green in the morning light.... And then I suddenly remembered that this liberty was still in some sense enlightening the world, one part of the world; was a lamp for one sort of wanderer, a star of one sort of seafarer.[13]

ANARCHY

"I WAS WAITING for you," said Gregory. "Might I have a moment's conversation?"

"Certainly. About what?" asked Syme in a sort of weak wonder.

Gregory struck out with his stick at the lamp-post, and then at the tree. "About this and this," he cried; "about order and anarchy. There is your precious order, that lean, iron lamp, ugly and barren; and there is anarchy, rich, living, reproducing itself—there is anarchy, splendid in green and gold."

"All the same," replied Syme patiently, "just at present you only see the tree by the light of the lamp. I wonder when you would ever see the lamp by the light of the tree."[14]

"WHAT IS IT really all about? What is it you object to? You want to abolish Government?"

"To abolish God!" said Gregory, opening the eyes of a fanatic. "We do not only want to upset a few despotisms and police regulations;

that sort of anarchism does exist, but it is a mere branch of the Nonconformists. We dig deeper and we blow you higher. We wish to deny all those arbitrary distinctions of vice and virtue, honour and treachery, upon which mere rebels base themselves. The silly sentimentalists of the French Revolution talked of the Rights of Man! We hate Rights as we hate Wrongs. We have abolished Right and Wrong."[15]

GABRIEL SYME WAS not merely a detective who pretended to be a poet; he was really a poet who had become a detective. Nor was his hatred of anarchy hypocritical. He was one of those who are driven early in life into too conservative an attitude by the bewildering folly of most revolutionists. He had not attained it by any tame tradition. His respectability was spontaneous and sudden, a rebellion against rebellion.[16]

"DO YOU SEE this lantern?" cried Syme in a terrible voice. "Do you see the cross carved on it, and the flame inside? You did not make it. You did not light it. Better men than you, men who could believe and obey, twisted the entrails of iron and preserved the legend of fire. There is not a street you walk on, there is not a thread you wear, that was not made as this lantern was, by denying your philosophy of dirt and rats. You can make nothing. You can only destroy. You will destroy mankind; you will destroy the world. Let that suffice you. Yet this one old Christian lantern you shall not destroy. It shall go where your empire of apes will never have the wit to find it."

He struck the Secretary once with the lantern so that he staggered; and then, whirling it twice round his head, sent it flying far out to sea, where it flared like a roaring rocket and fell.

"Swords!" shouted Syme, turning his flaming face to the three behind him. "Let us charge these dogs, for our time has come to die."[17]

THE FALLING FIRE in the great cresset threw a last long gleam, like a bar of burning gold, across the dim grass. Against this fiery band was outlined in utter black the advancing legs of a black-clad figure. He seemed to have a fine close suit with knee-breeches such as that which was worn by the servants of the house, only that it was not blue, but of this absolute sable. He had, like the servants, a kind of sword by his side. It was only when he had come quite close to the crescent of the seven and flung up his face to look at them, that Syme saw, with thunderstruck clearness, that the face was the broad, almost ape-like face of his old friend Gregory, with its rank red hair and its insulting smile.

"Gregory!" gasped Syme, half-rising from his seat. "Why, this is the real anarchist!"

"Yes," said Gregory, with a great and dangerous restraint, "I am the real anarchist."

"'Now there was a day,'" murmured Bull, who seemed really to have fallen asleep, "'when the sons of God came to present themselves before the Lord, and Satan came also among them.'"

"You are right," said Gregory, and gazed all round. "I am a destroyer. I would destroy the world if I could."[18]

ANONYMITY

ANONYMOUS JOURNALISM IS dangerous, and is poisonous in our existing life simply because it is so rapidly becoming an anonymous life. That is the horrible thing about our contemporary atmosphere. Society is becoming a secret society. The modern tyrant is evil because of his elusiveness. He is more nameless than his slave. He is not more of a bully than the tyrants of the past; but he is more of a coward.[19]

APHORISMS

DESPAIR DOES NOT lie in being weary of suffering, but in being weary of joy.[20]

IT IS ALWAYS simple to fall; there are an infinity of angles at which one falls, only one at which one stands.[21]

YOU SHOULD NOT look a gift universe in the mouth.[22]

NO AMOUNT OF tragedy need amount to treason.[23]

IT IS BETTER to speak wisdom foolishly, like the Saints, rather than to speak folly wisely, like the Dons.[24]

THERE IS A spirit abroad among the nations of the earth which drives men incessantly on to destroy what they cannot understand, and to capture what they cannot enjoy.[25]

IT IS ONE of the simplest and silliest of the modern mistakes to connect the word "old" with the word "stale" or the word "weary."[26]

A DEAD THING can go with the stream, but only a living thing can go against it.[27]

THERE ARE TWO kinds of men who monopolise conversation. The first kind are those who like the sound of their own voice; the second are those who do not know what the sound of their own voice is like.[28]

THE BIBLE TELLS us to love our neighbours, and also to love our enemies, probably because they are generally the same people.[29]

ALL MEN ARE ordinary men; the extraordinary men are those who know it.[30]

THERE IS MORE of the song and music of mankind in a clerk putting on his Sunday clothes, than in a fanatic running down Cheapside.[31]

IT IS ABSURD to call a man cynical whose object it is to show that goodness, even when it is silly, is a healthier thing than wickedness when it is sensible.[32]

WHEN A MAN begins to think that the grass will not grow at night unless he lies awake to watch it, he generally ends either in an asylum or on the throne of an Emperor.[33]

APOLOGETICS

THERE IS IN modern discussions of religion and philosophy an absurd assumption that a man is in some way just and well-poised because he has come to no conclusion; and that a man is in some way knocked off the list of fair judges because he has come to a conclusion. It is assumed that the sceptic has no bias; whereas he has a very obvious bias in favour of scepticism.

I remember once arguing with an honest young atheist, who was very much shocked at my disputing some of the assumptions which were absolute sanctities to him (such as the quite unproved proposition of the independence of matter and the quite improbable proposition of its power to originate mind), and he at length fell back upon this question, which he delivered with an honourable heat of defiance and indignation: "Well, can you tell me any man of intellect, great in science or philosophy, who accepted the miraculous?" I said, "With pleasure. Descartes, Dr. Johnson, Newton, Faraday, Newman, Gladstone, Pasteur, Browning, Brunetière—as many more as you please." To which that quite admirable and idealistic young man made this astonishing reply—"Oh, but of course they *had* to say that; they were Christians." First he challenged me to find a black swan, and then he ruled out all my swans because they were black. The fact that all these great intellects had come to the Christian view was somehow or other a proof either that they were not great intellects or that they had not really come to that view. The argument thus stood in a charmingly convenient form: "All men that count have come to my conclusion; for if they come to your conclusion they do not count."[34]

[AT ONE POINT in my life] I was much moved by the eloquent attack on Christianity as a thing of inhuman gloom; for I thought (and still think) sincere pessimism the unpardonable sin. Insincere pessimism is a social accomplishment, rather agreeable than otherwise; and fortunately nearly all pessimism is insincere. But if Christianity was, as these people said, a thing purely pessimistic and opposed to life, then I was quite prepared to blow up St. Paul's Cathedral. But the extraordinary thing is this. They did prove to me in Chapter I. (to my complete satisfaction) that Christianity was too pessimistic; and then, in Chapter II., they began to prove to me that it was a great deal too optimistic. One accusation against Christianity was that it prevented men, by morbid tears and terrors, from seeking joy and liberty in the bosom of Nature. But another accusation was that it comforted men with a fictitious providence, and put them in a pink-and-white nursery. One great agnostic asked why Nature was not beautiful enough, and why it was hard to be free. Another great agnostic objected that Christian optimism, "the garment of make-believe woven by pious hands," hid from us the fact that Nature was ugly, and that it was impossible to be free. One rationalist had hardly done calling Christianity a nightmare before another began to call it a fool's paradise.

This puzzled me; the charges seemed inconsistent. Christianity could not at once be the black mask on a white world, and also the white mask on a black world. The state of the Christian could not be at once so comfortable that he was a coward to cling to it, and so uncomfortable that he was a fool to stand it. If it falsified human vision it must falsify it one way or another; it could not wear both green and rose-coloured spectacles.[35]

IT WAS HUXLEY and Herbert Spencer and Bradlaugh who brought me back to orthodox theology. They sowed in my mind my first wild doubts of doubt. Our grandmothers were quite right when they said that Tom Paine and the free-thinkers unsettled the mind. They do. They unsettled mine horribly. The rationalist made me question whether reason was of any use whatever; and when I had finished Herbert Spencer I had got as far as doubting (for the first time) whether evolution had occurred at all. As I laid down the last of Colonel Ingersoll's atheistic lectures the dreadful thought broke across my mind, "Almost thou persuadest me to be a Christian." I was in a desperate way.

This odd effect of the great agnostics in arousing doubts deeper than their own might be illustrated in many ways. I take only one. As I read and re-read all the non-Christian or anti-Christian accounts of the faith, from Huxley to Bradlaugh, a slow and awful impression grew gradually but graphically upon my mind—the impression that Christianity must be a most extraordinary thing. For not only (as I understood) had Christianity the most flaming vices, but it had apparently a mystical talent for combining vices which seemed inconsistent with each other. It was attacked on all sides and for all contradictory reasons. No sooner had one rationalist demonstrated that it was too far to the east than another demonstrated with equal clearness that it was much too far to the west. No sooner had my indignation died down at its angular and aggressive squareness than I was called up again to notice and condemn its enervating and sensual roundness.[36]

REASONS FOR HIS HOPE

Chesterton the Apologist

To the young people of my generation G. K. C. was a kind of Christian liberator. Like a beneficent bomb, he blew out of the Church a quantity of stained glass of a very poor period, and let in gusts of fresh air in which the dead leaves of doctrine danced with all the energy and indecorum of Our Lady's Tumbler."[1] So wrote Dorothy Sayers in 1952, in a preface to Chesterton's play *The Surprise*.

Such a tribute was wholly fitting, not least because Sayers herself was so much like Chesterton. Indeed, she possessed many of his gifts. She had an incandescent intellect; a vital, unconventional faith; and was an accomplished poet, essayist, and mystery writer. She knew well how to rightly acknowledge her indebtedness to a kindred spirit—one who had not only shaped her faith commitment, but given her (and so many others) vibrant reasons for their hope that lingered in memory.

More recently Frederick Buechner has penned one of the best summations of how Chesterton's faith infused his art. The setting was as follows. For a time during Chesterton's years at art college (summer 1893 through the summer of 1894), he endured a searing period of darkness and despair. Separated from close friends who had gone to university, and amid a welter of confusing and conflicting emotions about his sense of himself and the world, he became deeply depressed. These feelings of desolation were heightened by dabbling in spiritualism and the occult, largely through the use of a ouija board. In his posthumously published *Autobiography*, he described this time of his life as one in which he was "playing with hellfire." He began to experience headaches and what he described as "a bad smell in the mind." All of these experiences conspired together to make him feel as though he were "plunging deeper and deeper in a blind spiritual suicide." Concerned friends began to fear for Chesterton's sanity.

But then he was, as C. S. Lewis famously would be later, surprised by joy. Recoiling with horror from the abyss into which he had stared during his time of despair, he embarked on a quest for truth. "One searches for truth," he would later write, "but it may be that one pursues instinctively the more extraordinary truths."[2]

This search culminated in his embrace of the most extraordinary truth of all—found at the feet of a risen Christ with healing in his wings. He later described how this dawn of truth lightened his darkness:

> Satan was the most celebrated of Alpine guides, when he took Jesus to the top of an exceeding high mountain and showed him all the kingdoms of the earth. But the joy of Satan in standing on a peak is not a joy in largeness, but a joy in beholding smallness, in the fact that all men look like insects at his feet. It is from the valley that things look large; it is from the level that things look high; I am a child of the level and have no need of that celebrated Alpine guide. I will lift up my eyes to the hills, from whence cometh my help.[3]

It is here that Buechner offers a crucial insight: "having been given back his life and his sanity, [Chesterton] was filled both with an enormous sense of thankfulness and an enormous need for someone or something to thank."[4]

Following his embrace of Christianity, Chesterton's art could not help but reflect this overarching reality.[5] In saying this, Buechner also rendered a lasting service in helping readers see that while the novel *The Man Who Was Thursday* is a literary masterpiece, it was no less a fictional recasting of Chesterton's own journey from despair to hope. It is a work of art that also serves as a powerful *apologia*, and should be celebrated on both levels.

Chesterton wrote two books, *Heretics* and *Orthodoxy*, that have become classics and that serve as twin pillars of his apologetic. *Heretics* (published in June 1905) was born out of the conviction "that the most practical and important thing about a man is still his view of the universe." And so he took the measure of worldviews championed by George Bernard Shaw, H. G. Wells, and prominent artists such as James Whistler, crafting a critique that was simultaneously colorful, trenchant, and winsome. The fame resulting from this *tour de force* was such that readers clamored for a sequel setting forth Chesterton's own philosophy. *Orthodoxy* (published in September 1908) was the result, a book in which Chesterton assayed "to state the philosophy in which I have come to believe. I will not call it my philosophy," he stated, "for I did not make it. God and humanity made it; and it made me."[6]

The capstone of Chesterton's writings as an apologist was *The Everlasting Man* (published in September 1925). This work has also become a classic, and it is little less famous as a book that served as a catalyst for C. S. Lewis's embrace of Christianity. Lewis never forgot his first reading of this book:

> Then I read Chesterton's *Everlasting Man* and for the first time saw the whole Christian outline of history set out in a form that seemed to me to make sense. Somehow I contrived not to be too badly shaken. You will remember that I already thought Chesterton the most sensible man alive "apart from his Christianity." Now, I veritably believe, I thought—I didn't of course *say*; words would have revealed the nonsense—that Christianity itself was very sensible.[7]

On another occasion, when writing to his friend Sheldon Vanauken in December 1950, Lewis described *The Everlasting Man* as "the best popular apologetic I know."[8]

Lewis's affirmation of Chesterton's influence upon him is one supreme reason, among many, as to why Chesterton the apologist matters today. As an apologist, he helped to give the world C. S. Lewis, perhaps the most influential Christian apologist of all time. Lewis later underscored Chesterton's influence upon him as an apologist when he wrote: "The case for Christianity in general is well given by Chesterton; and I tried to do something [along the same lines] in my *Broadcast Talks*."[9] Lewis's *Broadcast Talks* later became the basis for his classic treatise, *Mere Christianity*. And so the streams that Chesterton set in motion when giving the reasons for his hope are very much with us still—in his own writings, and also in the works of Lewis. Bless God for that.

Apotheosis (the ultimate)

IT IS CONCEIVABLE that we are going more and more to keep our hands off things: not to drive horses; not to pick flowers. We may eventually be bound not to disturb a man's mind even by argument; not to disturb the sleep of birds even by coughing. The ultimate apotheosis would appear to be that of a man sitting quite still, not daring to stir for fear of disturbing a fly, nor to eat for fear of incommoding a microbe. To so crude a consummation as that we might perhaps unconsciously drift. But do we want so crude a consummation?[37]

Architecture

I SOMETIMES FANCY that every great city must have been built by night. At least, it is only at night that every part of a great city is great. All architecture is great architecture after sunset; perhaps architecture is really a nocturnal art, like the art of fireworks. At least, I think many people of those nobler trades that work by night (journalists, policemen, burglars, coffee-stall keepers, and such mistaken enthusiasts as refuse to go home till morning) must often have stood admiring some black bulk of building with a crown of battlements or a crest of spires and then burst into tears at daybreak to discover that it was only a haberdasher's shop with huge gold letters across the face of it.[38]

THERE ARE SOUNDS in music that are more ancient and awful than the cry of the strangest beast at night. And so also there are buildings that are shapeless in their strength, seeming to lift themselves slowly like monsters from the primal mire, and there are spires that seem to fly up suddenly like a startled bird.[39]

ARISTOCRACY

THE EVIL OF aristocracy is not that it leads to the infliction of bad things or the suffering of sad ones; the evil of aristocracy is that it places everything in the hands of a class of people who can always inflict what they can never suffer.[40]

THE GOD OF the aristocrats is not tradition, but fashion, which is the opposite of tradition. If you wanted to find an old-world Norwegian head-dress, would you look for it in the Scandinavian Smart Set? No; the aristocrats never have customs; at the best they have habits.[41]

IT MAY BE a mere patriotic bias, though I do not think so, but it seems to me that the English aristocracy is not only the type, but is the crown and flower of all actual aristocracies; it has all the oligarchical virtues as well as all the defects. It is casual, it is kind, it is courageous in obvious matters; but it has one great merit that overlaps even these. The great and very obvious merit of the English aristocracy is that nobody could possibly take it seriously.[42]

ARNOLD, MATTHEW

HE WAS A sort of Heaven-sent courier. His frontal attack on the vulgar and sullen optimism of Victorian utility may be summoned up in the admirable sentence, in which he asked the English what was the use of a train taking them quickly from Islington to Camberwell, if it only took them "from a dismal and illiberal life in Islington to a dismal and illiberal life in Camberwell?"[43]

ARROGANCE

IF HUMILITY HAS been discredited as a virtue at the present day, it is not wholly irrelevant to remark that this discredit has arisen at the same time as a great collapse of joy in current literature and philosophy. Men have revived the splendour of Greek self-assertion at the same time that they have revived the bitterness of Greek pessimism. A literature has arisen which commands us all to arrogate to ourselves the liberty of self-sufficing deities.[44]

ART

WE TALK OF art as something artificial in comparison with life. But I sometimes fancy that the very highest art is more real than life itself. At least this is true; that in proportion as passions become real they become poetical; the lover is always trying to be the poet.[45]

NOTHING SUBLIMELY ARTISTIC has ever arisen out of mere art, any more than anything essentially reasonable has arisen out of pure reason. There must always be a rich moral soil for any great aesthetic growth. The principle of art for art's sake is a very good principle if it means that there is a vital distinction between the earth and the tree that has its root in the earth; but it is a very bad principle if it means that the tree could grow just as well with its roots in the air.[46]

AND THIS, I think, is the mistake that people make about the old poets who lived before Wordsworth, and were supposed not to care very much about Nature because they did not describe it much.

They preferred writing about great men to writing about great hills; but they sat on the great hills to write it. They gave out much less about Nature, but they drank in, perhaps, much more. They painted the white robes of their holy virgins with the blinding snow, at which they had stared all day. They blazoned the shields of their paladins with the purple and gold of many heraldic sunsets. The greenness of a thousand green leaves clustered into the live green figure of Robin Hood. The blueness of a score of forgotten skies became the blue robes of the Virgin. The inspiration went in like sunbeams and came out like Apollo.[47]

WHEN I WAS in Paris a short time ago, I went with an English friend of mine to an extremely brilliant and rapid succession of French plays, each occupying about twenty minutes. They were all astonishingly effective; but there was one of them which was so effective that my friend and I fought about it outside, and had almost to be separated by the police. It was intended to indicate how men really behaved in a wreck or naval disaster, how they break down, how they scream, how they fight each other without object and in a mere hatred of everything. And then there was added, with all that horrible irony which Voltaire began, a scene in which a great statesman made a speech over their bodies, saying that they were all heroes and had died in a fraternal embrace. My friend and I came out of this theatre, and as he had lived long in Paris, he said, like a Frenchman: "What admirable artistic arrangement! Is it not exquisite?"

"No," I replied, assuming as far as possible the traditional attitude of John Bull in the pictures in *Punch*—"No, it is not exquisite. Perhaps it is unmeaning; if it is unmeaning I do not mind. But if it has a meaning I know what the meaning is; it is that under all their pageant of chivalry men are not only beasts, but even hunted beasts. I do not know much of humanity, especially when humanity talks in French. But I know when a thing is meant to uplift the human soul, and when it is meant to depress it."[48]

IF [PEOPLE] TAKE it for granted that an art must always be enjoyed in the most comfortable conditions, as if they were the most inspiring conditions, I think they are wrong about the whole psychology of art. A man who climbs a mountain to see the sunrise sees something quite different from that which is shown in a magic lantern to a man sitting in an armchair. Let us be kind to the man in the armchair when he cannot get out of the armchair; but let us not assume that there are no peaks worth climbing or no theatres good enough to go to. I remembered even in my childhood all the pleasures of going to the theatre; and one of the greatest pleasures was simply going there.[49]

ATHEISM

ROSSETTI MAKES THE remark somewhere, bitterly but with great truth, that the worst moment for the atheist is when he is really thankful and has nobody to thank.[50]

IT IS VAIN for eloquent atheists to talk of the great truths that will be revealed if once we see free thought begin. We have seen it end. It has no more questions to ask; it has questioned itself. You cannot call up any wilder vision than a city in which men ask themselves if they have any selves. You cannot fancy a more sceptical world than that in which men doubt if there is a world. It might certainly have reached its bankruptcy more quickly and cleanly if it had not been feebly hampered by the application of indefensible laws of blasphemy or by the absurd pretence that modern England is Christian. But it would have reached the bankruptcy anyhow. Militant atheists are still unjustly persecuted; but rather because they are an old minority than because they are a new one. Free thought has exhausted its own freedom. It is weary of its own success. If any eager freethinker now hails philosophic freedom as the dawn, he is only like the man in Mark Twain who came out wrapped in blankets to see the sun rise and was just in time to see it set.[51]

Austen, Jane

JANE AUSTEN WAS born before those bonds which (we are told) protected woman from truth, were burst by the Brontës or elaborately untied by George Eliot. Yet the fact remains that Jane Austen knew much more about men than either of them. Jane Austen may have been protected from truth: but it was precious little of truth that was protected from her.[52]

B

BALLADS

THE CHORUS OF a song, even of a comic song, has the same purpose as the chorus in a Greek tragedy. It reconciles men to the gods. It connects this one particular tale with the cosmos and the philosophy of common things. Thus we constantly find in the old ballads, especially the pathetic ballads, some refrain about the grass growing green, or the birds singing, or the woods being merry in spring. These are windows opened in the house of tragedy; momentary glimpses of larger and quieter scenes, of more ancient and enduring landscapes.[1]

BARBARISM

I AM INCLINED to think now that the chief modern danger is that of a slow return towards barbarism, just such a return towards barbarism as is indicated in the suggestions of barbaric retaliation of which I have just spoken. Civilisation in the best sense merely means the full authority of the human spirit over all externals. Barbarism means the worship of those externals in their crude and unconquered state. Barbarism means the worship of Nature; and in recent poetry, science, and philosophy there has been too much of the worship of Nature. Wherever men begin to talk much and with great solemnity about the forces outside man, the note of it is barbaric. When men talk much about heredity and environment they are almost barbarians.[2]

Beauty

ONE OF THE deepest and strangest of all human moods is the mood which will suddenly strike us perhaps in a garden at night, or deep in sloping meadows, the feeling that every flower and leaf has just uttered something stupendously direct and important, and that we have by a prodigy of imbecility not heard or understood it. There is a certain poetic value, and that a genuine one, in this sense of having missed the full meaning of things. There is beauty, not only in wisdom, but in this dazed and dramatic ignorance.[3]

HE STARED AND talked at the girl's red hair and amused face for what seemed to be a few minutes; and then, feeling that the groups in such a place should mix, rose to his feet. To his astonishment, he discovered the whole garden empty. Everyone had gone long ago, and he went himself with a rather hurried apology. He left with a sense of champagne in his head, which he could not afterwards explain. In the wild events which were to follow this girl had no part at all; he never saw her again until all his tale was over. And yet, in some indescribable way, she kept recurring like a motive in music through all his mad adventures afterwards, and the glory of her strange hair ran like a red thread through those dark and ill-drawn tapestries of the night.[4]

DAWN WAS BREAKING over everything in colours at once clear and timid; as if Nature made a first attempt at yellow and a first attempt at rose. A breeze blew so clean and sweet, that one could not think that it blew from the sky; it blew rather through some hole in the sky. Syme felt a simple surprise when he saw rising all round him on both sides of the road the red, irregular buildings of Saffron Park. He had no idea that he had walked so near London. He walked by instinct along one white road, on which early birds hopped and sang, and found himself outside a fenced garden. There he saw the sister of Gregory, the girl with the gold-red hair, cutting lilac before breakfast, with the great unconscious gravity of a girl.[5]

BEER

LET A MAN walk ten miles steadily on a hot summer's day along a dusty English road, and he will soon discover why beer was invented.[6]

BEGINNING ANEW

THE OBJECT OF a New Year is not that we should have a new year. It is that we should have a new soul and a new nose; new feet, a new backbone, new ears, and new eyes. Unless a particular man made New Year resolutions, he would make no resolutions. Unless a man starts afresh about things, he will certainly do nothing effective. Unless a man starts on the strange assumption that he has never existed before, it is quite certain that he will never exist afterwards. Unless a man be born again, he shall by no means enter into the Kingdom of Heaven.[7]

BENEFIT OF THE DOUBT

SMITH. I stick up for the thing every man has a right to.
   Perhaps the only thing that every man has a right to.
MORRIS. And what is that?
SMITH. The benefit of the doubt. Even your master, the
   petroleum millionaire, has a right to that. And I think
   he needs it more.[8]

BIG THINGS

IN THIS WORLD of ours we do not go on and discover small things: rather we go on and discover big things. It is the detail that we see first: it is the design that we only see very slowly and some men die never having seen it at all.[9]

BIGOTRY

BIGOTRY IS AN incapacity to conceive seriously the alternative to a proposition.[10]

IN REAL LIFE the people who are the most bigoted are the people who have no convictions at all.[11]

BLASPHEMIES

IN OUR TIME the blasphemies are threadbare. Pessimism is now patently, as it always was essentially, more commonplace than piety. Profanity is now more than an affectation—it is a convention. The curse against God is Exercise I. in the primer of minor poetry.[12]

BLATCHFORD, ROBERT

I MEAN NO disrespect to Mr. Blatchford in saying that our difficulty very largely lies in the fact that he, like masses of clever people nowadays, does not understand what theology is. To make mistakes in a science is one thing, to mistake its nature another. And as I read [his book] *God and My Neighbour*, the conviction gradually dawns on me that he thinks theology is the study of whether a lot of tales about God told in the Bible are historically demonstrable. This is as if he were trying to prove to a man that Socialism was sound Political Economy, and began to realise half-way through that the man thought that Political Economy meant the study of whether politicians were economical.[13]

IF ONLY MR. Blatchford would ask the real question. It is not, "Why is Christianity so bad when it claims to be so good?" The real question is, "Why are all human beings so bad when they claim to be so good?" Why is not the most noble scheme a guarantee against corruption?[14]

LET [MR. BLATCHFORD] doubt more, and he will believe more; for belief was always born out of doubt. Once before, the world went through an equinox of doubt, of cultured, serious, philosophical, cosmopolitan doubt; the result was Christianity.[15]

THE TRUE RELIGION is not that which has no difficulties. We have to swallow mysteries with it. But we have to swallow the same mysteries without it.[16]

BOSTON

THE ACADEMIC ARISTOCRACY of Boston, which Oliver Wendell Holmes called the Brahmins, is still a reality—though it was always a minority and is now a very small minority. An epigram, invented by Yale at the expense of Harvard, describes it as very small indeed—

> Here is to jolly old Boston, the home of the bean and the cod,
> Where Cabots speak only to Lowells, and Lowells speak only
> to God.

But an aristocracy must be a minority, and it is arguable that the smaller it is the better.[17]

BRITAIN AND AMERICA

THE OLD ANGLO-AMERICAN quarrel was much more fundamentally friendly than most Anglo-American alliances. Each nation understood the other enough to quarrel. In our time, neither nation understands itself even enough to quarrel.[18]

The Brontës

WHAT THE BRONTËS really brought into fiction was exactly what Carlyle brought into history; the blast of the mysticism of the North. They were of Irish blood settled on the windy heights of Yorkshire; in that country where Catholicism lingered latest, but in a superstitious form; where modern industrialism came earliest and was more superstitious still. The strong winds and sterile places, the old tyranny of barons and the new and blacker tyranny of manufacturers, has made and left that country a land of barbarians. All Charlotte Brontë's earlier work is full of that sullen and unmanageable world.[19]

Browning, Elizabeth Barrett

SHE EXCELLED IN . . . epigram, almost as much as Voltaire in his. Pointed phrases like: "Are Martyrs by the pang without the palm" or "Incense to sweeten a crime and myrrh to embitter a curse," these expressions, which are witty after the old fashion of the conceit, came quite freshly and spontaneously to her quite modern mind. But the first fact is this, that these epigrams of hers were never so true as when they turned on one of the two or three pivots on which contemporary Europe was really turning. She is by far the most European of all the English poets of that age; all of them, even her own much greater husband, look local beside her. Tennyson and the rest are nowhere.[20]

MRS. BROWNING KNEW no more facts about Napoleon, perhaps, than Tennyson did; but she knew the truth. Her epigram on Napoleon's fall is in one line

"And kings crept out again to feel the sun."

Talleyrand would have clapped his horrible old hands at that. Her instinct about the statesman and the soldier was very like Jane Austen's instinct for the gentleman and the man.[21]

SHE HAD ONE of the peculiar talents of true rhetoric, that of a powerful concentration. As to the critic who thinks her poetry owed anything to the great poet who was her husband, he can go and live in the same hotel with the man who can believe that George Eliot owed anything to the extravagant imagination of Mr. George Henry Lewes.[22]

BROWNING, ROBERT

THOUGH THIS WORLD is the only world that we have known, or of which we could even dream, the fact remains that we have named it "a strange world." In other words, we have certainly felt that this world did not explain itself, that something in its complete and patent picture has been omitted. And Browning was right in saying that in a cosmos where incompleteness implies completeness, life implies immortality.[23]

BROWNING ALSO WAS at once romantic and Puritan; but he belonged to no group, and worked against materialism in a manner entirely his own. Though as a boy he bought eagerly Shelley's revolutionary poems, he did not think of becoming a revolutionary poet. He concentrated on the special souls of men; seeking God in a series of private interviews. Hence Browning, great as he is, is rather one of the Victorian novelists than wholly of the Victorian poets.[24]

BROWNING . . . GOT ON much better [than Tennyson did] with eccentric and secluded England because he treated it as eccentric and secluded; a place where one could do what one liked. To a considerable extent he did do what he liked; arousing not a few complaints; and many doubts and conjectures as to why on earth he liked it.[25]

[BROWNING] DID ONE really original and admirable thing: he managed the real details of modern love affairs in verse, and love is the most realistic thing in the world. He substituted the street with the green blind for the faded garden of Watteau, and the "blue spirt of a lighted match" for the monotony of the evening star.[26]

[BROWNING] WAS A keen artist, a keen scholar, he could put his finger on anything, and he had a memory like the British Museum Library.[27]

DO THE PEOPLE who call one of Browning's poems scientific in its analysis realise the meaning of what they say? One is tempted to think that they know a scientific analysis when they see it as little as they know a good poem. The one supreme difference between the scientific method and the artistic method is, roughly speaking, simply this: that a scientific statement means the same thing wherever and whenever it is uttered, and that an artistic statement means something entirely different, according to the relation in which it stands to its surroundings.[28]

BROWNING GREW UP, then, with the growing fame of Shelley and Keats, in the atmosphere of literary youth, fierce and beautiful, among new poets who believed in a new world. It is important to remember this, because the real Browning was a quite different person from the grim moralist and metaphysician who is seen through the spectacles of Browning Societies and University Extension Lecturers. Browning was first and foremost a poet, a man made to enjoy all things visible and invisible, a priest of the higher passions.[29]

IT WOULD HAVE been hard, therefore, for Browning to have chosen a better example for his study of intellectual egotism than Paracelsus. Modern life accuses the mediæval tradition of crushing the intellect; Browning, with a truer instinct, accuses that tradition of over-glorifying it.[30]

THE USUAL ACCUSATION against Browning is that he was con-
sumed with logic; that he thought all subjects to be the proper
pabulum of intellectual disquisition; that he gloried chiefly in his
own power of plucking knots to pieces and rending fallacies in two;
and that to this method he sacrificed deliberately, and with complete self-complacency, the element of poetry and sentiment. To
people who imagine Browning to have been this frigid believer in
the intellect there is only one answer necessary or sufficient. It is
the fact that he wrote a play designed to destroy the whole of this
intellectualist fallacy at the age of twenty-three.[31]

WITH BROWNING, AS with all true poets, passion came first and
made intellectual expression, the hunger for beauty making literature as the hunger for bread made a plough.[32]

IN THE CHARACTER of Paracelsus, Browning wished to paint the
dangers and disappointments which attend the man who believes
merely in the intellect. He wished to depict the fall of the logician;
and with a perfect and unerring instinct he selected a man who
wrote and spoke in the tradition of the Middle Ages, the most
thoroughly and even painfully logical period that the world has
ever seen.[33]

Buildings

THERE IS SOMETHING strangely primary and poetic about this
sight of the scaffolding and main lines of a human building.... One
seems to see domestic life as the daring and ambitious thing that
it is, when one looks at those open staircases and empty chambers, those spirals of wind and open halls of sky. Ibsen said that
the art of domestic drama was merely to knock one wall out of the
four walls of a drawing-room. I find the drawing-room even more
impressive when all four walls are knocked out.[34]

I CANNOT UNDERSTAND people at present making such a fuss about flying ships and aviation, when men ever since Stonehenge and the Pyramids have done something so much more wild than flying. A grasshopper can go astonishingly high up in the air; his biological limitation and weakness is that he cannot stop there. Hosts of unclean birds and crapulous insects can pass through the sky, but they cannot pass any communication between it and the earth. But the army of man has advanced vertically into infinity, and not been cut off. It can establish outposts in the ether, and yet keep open behind it its erect and insolent road. It would be grand (as in Jules Verne) to fire a cannonball at the moon; but would it not be grander to build a railway to the moon? Yet every building of brick or wood is a hint of that high railroad; every chimney points to some star, and every tower is a Tower of Babel. Man rising on these awful and unbroken wings of stone seems to me more majestic and more mystic than man fluttering for an instant on wings of canvas and sticks of steel.[35]

BUNYAN, JOHN

[BUNYAN] WROTE GRACE *Abounding to the Chief of Sinners*, perhaps the most powerful work ever wrought by genius with the materials of morbidity.[36]

NO ONE . . . CAN ever forget the impression of that awful chapter [of Bunyan's autobiography] *Grace Abounding*, in which the sinner takes refuge in place after place only to expect that roof after roof will crash down upon him, and that he is safe nowhere if the very Universe that he inherits belongs to one who is his enemy. Nor will anyone forget the chapter in which the sinner is reconciled to the Universe, and walks about the fields and cannot forbear from talking to the birds about the great mercy of God.[37]

C

Calling things by their real names

WHITE IS A colour. It is not a mere absence of colour; it is a shining and affirmative thing, as fierce as red, as definite as black. When, so to speak, your pencil grows red-hot, it draws roses; when it grows white-hot, it draws stars. And one of the two or three defiant verities of the best religious morality, of real Christianity, for example, is exactly this same thing; the chief assertion of religious morality is that white is a colour. Virtue is not the absence of vices or the avoidance of moral dangers; virtue is a vivid and separate thing, like pain or a particular smell. Mercy does not mean not being cruel or sparing people revenge or punishment; it means a plain and positive thing like the sun, which one has either seen or not seen.[1]

Capricious divorce

THE ORDINARY EMANCIPATED prig or poet who urges this side of the question [ease in obtaining divorces] always talks to one tune. "Marriage may be best for most men," he says, "but there are exceptional natures that demand a more undulating experience; constancy will do for the common herd, but there are complex natures and complex cases where no one could recommend constancy."[2]

Caricature

CARICATURE IS A serious thing; it is almost blasphemously serious. Caricature really means making a pig more like a pig than even God has made him.[3]

"CARICATURE," SAID SIR Willoughby Patterne, in his fatuous way, "is rough truth." It is not; it is subtle truth. This is what gives Dickens his unquestionable place among artists. He realised thoroughly a certain phase or atmosphere of existence, and he knew the precise strokes and touches that would bring it home to the reader.[4]

DICKENS WAS, OF course, as is repeated *ad nauseam*, a caricaturist, and when we have understood this word we have understood the whole matter; but in truth the word, caricaturist, is commonly misunderstood; it is even, in the case of men like Dickens, used as implying a reproach. Whereas it has no more reproach in it than the word organist. Caricature is not merely an important form of art: it is a form of art which is often most useful for purposes of profound philosophy and powerful symbolism. The age of scepticism put caricature into ephemeral feuilletons; but the ages of faith built caricatures into their churches of everlasting stone.[5]

CATHEDRALS

CATHEDRALS AND COLUMNS of triumph were meant, not for people more cultured and self-conscious than modern tourists, but for people much rougher and more casual. Those heaps of live stone like frozen fountains, were so placed and poised as to catch the eye of ordinary inconsiderate men going about their daily business; and when they are so seen they are never forgotten. The true way of reviving the magic of our great minsters and historic sepulchres is not the one which Ruskin was always recommending. It is not to be more careful of historic buildings. Nay, it is rather to be more careless of them. Buy a bicycle in Maidstone to visit an aunt in Dover, and you will see Canterbury Cathedral as it was built to be seen.... For it was for the simple and laborious generations of men, practical, troubled about many things, that our fathers reared those portents.[6]

THE SEALED AND sullen sunset behind the dark dome of St. Paul's had in it smoky and sinister colours—colours of sickly green, dead red or decaying bronze, that were just bright enough to emphasise the solid whiteness of the snow. But right up against these dreary colours rose the black bulk of the cathedral; and upon the top of the cathedral was a random splash and great stain of snow, still clinging as to an Alpine peak. It had fallen accidentally, but just so fallen as to half drape the dome from its very topmost point, and to pick out in perfect silver the great orb and the cross. When Syme saw it he suddenly straightened himself, and made with his sword-stick an involuntary salute.

He knew that that evil figure, his shadow, was creeping quickly or slowly behind him, and he did not care. It seemed a symbol of human faith and valour that while the skies were darkening that high place of the earth was bright. The devils might have captured heaven, but they had not yet captured the cross.[7]

CHARITY

CHARITY IS A fashionable virtue in our time; it is lit up by the gigantic firelight of Dickens. Hope is a fashionable virtue to-day; our attention has been arrested for it by the sudden and silver trumpet of Stevenson. But faith is unfashionable, and it is customary on every side to cast against it the fact that it is a paradox. Everybody mockingly repeats the famous childish definition that faith is "the power of believing that which we know to be untrue." Yet it is not one atom more paradoxical than hope or charity. Charity is the power of defending that which we know to be indefensible. Hope is the power of being cheerful in circumstances which we know to be desperate.[8]

CHAUCER, GEOFFREY

CHAUCER'S KNIGHT RODE with a cook quite naturally; because the thing they were all seeking together was as much above knighthood as it was above cookery. Soldiers and swindlers and bullies and outcasts, they were all going to the shrine of a distant saint.[9]

Cheese

POETS HAVE BEEN mysteriously silent on the subject of cheese.[10]

ONCE IN ENDEAVOURING to lecture in several places at once, I made an eccentric journey across England, a journey of so irregular and even illogical shape that it necessitated my having lunch on four successive days in four roadside inns in four different counties. In each inn they had nothing but bread and cheese; nor can I imagine why a man should want more than bread and cheese, if he can get enough of it. In each inn the cheese was good; and in each inn it was different. There was a noble Wensleydale cheese in Yorkshire, a Cheshire cheese in Cheshire, and so on.[11]

Children

THE WHOLE DIFFERENCE between construction and creation is exactly this: that a thing constructed can only be loved after it is constructed; but a thing created is loved before it exists, as the mother can love the unborn child.[12]

I DOUBT IF anyone of any tenderness of imagination can see the hand of a child and not be a little frightened of it. It is awful to think of the essential human energy moving so tiny a thing; it is like imagining that human nature could live in the wing of a butterfly, or the leaf of a tree.[13]

BUT THE INFLUENCE of children goes further than its first trifling effort of remaking heaven and earth. It forces us actually to remodel our conduct in accordance with this revolutionary theory of the marvellousness of all things. We do (even when we are perfectly simple or ignorant)—we do actually treat talking in children as marvellous, walking in children as marvellous, common intelligence in children as marvellous. The cynical philosopher fancies he has a victory in this matter—that he can laugh when he shows that the words or antics of the child, so much admired by its worshippers, are common enough. The fact is that this is precisely where baby-worship is so profoundly right. Any words and any antics in a lump of clay are wonderful, the child's words and antics are wonderful, and it is only fair to say that the philosopher's words and antics are equally wonderful.[14]

THE FASCINATION OF children lies in this: that with each of them all things are remade, and the universe is put again upon its trial. As we walk the streets and see below us those delightful bulbous heads, three times too big for the body, which mark these human mushrooms, we ought always primarily to remember that within every one of these heads there is a new universe, as new as it was on the seventh day of creation. In each of those orbs there is a new system of stars, new grass, new cities, a new sea.[15]

> For every tiny town or place
> God made the stars especially;
> Babies look up with owlish face
> And see them tangled in a tree.[16]

CHILTERN HILLS

THE OTHER DAY on a stray spur of the Chiltern Hills I climbed up upon one of those high, abrupt, windy churchyards from which the dead seem to look down upon all the living. It was a mountain of ghosts as Olympus was a mountain of gods. In that church lay the bones of great Puritan lords, of a time when most of the power of England was Puritan, even of the Established Church. And below these uplifted bones lay the huge and hollow valleys of the English countryside, where the motors went by every now and then like meteors. . . . And looking over that deep green prospect on that luminous yellow evening, a lovely and austere thought came into my mind, a thought as beautiful as the green wood and as grave as the tombs. The thought was this: that I should like to go into Parliament, quarrel with my party, accept the Stewardship of the Chiltern Hundreds, and then refuse to give it up.[17]

CHRIST

There was a man who dwelt in the east centuries ago,
And now I cannot look at a sheep or a sparrow,
A lily or a cornfield, a raven or a sunset,
A vineyard or a mountain, without thinking of him.[18]

CHRIST DID NOT tell his apostles that they were only the excellent people, or the only excellent people, but that they were the exceptional people; the permanently incongruous and incompatible people; and the text about the salt of the earth is really as sharp and shrewd and tart as the taste of salt. It is because they were the exceptional people, that they must not lose their exceptional quality.[19]

"THEN, WHAT," ASKED Turnbull, very slowly, as he softly picked a flower, "what is the difference between Christ and Satan?"

"It is quite simple," replied the Highlander. "Christ descended into hell; Satan fell into it."

"Does it make much odds?" asked the free thinker.

"It makes all the odds," said the other. "One of them wanted to go up and went down; the other wanted to go down and went up."[20]

Christian theism

AND THE ROOT phrase for all Christian theism was this, that God was a creator, as an artist is a creator.[21]

Christian virtues

AS THE WORD "unreasonable" is open to misunderstanding, the matter may be more accurately put by saying that each one of these Christian or mystical virtues involves a paradox in its own nature, and that this is not true of any of the typically pagan or rationalist virtues. Justice consists in finding out a certain thing due to a certain man and giving it to him. Temperance consists in finding out the proper limit of a particular indulgence and adhering to that. But charity means pardoning what is unpardonable, or it is no virtue at all. Hope means hoping when things are hopeless, or it is no virtue at all. And faith means believing the incredible, or it is no virtue at all.[22]

THE ACT OF defending any of the cardinal virtues has to-day all the exhilaration of a vice. Moral truisms have been so much disputed that they have begun to sparkle like so many brilliant paradoxes. And especially (in this age of egoistic idealism) there is about one who defends humility something inexpressibly rakish.[23]

Christianity

CHRISTIANITY EVEN WHEN watered down is hot enough to boil all modern society to rags. The mere minimum of the Church would be a deadly ultimatum to the world.[24]

CHRISTIANITY AROSE AND spread in a very cultured and very cynical world—in a very modern world. Lucretius was as much a materialist as Haeckel, and a much more persuasive writer.[25]

THE CHRISTIAN OPTIMISM is based on the fact that we do *not* fit in to the world. I had tried to be happy by telling myself that man is an animal, like any other which sought its meat from God. But now I really was happy, for I had learnt that man is a monstrosity. I had been right in feeling all things as odd, for I myself was at once worse and better than all things. The optimist's pleasure was prosaic, for it dwelt on the naturalness of everything; the Christian pleasure was poetic, for it dwelt on the unnaturalness of everything in the light of the supernatural. The modern philosopher had told me again and again that I was in the right place, and I had still felt depressed even in acquiescence. But I had heard that I was in the *wrong* place, and my soul sang for joy, like a bird in spring. The knowledge found out and illuminated forgotten chambers in the dark house of infancy. I knew now why grass had always seemed to me as queer as the green beard of a giant, and why I could feel homesick at home.[26]

AND MY HAUNTING instinct that somehow good was not merely a tool to be used, but a relic to be guarded, like the goods from Crusoe's ship—even that had been the wild whisper of something originally wise, for, according to Christianity, we were indeed the survivors of a wreck, the crew of a golden ship that had gone down before the beginning of the world.[27]

AND THEN FOLLOWED an experience impossible to describe. It was as if I had been blundering about since my birth with two huge and unmanageable machines, of different shapes and without apparent connection—the world and the Christian tradition. I had found this hole in the world: the fact that one must somehow find a way of loving the world without trusting it; somehow one must love the world without being worldly. I found this projecting feature of Christian theology, like a sort of hard spike, the dogmatic insistence that God was personal, and had made a world separate from Himself. The spike of dogma fitted exactly into the hole in the world—it had evidently been meant to go there—and then the strange thing began to happen. When once these two parts of the two machines had come together, one after another, all the other parts fitted and fell in with an eerie exactitude. I could hear bolt after bolt over all the machinery falling into its place with a kind of click of relief. Having got one part right, all the other parts were repeating that rectitude, as clock after clock strikes noon. Instinct after instinct was answered by doctrine after doctrine. Or, to vary the metaphor, I was like one who had advanced into a hostile country to take one high fortress. And when that fort had fallen the whole country surrendered and turned solid behind me. The whole land was lit up, as it were, back to the first fields of my childhood.[28]

POETS WILL TEND towards Christian orthodoxy for a perfectly plain reason: because it is about the simplest and freest thing now left in the world.[29]

CHRISTIANITY IS ALWAYS out of fashion because it is always sane; and all fashions are mild insanities.[30]

AS WE HAVE taken the circle as the symbol of reason and madness, we may very well take the cross as the symbol at once of mystery and of health. Buddhism is centripetal, but Christianity is centrifugal: it breaks out. For the circle is perfect and infinite in its nature; but it is fixed for ever in its size; it can never be larger or smaller. But the cross, though it has at its heart a collision and contradiction, can extend its four arms for ever without altering its shape. Because it has a paradox in its centre it can grow without changing. The circle returns upon itself and is bound. The cross opens its arms to the four winds; it is a sign-post for free travellers.[31]

I WAS THOROUGHLY annoyed with Christianity for suggesting (as I supposed) that whole ages and empires of men had utterly escaped this light of justice and reason. But then I found an astonishing thing. I found that the very people who said that mankind was one church from Plato to Emerson were the very people who said that morality had changed altogether, and that what was right in one age was wrong in another. If I asked, say, for an altar, I was told that we needed none, for men our brothers gave us clear oracles and one creed in their universal customs and ideals. But if I mildly pointed out that one of men's universal customs was to have an altar, then my agnostic teachers turned clean round and told me that men had always been in darkness and the superstitions of savages. I found it was their daily taunt against Christianity that it was the light of one people and had left all others to die in the dark. But I also found that it was their special boast for themselves that science and progress were the discovery of one people, and that all other peoples had died in the dark. Their chief insult to Christianity was actually their chief compliment to themselves, and there seemed to be a strange unfairness about all their relative insistence on the two things. When considering some pagan or agnostic, we were to remember that all men had one religion; when considering some mystic or spiritualist, we were only to consider what absurd religions some men had.[32]

THE PAGANS INSISTED upon self-assertion because it was the essence of their creed that the gods, though strong and just, were mystic, capricious, and even indifferent. But the essence of Christianity was in a literal sense the New Testament—a covenant with God which opened to men a clear deliverance. They thought themselves secure . . . they believed themselves rich with an irrevocable benediction which set them above the stars; and immediately they discovered humility.[33]

NOW, THIS IS exactly the claim which I have since come to propound for Christianity. Not merely that it deduces logical truths, but that when it suddenly becomes illogical, it has found, so to speak, an illogical truth. It not only goes right about things, but it goes wrong (if one may say so) exactly where the things go wrong. Its plan suits the secret irregularities, and expects the unexpected. It is simple about the simple truth; but it is stubborn about the subtle truth.[34]

CHRISTIANS

THESE ARE THE days when the Christian is expected to praise every creed except his own.[35]

CHRISTMAS

There fared a mother driven forth
Out of an inn to roam;
In the place where she was homeless
All men are at home.
The crazy stable close at hand,
With shaking timber and shifting sand,
Grew a stronger thing to abide and stand
Than the square stones of Rome.
For men are homesick in their homes,
And strangers under the sun,
And they lay their heads in a foreign land
Whenever the day is done.
Here we have battle and blazing eyes,
And chance and honour and high surprise,
But our homes are under miraculous skies
Where the yule tale was begun.
A Child in a foul stable,
Where the beasts feed and foam;
Only where He was homeless
Are you and I at home;
We have hands that fashion and heads that know,
But our hearts we lost—how long ago!

In a place no chart nor ship can show
Under the sky's dome.
This world is wild as an old wives' tale,
And strange the plain things are,
The earth is enough and the air is enough
For our wonder and our war;
But our rest is as far as the fire-drake swings
And our peace is put in impossible things
Where clashed and thundered unthinkable wings
Round an incredible star.
To an open house in the evening
Home shall men come,
To an older place than Eden
And a taller town than Rome.
To the end of the way of the wandering star,
To the things that cannot be and that are,
To the place where God was homeless
And all men are at home.[36]

Chronological snobbery

An imbecile habit has arisen in modern controversy of saying that such and such a creed can be held in one age but cannot be held in another. Some dogma, we are told, was credible in the twelfth century, but is not credible in the twentieth. You might as well say that a certain philosophy can be believed on Mondays, but cannot be believed on Tuesdays. You might as well say of a view of the cosmos that it was suitable to half-past three, but not suitable to half-past four. What a man can believe depends upon his philosophy, not upon the clock or the century.[37]

We choose to call the great mass of the history of mankind bad, not because it is bad, but because we [think we] are better.[38]

THE WHOLE CURSE of the last century has been what is called the Swing of the Pendulum; that is, the idea that Man must go alternately from one extreme to the other.[39]

WE MUST HAVE our own vision. But the attempts of most moderns to express it are highly vague.

Some fall back simply on the clock: they talk as if mere passage through time brought some superiority; so that even a man of the first mental calibre carelessly uses the phrase that human morality is never up to date. How can anything be up to date?—a date has no character.[40]

THE CHURCH

THE CHURCH ALWAYS seems behind the times, when it is really beyond the times; it is waiting till the last fad shall have seen its last summer. It keeps the key of a permanent virtue.[41]

WHEN PEOPLE IMPUTE special vices to the Christian Church, they seem entirely to forget that the world (which is the only other thing there is) has these vices much more. The Church has been cruel; but the world has been much more cruel. The Church has plotted; but the world has plotted much more. The Church has been superstitious; but it has never been so superstitious as the world is when left to itself.[42]

MACIAN BURST OUT like a man driven back and explaining everything.

"The Church is not a thing like the Athenaeum Club," he cried. "If the Athenaeum Club lost all its members, the Athenaeum Club would dissolve and cease to exist. But when we belong to the Church we belong to something which is outside all of us; which is outside everything you talk about, outside the Cardinals and the Pope. They belong to it, but it does not belong to them. If we all fell dead suddenly, the Church would still somehow exist in God."[43]

CIVILISATION

"MANY CLEVER MEN like you have trusted to civilisation. Many clever Babylonians, many clever Egyptians, many clever men at the end of Rome. Can you tell me, in a world that is flagrant with the failures of civilisation, what there is particularly immortal about yours?"[44]

CLEVERNESS

CLEVERNESS KILLS WISDOM: that is one of the few sad and certain things.[45]

IN THE BEGINNING of the twentieth century you could not see the ground for clever men. They were so common that a stupid man was quite exceptional, and when they found him, they followed him in crowds down the street and treasured him up and gave him some high post in the State. And all these clever men were at work giving accounts of what would happen in the next age, all quite clear, all quite keen-sighted and ruthless, and all quite different.[46]

COLOURS

GOD HAS GIVEN us not so much the colours of a picture as the colours of a palette. But He has also given us a subject, a model, a fixed vision. We must be clear about what we want to paint.[47]

IT IS NOT for nothing that the very nature of local character has gained the nickname of local colour. Colour runs through all our experience; and we all know that our childhood found talismanic gems in the very paints in the paint-box, or even in their very names. And just as the very name of "crimson lake" really suggested to me some sanguine and mysterious mere, dark yet red as blood, so the very name of "burnt sienna" became afterwards tangled up in my mind with the notion of something traditional and tragic; as if some such golden Italian city had really been darkened by many conflagrations in the wars of mediaeval democracy.[48]

COMEDY

MY FRIEND HAD met me in his car . . . at the little painted station in the middle of the warm wet woods and hop-fields of that western country. He proposed to drive me first to his house beyond the village before starting for a longer spin of adventure, and we rattled through those rich green lanes which have in them something singularly analogous to fairy tales; whether the lanes produced the fairies or (as I believe) the fairies produced the lanes. All around in the glimmering hop-yards stood those little hop-kilns like stunted and slanting spires. They look like dwarfish churches in fact, rather like many modern churches I could mention, churches all of them small and each of them a little crooked.

In this elfin atmosphere we swung round a sharp corner and half-way up a steep, white hill, and saw what looked at first like a tall, black monster against the sun. It appeared to be a dark and dreadful woman walking on wheels and waving long ears like a bat's. A second glance told me that she was not the local witch in a state of transition; she was only one of the million tricks of perspective. She stood up in a small wheeled cart drawn by a donkey; the donkey's ears were just behind her head, and the whole was black against the light. Perspective is really the comic element in everything.[49]

COMIC (THINGS THAT ARE)

WHEN I WAS a very young journalist I used to be irritated at a peculiar habit of printers, a habit which most persons of a tendency similar to mine have probably noticed also. It goes along with the fixed belief of printers that to be a Rationalist is the same thing as to be a Nationalist. I mean the printer's tendency to turn the word "cosmic" into the word "comic." It annoyed me at the time. But since then I have come to the conclusion that the printers were right. The democracy is always right. Whatever is cosmic is comic.[50]

SO FAR AS a thing is universal it is serious. And so far as a thing is universal it is full of comic things. If you take a small thing, it may be entirely serious: Napoleon, for instance, was a small thing, and he was serious: the same applies to microbes. If you isolate a thing, you may get the pure essence of gravity. But if you take a large thing (such as the Solar System) it *must* be comic, at least in parts. The germs are serious, because they kill you. But the stars are funny, because they give birth to life, and life gives birth to fun. If you have, let us say, a theory about man, and if you can only prove it by talking about Plato and George Washington, your theory may be a quite frivolous thing. But if you can prove it by talking about the butler or the postman, then it is serious, because it is universal. So far from it being irreverent to use silly metaphors on serious questions, it is one's duty to use silly metaphors on serious questions. It is the test of one's seriousness. It is the test of a responsible religion or theory whether it can take examples from pots and pans and boots and butter-tubs. It is the test of a good philosophy whether you can defend it grotesquely. It is the test of a good religion whether you can joke about it.[51]

COMMANDMENTS AND CONVENTIONS

IF HE CAN defy the conventions, it is just because he can keep the commandments.[52]

COMMON FOLK

WHEN A MAN says that democracy is false because most people are stupid, there are several courses which the philosopher may pursue.

The most obvious is to hit him smartly and with precision on the exact tip of the nose. But if you have scruples (moral or physical) about this course, you may proceed to employ Reason, which in this case has all the savage solidity of a blow with the fist. It is stupid to say that "most people" are stupid. It is like saying "most people are tall," when it is obvious that "tall" can only mean taller than most people. It is absurd to denounce the majority of mankind as below the average of mankind. Should the man have been hammered on the nose and brained with logic, and should he still remain cold, a third course opens: lead him by the hand (himself half-willing) towards some sunlit and yet secret meadow and ask him who made the names of the common wild flowers. They were ordinary people, so far as any one knows, who gave to one flower the name of the Star of Bethlehem and to another and much commoner flower the tremendous title of the Eye of Day. If you cling to the snobbish notion that common people are prosaic, ask any common person for the local names of the flowers, names which vary not only from county to county, but even from dale to dale.[53]

THERE IS HOPE for people who have gone down into the hells of greed and economic oppression (at least, I hope there is, for we are such a people ourselves), but there is no hope for a people that does not exult in the abstract idea of the peasant scoring off the prince.[54]

COMMON THINGS

ORDINARY THINGS ARE more valuable than extraordinary things; nay, they are more extraordinary. Man is something more awful than men; something more strange. The sense of the miracle of humanity itself should be always more vivid to us than any marvels of power, intellect, art, or civilization. The mere man on two legs, as such, should be felt as something more heartbreaking than any music and more startling than any caricature.[55]

LET US EXERCISE the eye until it learns to see the startling facts that run across the landscape as plain as a painted fence. . . . Let us learn to write essays on a stray cat or a coloured cloud.[56]

IT IS ADMITTED, one may hope, that common things are never commonplace. Birth is covered with curtains precisely because it is a staggering and monstrous prodigy. Death and first love, though they happen to everybody, can stop one's heart with the very thought of them. But while this is granted, something further may be claimed. It is not merely true that these universal things are strange; it is moreover true that they are subtle. In the last analysis most common things will be found to be highly complicated. Some men of science do indeed get over the difficulty by dealing only with the easy part of it: thus, they will call first love the instinct of sex, and the awe of death the instinct of self-preservation. But this is only getting over the difficulty of describing peacock green by calling it blue. There is blue in it. That there is a strong physical element in both romance and the *Memento Mori* makes them if possible more baffling than if they had been wholly intellectual. No man could say exactly how much his sexuality was colored by a clean love of beauty, or by the mere boyish itch for irrevocable adventures, like running away to sea. No man could say how far his animal dread of the end was mixed up with mystical traditions touching morals and religion. It is exactly because these things are animal, but not quite animal, that the dance of all the difficulties begins. The materialists analyze the easy part, deny the hard part and go home to their tea.[57]

COMMUNALISM

A CORRESPONDENT HAS written me an able and interesting letter in the matter of some allusions of mine to the subject of communal kitchens. He defends communal kitchens very lucidly from the standpoint of the calculating collectivist; but, like many of his school, he cannot apparently grasp that there is another test of the whole matter, with which such calculation has nothing at all to do. He knows it would be cheaper if a number of us ate at the same time, so as to use the same table. So it would. It would also be cheaper if a number of us slept at different times, so as to use the same pair of trousers. But the question is not how cheap are we buying a thing, but what are we buying? It is cheap to own a slave. And it is cheaper still to be a slave.[58]

Conservatives

HE IS A very shallow critic who cannot see an eternal rebel in the heart of a conservative.[59]

Convictions

EVERY ACT OF will is an act of self-limitation. To desire action is to desire limitation. In that sense, every act is an act of self-sacrifice. When you choose anything, you reject everything else.[60]

NO ONE WORTH calling a man allows his moods to change his convictions; but it is by moods that we understand other men's convictions.[61]

Corruption

AN ENORMOUS AMOUNT of modern ingenuity is expended on finding defences for the indefensible conduct of the powerful.[62]

POWERFUL MEN WHO have powerful passions use much of their strength in forging chains for themselves; they alone know how strong the chains need to be.[63]

Courage

PAGANISM DECLARED THAT virtue was in a balance; Christianity declared it was in a conflict; the collision of two passions apparently opposite. Of course they were not really inconsistent; but they were such that it was hard to hold [both] simultaneously. Let us . . . take the case of courage. No quality has ever so much addled the brains and tangled the definitions of merely rational sages. Courage is almost a contradiction in terms. It means a strong desire to live taking the form of a readiness to die. "He that will lose his life, the same shall save it," is not a piece of mysticism for saints and heroes. It is a piece of everyday advice for sailors or mountaineers.[64]

Creation

WHAT CHRISTIANITY SAYS is merely this. That this repetition in Nature has its origin not in a thing resembling a law but a thing resembling a will. . . . Christianity holds that the world and its repetition came by will or Love as children begotten by a father, and therefore that other and different things might come by it.[65]

Creeds

BUT, ODDLY ENOUGH, there really is a sense in which a creed, if it is believed at all, can be believed more fixedly in a complex society than in a simple one. If a man finds Christianity true in Birmingham, he has actually clearer reasons for faith than if he had found it true in Mercia. For the more complicated seems the coincidence, the less it can be a coincidence. If snowflakes fell in the shape, say, of the heart of Midlothian, it might be an accident. But if snow-flakes fell in the exact shape of the maze at Hampton Court, I think one might call it a miracle. It is exactly as of such a miracle that I have since come to feel of the philosophy of Christianity. The complication of our modern world proves the truth of the creed more perfectly than any of the plain problems of the ages of faith. It was in Notting Hill and Battersea that I began to see that Christianity was true. This is why the faith has that elaboration of doctrines and details which so much distresses those who admire Christianity without believing in it. When once one believes in a creed, one is proud of its complexity, as scientists are proud of the complexity of science. It shows how rich it is in discoveries. If it is right at all, it is a compliment to say that it's elaborately right. A stick might fit a hole or a stone a hollow by accident. But a key and a lock are both complex. And if a key fits a lock, you know it is the right key.[66]

CRIMINOLOGY

IN A POPULAR magazine there is one of the usual articles about criminology; about whether wicked men could be made good if their heads were taken to pieces. As by far the wickedest men I know of are much too rich and powerful ever to submit to the process, the speculation leaves me cold.[67]

THE TROUBLE WITH most sociologists, criminologists, etc., is that while their knowledge of their own details is exhaustive and subtle, their knowledge of man and society, to which these are to be applied, is quite exceptionally superficial and silly. They know everything about biology, but almost nothing about life.[68]

CRITICS

CRITICS WERE ALMOST entirely complimentary to what they were pleased to call my brilliant paradoxes; *until* they discovered that I really meant what I said.[69]

BY A CURIOUS confusion, many modern critics have passed from the proposition that a masterpiece may be unpopular to the other proposition that unless it is unpopular it cannot be a masterpiece.[70]

WE OFTEN READ nowadays of the valour or audacity with which some rebel attacks a hoary tyranny or an antiquated superstition. There is not really any courage at all in attacking hoary or antiquated things, any more than in offering to fight one's grandmother. The really courageous man is he who defies tyrannies young as the morning and superstitions fresh as the first flowers.[71]

IT IS SOMETIMES curious to notice how a critic, possessing no little cultivation and fertility, will, in speaking of a work of art, let fall almost accidentally some apparently trivial comment, which reveals to us with an instantaneous and complete mental illumination the fact that he does not, so far as that work of art is concerned, in the smallest degree understand what he is talking about. He may have intended to correct merely some minute detail of the work he is studying, but that single movement is enough to blow him and all his diplomas into the air.[72]

The Cross

TURNBULL GLANCED AT the crucifix with a sort of scowling good-humour and then said: "He may look and see His cross defeated."

"The cross cannot be defeated," said MacIan, "for it is Defeat."[73]

Culture

THE TRUE TASK of culture to-day is not a task of expansion, but very decidedly of selection and rejection.[74]

HOW MANY EXCELLENT thinkers have pointed out that political reform is useless until we produce a cultured populace.[75]

Cynicism

CYNICISM DENOTES THAT condition of mind in which we hold that life is in its nature mean and arid; that no soul contains genuine goodness, and no state of things genuine reliability.[76]

D

Darkness

WE HAVE IN our great cities abolished the clean and sane darkness of the country. We have outlawed Night and sent her wandering in wild meadows; we have lit eternal watch-fires against her return. We have made a new cosmos, and as a consequence our own sun and stars. And as a consequence also, and most justly, we have made our own darkness. Just as every lamp is a warm human moon, so every fog is a rich human nightfall. If it were not for this mystic accident we should never see darkness: and he who has never seen darkness has never seen the sun.[1]

Darwin, Charles

DARWINISM CAN BE used to back up two mad moralities, but it cannot be used to back up a single sane one. The kinship and competition of all living creatures can be used as a reason for being insanely cruel or insanely sentimental; but not for a healthy love of animals. On the evolutionary basis you may be inhumane, or you may be absurdly humane; but you cannot be human. That you and a tiger are one may be a reason for being tender to a tiger. Or it may be a reason for being as cruel as the tiger. It is one way to train the tiger to imitate you, it is a shorter way to imitate the tiger. But in neither case does evolution tell you how to treat a tiger reasonably, that is, to admire his stripes while avoiding his claws.[2]

ON THE ONE hand Darwin, especially through the strong journalistic genius of Huxley, had won a very wide spread though an exceedingly vague victory. I do not mean that Darwin's own doctrine was vague; his was merely one particular hypothesis about how animal variety might have arisen; and that particular hypothesis, though it will always be interesting, is now very much the reverse of secure.[3]

I WISH, INDEED, that in such a rude summary as this, I had space to do justice to Huxley as a literary man and a moralist. He had a live taste and talent for the English tongue, which he devoted to the task of keeping Victorian rationalism rational. He did not succeed. As so often happens when a rather unhealthy doubt is in the atmosphere, the strongest words of their great captain could not keep the growing crowds of agnostics back from the most hopeless and inhuman extremes of destructive thought. Nonsense not yet quite dead about the folly of allowing the unfit to survive began to be more and more wildly whispered. Such helpless specimens of "advanced thought" are, of course, quite as inconsistent with Darwinism as they are with democracy or with any other intelligent proposition ever offered.[4]

BUT THESE UNINTELLIGENT propositions were offered; and the ultimate result was this rather important one: that the harshness of Utilitarianism began to turn into downright tyranny. That beautiful faith in human nature and in freedom which had made delicate the dry air of John Stuart Mill; that robust, romantic sense of justice which had redeemed even the injustices of Macaulay— all that seemed slowly and sadly to be drying up. Under the shock of Darwinism all that was good in the Victorian rationalism shook and dissolved like dust. All that was bad in it abode and clung like clay. The magnificent emancipation evaporated; the mean calculation remained. One could still calculate in clear statistical tables, how many men lived, how many men died. One must not ask how they lived; for that is politics. One must not ask how they died; for that is religion. And religion and politics were ruled out of all the Later Victorian debating clubs; even including the debating club at Westminster.[5]

IN ANY CASE it is clear that a change had begun to pass over scientific inquiry, of which we have seen the culmination in our own day. There had begun that easy automatic habit, of science as an oiled and smooth-running machine, that habit of treating things as obviously unquestionable, when, indeed, they are obviously questionable. This began with vaccination in the Early Victorian Age; it extended to the early licence of vivisection in its later age; it has found a sort of fitting foolscap, or crown of crime and folly, in the thing called Eugenics. In all three cases the point was not so much that the pioneers had not proved their case; it was rather that, by an unexpressed rule of respectability, they were not required to prove it. This rather abrupt twist of the rationalistic mind in the direction of arbitrary power, certainly weakened the Liberal movement from within. And meanwhile it was being weakened by heavy blows from without.[6]

Debate

GENUINE CONTROVERSY, FAIR cut and thrust before a common audience, has become in our special epoch very rare. For the sincere controversialist is above all things a good listener. The really burning enthusiast never interrupts; he listens to the enemy's arguments as eagerly as a spy would listen to the enemy's arrangements.[7]

Decision and indecision

BUT WHATEVER BE the truth about exceptional intelligence and the masses, it is manifestly most unreasonable that intelligent men should be divided upon the absurd modern principle of regarding every clever man who cannot make up his mind as an impartial judge, and regarding every clever man who can make up his mind as a servile fanatic. As it is, we seem to regard it as a positive objection to a reasoner that he has taken one side or the other. We regard it (in other words) as a positive objection to a reasoner that he has contrived to reach the object of his reasoning. We call a man a bigot or a slave of dogma because he is a thinker who has thought thoroughly and to a definite end. We say that the juryman is not a juryman because he has brought in a verdict. We say that the judge is not a judge because he gives judgment. We say that the sincere believer has no right to vote, simply because he has voted.[8]

IF WE WALK down the street, taking all the jurymen who have not formed opinions and leaving all the jurymen who have formed opinions, it seems highly probable that we shall only succeed in taking all the stupid jurymen and leaving all the thoughtful ones.[9]

DEMOCRACY

NOTHING SO MUCH threatens the safety of democracy as assuming that democracy is safe. And that is another version of the same arrogant error; that, because you and I are democrats (if we are) we assume that all thinking people of all schools of thought must believe in democracy. If we go on assuming it much longer, there will be nobody left who does believe in democracy.[10]

I HAVE FIRST to say, therefore, that if I have had a bias, it was always a bias in favour of democracy, and therefore of tradition. . . . I have always been more inclined to believe the ruck of hardworking people than to believe that special and troublesome literary class to which I belong.[11]

I WAS BROUGHT up a Liberal, and have always believed in democracy, in the elementary liberal doctrine of a self-governing humanity.[12]

BUT THERE IS one thing that I have never from my youth up been able to understand. I have never been able to understand where people got the idea that democracy was in some way opposed to tradition. It is obvious that tradition is only democracy extended through time.[13]

THE OLD DEMOCRATIC doctrine was that the more light that was let in to all departments of State, the easier it was for a righteous indignation to move promptly against wrong. In other words, monarchs were to live in glass houses, that mobs might throw stones. Again, no admirer of existing English politics (if there is any admirer of existing English politics) will really pretend that this ideal of publicity is exhausted, or even attempted. Obviously public life grows more private every day.[14]

NOW, ONE MAY believe in democracy or disbelieve in it. It would be grossly unfair to conceal the fact that there are difficulties on both sides. The difficulty of believing in democracy is that it is so hard to believe—like God and most other good things. The difficulty of disbelieving in democracy is that there is nothing else to believe in. I mean there is nothing else on earth or in earthly politics. Unless an aristocracy is selected by gods, it must be selected by men. It may be negatively and passively permitted, but either heaven or humanity must permit it; otherwise it has no more moral authority than a lucky pickpocket. It is baby talk to talk about "Superman" or "Nature's Aristocracy" or "The Wise Few." "The Wise Few" must be either those whom others think wise who are often fools; or those who think themselves wise who are always fools.[15]

NOW PEOPLE TALK of democracy as being coarse and turbulent: it is a self-evident error in mere history. Aristocracy is the thing that is always coarse and turbulent: for it means appealing to the self-confident people. Democracy means appealing to the different people. Democracy means getting those people to vote who would never have the cheek to govern: and (according to Christian ethics) the precise people who ought to govern are the people who have not the cheek to do it.[16]

THE PRINCIPLE OF democracy, as I mean it, can be stated in two propositions. The first is this: that the things common to all men are more important than the things peculiar to any men.[17]

"THE OLD IDEALISTIC republicans used to found democracy on the idea that all men were equally intelligent. Believe me, the sane and enduring democracy is founded on the fact that all men are equally idiotic."[18]

THE OLD GENTLEMAN opened his eyes with some surprise.
   "Are you, then," he said, "no longer a democracy in England?"
   Barker laughed.
   "The situation invites paradox," he said. "We are, in a sense, the purest democracy. We have become a despotism. Have you not noticed how continually in history democracy becomes despotism? People call it the decay of democracy. It is simply its fulfilment."[19]

DEMOCRATS

IF YOU ARE a democrat who likes to be an honest man ... you want to know what the people want and not merely what you can somehow induce them to ask for.[20]

DERISION AND IRONY

TO BATTER THE worldly castle with the artillery of open derision is a much swifter task than to blow it up from within with one carefully constructed bomb of irony.[21]

Despotism (the subtle origins of)

IT IS WHEN men begin to grow desperate in their love for the people, when they are overwhelmed with the difficulties and blunders of humanity, that they fall back upon a wild desire to manage everything themselves. Their faith in themselves is only a disillusionment with mankind. They are in that most dreadful position, dreadful alike in personal and public affairs—the position of the man who has lost faith and not lost love. This belief that all would go right if we could only get the strings into our own hands is a fallacy almost without exception, but nobody can justly say that it is not public-spirited. The sin and sorrow of despotism is not that it does not love men, but that it loves them too much and trusts them too little.[22]

Detective stories

THERE IS, HOWEVER, another good work that is done by detective stories. While it is the constant tendency of the Old Adam to rebel against so universal and automatic a thing as civilisation, to preach departure and rebellion, the romance of police activity keeps in some sense before the mind the fact that civilisation itself is the most sensational of departures and the most romantic of rebellions. By dealing with the unsleeping sentinels who guard the outposts of society, it tends to remind us that we live in an armed camp, making war with a chaotic world.[23]

THE CHIEF DIFFICULTY is that the detective story is, after all, a drama of masks and not of faces. It depends on men's false characters rather than their real characters. The author cannot tell us until the last chapter any of the most interesting things about the most interesting people. It is a masquerade ball in which everybody is disguised as somebody else, and there is no true personal interest until the clock strikes twelve. That is, as I have said, we cannot really get at the psychology and philosophy, the morals and the religion, of the thing until we have read the last chapter. Therefore, I think it is best of all when the first chapter is also the last chapter.[24]

Determinism (scientific fatalism)

I FOUND THE whole modern world talking scientific fatalism; saying that everything is as it must always have been, being unfolded without fault from the beginning. The leaf on the tree is green because it could never have been anything else. Now, the fairy-tale philosopher is glad that the leaf is green precisely because it might have been scarlet. He feels as if it had turned green an instant before he looked at it. He is pleased that snow is white on the strictly reasonable ground that it might have been black. Every colour has in it a bold quality as of choice; the red of garden roses is not only decisive but dramatic, like suddenly spilt blood. He feels that something has been *done*. But the great determinists of the nineteenth century were strongly against this native feeling that something had happened an instant before. In fact, according to them, nothing ever really had happened since the beginning of the world. Nothing ever had happened since existence had happened; and even about the date of that they were not very sure.[25]

Dickens, Charles

THE RISE OF Dickens is like the rising of a vast mob. This is not only because his tales are indeed as crowded and populous as towns: for truly it was not so much that Dickens appeared as that a hundred Dickens characters appeared. It is also because he was the sort of man who has the impersonal impetus of a mob: what Poe meant when he truly said that popular rumour, if really spontaneous, was like the intuition of the individual man of genius.[26]

BUT WE HAVE a long way to travel before we get back to what Dickens meant: and the passage is along a rambling English road, a twisting road such as Mr. Pickwick travelled. But this at least is part of what he meant; that comradeship and serious joy are not interludes in our travel; but that rather our travels are interludes in comradeship and joy, which through God shall endure for ever. The inn does not point to the road; the road points to the inn. And all roads point at last to an ultimate inn, where we shall meet Dickens and all his characters: and when we drink again it shall be from the great flagons in the tavern at the end of the world.[27]

"SIR," I ANSWERED, "there are certain writers to whom humanity owes much, whose talent is yet of so shy or delicate or retrospective a type that we do well to link it with certain quaint places or certain perishing associations. It would not be unnatural to look for the spirit of Horace Walpole at Strawberry Hill, or even for the shade of Thackeray in Old Kensington. But let us have no antiquarianism about Dickens, for Dickens is not an antiquity. Dickens looks not backward, but forward; he might look at our modern mobs with satire, or with fury, but he would love to look at them. He might lash our democracy, but it would be because, like a democrat, he asked much from it. We will not have all his books bound up under the title of *The Old Curiosity Shop*. Rather we will have them all bound up under the title of *Great Expectations*. Wherever humanity is he would have us face it and make something of it."[28]

HIS THIRST WAS for things as humble, as human, as laughable as that daily bread for which we cry to God. He had no particular plan of reform; or, when he had, it was startlingly petty and parochial compared with the deep, confused clamour of comradeship and insurrection that fills all his narrative.[29]

DICKENS DID NOT merely believe in the brotherhood of men in the weak modern way; he was the brotherhood of men, and knew it was a brotherhood in sin as well as in aspiration.[30]

THIS IS THE artistic greatness of Dickens, before and after which there is really nothing to be said. He had the power of creating people, both possible and impossible, who were simply precious and priceless people; and anything subtler added to that truth really only weakens it.[31]

SMOLLETT WAS COARSE; but Smollett was also cruel. Dickens was frequently horrible; he was never cruel. The art of Dickens was the most exquisite of arts: it was the art of enjoying everybody. Dickens, being a very human writer, had to be a very human being; he had his faults and sensibilities in a strong degree; and I do not for a moment maintain that he enjoyed everybody in his daily life. But he enjoyed everybody in his books: and everybody has enjoyed everybody in those books even till to-day. His books are full of baffled villains stalking out or cowardly bullies kicked downstairs. But the villains and the cowards are such delightful people that the reader always hopes the villain will put his head through a side window and make a last remark; or that the bully will say one thing more, even from the bottom of the stairs.[32]

DICKENS (UNLIKE THE social reformers) really did sympathise with every sort of victim of every sort of tyrant. He did truly pray for all who are desolate and oppressed. If you try to tie him to any cause narrower than that Prayer Book definition, you will find you have shut out half his best work.[33]

IN EVERYDAY TALK, or in any of our journals, we may find the loose but important phrase, "Why have we no great men to-day? Why have we no great men like Thackeray, or Carlyle, or Dickens?" Do not let us dismiss this expression, because it appears loose or arbitrary. "Great" does mean something, and the test of its actuality is to be found by noting how instinctively and decisively we do apply it to some men and not to others; above all, how instinctively and decisively we do apply it to four or five men in the Victorian era, four or five men of whom Dickens was not the least. The term is found to fit a definite thing. Whatever the word "great" means, Dickens was what it means.[34]

THE TIME WILL come when the wildest upheaval of Zolaism, when the most abrupt and colloquial dialogue of Norwegian drama, will appear a fine old piece of charming affectation, a stilted minuet of literature, like little Nell in the churchyard, or the repentance of the white-haired Dombey. All their catchwords will have become catchwords; the professor's explanations of heredity will have the mellow, foolish sound of the villain's curses against destiny. And in that time men will for the first time become aware of the real truth and magnificence of Zola and Ibsen, just as we, if we are wise, are now becoming aware of the real truth and magnificence of Dickens.[35]

DIGNITY

BABIES ARE NOT always strong on the point of dignity, and grown-up men are quite unpresentable.[36]

DIPLOMATS

IT IS ONE of the tragedies of the diplomat that they are not allowed to admit either knowledge or ignorance.[37]

MANY MODERN INTERNATIONALISTS talk as if men of different nationalities had only to meet and mix and understand each other.[38]

DISCERNMENT

IT IS ALWAYS easy to let the age have its head; the difficult thing is to keep one's own.[39]

FALLACIES DO NOT cease to be fallacies because they become fashions.[40]

WHEN THE BUSINESS man rebukes the idealism of his office-boy, it is commonly in some such speech as this: "Ah, yes, when one is young, one has these ideals in the abstract and these castles in the air; but in middle age they all break up like clouds, and one comes down to a belief in practical politics, to using the machinery one has and getting on with the world as it is." Thus, at least, venerable and philanthropic old men now in their honoured graves used to talk to me when I was a boy. But since then I have grown up and have discovered that these philanthropic old men were telling lies. What has really happened is exactly the opposite of what they said would happen. They said that I should lose my ideals and begin to believe in the methods of practical politicians. Now, I have not lost my ideals in the least; my faith in fundamentals is exactly what it always was. What I have lost is my old childlike faith in practical politics. I am still as much concerned as ever about the Battle of Armageddon; but I am not so much concerned about the General Election.[41]

DISGUISE

[SYME] FELT A curious freedom and naturalness in his movements as the blue and gold garment fell about him; and when he found that he had to wear a sword, it stirred a boyish dream. As he passed out of the room he flung the folds across his shoulder with a gesture, his sword stood out at an angle, and he had all the swagger of a troubadour. For these disguises did not disguise, but reveal.[42]

THEY WERE LED out of another broad and low gateway into a very large old English garden, full of torches and bonfires, by the broken light of which a vast carnival of people were dancing in motley dress. Syme seemed to see every shape in Nature imitated in some crazy costume. There was a man dressed as a windmill with enormous sails, a man dressed as an elephant, a man dressed as a balloon; the two last, together, seemed to keep the thread of their farcical adventures. Syme even saw, with a queer thrill, one dancer dressed like an enormous hornbill, with a beak twice as big as himself—the queer bird which had fixed itself on his fancy like a living question while he was rushing down the long road at the Zoological Gardens. There were a thousand other such objects, however. There was a dancing lamp-post, a dancing apple tree, a dancing ship. One would have thought that the untamable tune of some mad musician had set all the common objects of field and street dancing an eternal jig. And long afterwards, when Syme was middle-aged and at rest, he could never see one of those particular objects—a lamppost, or an apple tree, or a windmill—without thinking that it was a strayed reveller from that revel of masquerade.[43]

Dogmas

LET US, AT least, dig and seek till we have discovered our own opinions. The dogmas we really hold are far more fantastic, and, perhaps, far more beautiful than we think.[44]

DOGMAS ARE OFTEN spoken of as if they were signs of the slowness or endurance of the human mind. As a matter of fact, they are marks of mental promptitude and lucid impatience. A man will put his meaning mystically because he cannot waste time in putting it rationally. Dogmas are not dark and mysterious; rather a dogma is like a flash of lightning—an instantaneous lucidity that opens across a whole landscape.[45]

IT IS QUAINT that people talk of separating dogma from education. Dogma is actually the only thing that cannot be separated from education. It *is* education. A teacher who is not dogmatic is simply a teacher who is not teaching.[46]

THERE ARE TWO kinds of people in the world, the conscious dogmatists and the unconscious dogmatists. I have always found myself that the unconscious dogmatists were by far the most dogmatic.[47]

SUDDENLY HE PULLED himself upright.

"Don't you really think the sacred Notting Hill at all absurd?"

"Absurd?" asked Wayne, blankly. "Why should I?"

The King stared back equally blankly.

"I beg your pardon," he said.

"Notting Hill," said the Provost, simply, "is a rise or high ground of the common earth, on which men have built houses to live, in which they are born, fall in love, pray, marry, and die. Why should I think it absurd?"

The King smiled.

"Because, my Leonidas—" he began, then suddenly, he knew not how, found his mind was a total blank. After all, why was it absurd? Why was it absurd? He felt as if the floor of his mind had given way. He felt as all men feel when their first principles are hit hard with a question.[48]

DOMESTIC AFFAIRS

MEN DO NOT now, any more than then [medieval times], become sinless by receiving a post in a bureaucracy; and if the domestic affairs of the poor were once put into the hands of mere lawyers and inspectors, the poor would soon find themselves in positions from which there is no exit save by the sword of Virginius and the hammer of Wat Tyler.[49]

DREAMS

Far from your sunny uplands set
I saw the dream; the streets I trod
The lit straight streets shot out and met
The starry streets that point to God.
This legend of an epic hour
A child I dreamed, and dream it still,
Under the great grey water-tower
That strikes the stars on Campden Hill.[50]

E

Ease

EASE IS THE worst enemy of happiness and civilisation, potentially the end of man.[1]

Eccentricity

TO ASK SOLELY for strange experiences of the soul is simply to let loose all the imbecile asylums about one's ears.[2]

TO ADVERTISE FOR exceptions is simply to advertise for egoists. To advertise for egoists is to advertise for idiots.[3]

Education

WITHOUT EDUCATION, WE are in a horrible and deadly danger of taking educated people seriously.[4]

FOR MY PART, I should be inclined to suggest that the chief object of education should be to restore simplicity. If you like to put it so, the chief object of education is not to learn things; nay, the chief object of education is to unlearn things. The chief object of education is to unlearn all the weariness and wickedness of the world and to get back into that state of exhilaration we all instinctively celebrate when we write by preference of children and of boys. If I were an examiner appointed to examine all examiners (which does not at present appear probable), I would not only ask the teachers how much knowledge they had imparted; I would ask them how much splendid and scornful ignorance they had erected, like some royal tower in arms. But, in any case, I would insist that people should have so much simplicity as would enable them to see things suddenly and to see things as they are.[5]

DURING THE PERIOD of what is commonly called education . . . I was being instructed by somebody I did not know, about something I did not want to know.[6]

EFFICIENCY

"EFFICIENCY," OF COURSE, is futile for the same reason that strong men, will-power and the superman are futile. That is, it is futile because it only deals with actions after they have been performed. It has no philosophy for incidents before they happen; therefore it has no power of choice.[7]

THIS ELDER LITERATURE

THE MODERNS, IN a word, describe life in short stories because they are possessed with the sentiment that life itself is an uncommonly short story, and perhaps not a true one. But in this elder literature, even in the comic literature (indeed, especially in the comic literature) the reverse is true. The characters are felt to be fixed things of which we have fleeting glimpses; that is, they are felt to be divine. Uncle Toby is talking for ever, as the elves are dancing for ever. We feel that whenever we hammer on the house of Falstaff, Falstaff will be at home. We feel it as a pagan would feel that, if a cry broke the silence after ages of unbelief, Apollo would still be listening in his temple.[8]

Elections

THE MAJORITY OF refined persons in our day may generally be heard abusing the practice of canvassing. In the same way the majority of refined persons (commonly the same refined persons) may be heard abusing the practice of interviewing celebrities. It seems a very singular thing to me that this refined world reserves all its indignation for the comparatively open and innocent element in both walks of life. There is really a vast amount of corruption and hypocrisy in our election politics; about the most honest thing in the whole mess is the canvassing. A man has not got a right to "nurse" a constituency with aggressive charities, to buy it with great presents of parks and libraries, to open vague vistas of future benevolence; all this, which goes on unrebuked, is bribery and nothing else.[9]

Eliot, George

I BEGIN WITH this great woman of letters for both the two reasons already mentioned. She represents the rationalism of the old Victorian Age at its highest. She and Mill are like two great mountains at the end of that long, hard chain which is the watershed of the Early Victorian time. They alone rise high enough to be confused among the clouds or perhaps confused among the stars. They certainly were seeking truth, as Newman and Carlyle were; the slow slope of the later Victorian vulgarity does not lower their precipice and pinnacle.[10]

THE STRENGTH AND subtlety of woman had certainly sunk deep into English letters when George Eliot began to write.[11]

IF LITERATURE MEANS anything more than a cold calculation of the chances, if there is in it, as I believe, any deeper idea of detaching the spirit of life from the dull obstacles of life, of permitting human nature really to reveal itself as human, if (to put it shortly) literature has anything on earth to do with being interesting then I think we would rather have a few more Marners than that rich maturity that gave us the analysed dust-heaps of *Daniel Deronda*.[12]

EMPIRE

"WHAT IS THIS, my people?" he said. "Is it altogether impossible to make a thing good without it immediately insisting on being wicked? The glory of Notting Hill in having achieved its independence, has been enough for me to dream of for many years, as I sat beside the fire. Is it really not enough for you, who have had so many other affairs to excite and distract you? Notting Hill is a nation. Why should it condescend to be a mere Empire?"[13]

ENGLAND

BUT WHEN, AFTER only a month's travelling, I did come back to England, I was startled to find that . . . England did break on me at once beautifully new and beautifully old. To land at Dover is the right way to approach England (most things that are hackneyed are right), for then you see first the full, soft gardens of Kent.[14]

IF I AM exiled from England I will go and live on an island somewhere and be as jolly as I can. I will not become a patriot of any other land.[15]

IT IS NEITHER blood nor rain that has made England, but hope— the thing all those dead men have desired. France was not France because she was made to be by the skulls of the Celts or by the sun of Gaul. France was France because she chose.[16]

AND YET HOWEVER high they went, the desert still blossomed like the rose. The fields were burnished in sun and wind with the colour of kingfisher and parrot and humming-bird; the hues of a hundred flowering flowers. There are no lovelier meadows and woodlands than the English; no nobler crests or chasms than those of Snowdon and Glencoe. But Ethel Harrogate had never before seen the southern parks tilted on the splintered northern peaks; the gorge of Glencoe laden with the fruits of Kent. There was nothing here of that chill and desolation that in Britain one associates with high and wild scenery. It was rather like a mosaic palace, rent with earthquakes.[17]

ENIGMA

"THERE ARE, AFTER all, enigmas," he said, "even to the man who has faith. There are doubts that remain even after the true philosophy is completed in every rung and rivet. And here is one of them. Is the normal human need, the normal human condition, higher or lower than those special states of the soul which call out a doubtful and dangerous glory? those special powers of knowledge or sacrifice which are made possible only by the existence of evil? Which should come first to our affections, the enduring sanities of peace or the half-maniacal virtues of battle? Which should come first, the man great in the daily round or the man great in emergency?"[18]

EQUALITY

EQUALITY IS NOT some crude fairy tale about all men being equally tall or equally tricky; which we not only cannot believe but cannot believe in anybody believing. It is an absolute of morals by which all men have a value invariable and indestructible and a dignity as intangible as death.[19]

Eternity

IF SEEDS IN the black earth can turn into such beautiful roses, what might not the heart of man become in its long journey towards the stars?[20]

Eternity of Joy

IT IS ABSURD indeed that Christians should be called the enemies of life because they wish life to last for ever; it is more absurd still to call the old comic writers dull because they wished their unchanging characters to last for ever. Both popular religion with its endless joys, and the old comic story, with its endless jokes, have in our time faded together. We are too weak to desire that undying vigour. We believe that you can have too much of a good thing—a blasphemous belief, which at one blow wrecks all the heavens that men have hoped for. The grand old defiers of God were not afraid of an eternity of torment. We have come to be afraid of an eternity of joy.[21]

Eugenics

THE EUGENIC PROFESSOR may or may not succeed in choosing a baby's parents; it is quite certain that he cannot succeed in choosing his own parents. All his thoughts, including his Eugenic thoughts, are, by the very principle of those thoughts, flowing from a doubtful or tainted source. In short, we should need a perfectly Wise Man to do the thing at all. And if he were a Wise Man he would not do it.[22]

IN PRACTICE NO one is mad enough to legislate or educate upon dogmas of physical inheritance; and even the language of the thing is rarely used except for special modern purposes, such as the endowment of research or the oppression of the poor.[23]

Evil

MEN MAY KEEP a sort of level of good, but no man has ever been able to keep on one level of evil.[24]

Exhilaration

EXHILARATION CAN BE infinite, like sorrow; a joke can be so big that it breaks the roof of the stars. By simply going on being absurd, a thing can become godlike; there is but one step from the ridiculous to the sublime.[25]

F

Failure

BUT I DO not believe that a nation dies save by suicide. To the very last every problem is a problem of will; and if we will we can be whole. But it involves facing our own failures as well as counting our successes.[1]

Fairy tales

THE OLD FABLES of mankind, are, indeed, unfathomably wise.[2]

FAIRY TALES, THEN, are not responsible for producing in children fear, or any of the shapes of fear; fairy tales do not give the child the idea of the evil or the ugly; that is in the child already, because it is in the world already. Fairy tales do not give the child his first idea of bogey. What fairy tales give the child is his first clear idea of the possible defeat of bogey. The baby has known the dragon intimately ever since he had an imagination. What the fairy tale provides for him is a St. George to kill the dragon.

Exactly what the fairy tale does is this: it accustoms him for a series of clear pictures to the idea that these limitless terrors had a limit, that these shapeless enemies have enemies in the knights of God, that there is something in the universe more mystical than darkness, and stronger than strong fear.[3]

IN THE FAIRY tale an incomprehensible happiness rests upon an incomprehensible condition. A box is opened, and all evils fly out.

A word is forgotten, and cities perish. A lamp is lit, and love flies away. A flower is plucked, and human lives are forfeited. An apple is eaten, and the hope of God is gone.[4]

FOR THIS THIN glitter of glass everywhere is the expression of the fact that the happiness is bright but brittle, like the substance most easily smashed by a housemaid or a cat. And this fairy-tale sentiment also sank into me and became my sentiment towards the whole world. I felt and feel that life itself is as bright as the diamond, but as brittle as the window-pane; and when the heavens were compared to the terrible crystal I can remember a shudder. I was afraid that God would drop the cosmos with a crash.

Remember, however, that to be breakable is not the same as to be perishable. Strike a glass, and it will not endure an instant; simply do not strike it, and it will endure a thousand years. Such, it seemed, was the joy of man, either in elfland or on earth.[5]

WELL, I LEFT the fairy tales lying on the floor of the nursery, and I have not found any books so sensible since. I left the nurse guardian of tradition and democracy, and I have not found any modern type so sanely radical or so sanely conservative. But the matter for important comment was here: that when I first went out into the mental atmosphere of the modern world, I found that the modern world was positively opposed on two points to my nurse and to the nursery tales. It has taken me a long time to find out that the modern world is wrong and my nurse was right. The really curious thing was this: that modern thought contradicted this basic creed of my boyhood on its two most essential doctrines. I have explained that the fairy tales founded in me two convictions; first, that this world is a wild and startling place, which might have been quite different, but which is quite delightful; second, that before this wildness and delight one may well be modest and submit to the queerest limitations of so queer a kindness. But I found the whole

modern world running like a high tide against both my tendernesses; and the shock of that collision created two sudden and
spontaneous sentiments, which I have had ever since and which,
crude as they were, have since hardened into convictions.[6]

HERE [ON OUR road through fairyland] I am only trying to describe
the enormous emotions which cannot be described. And the strongest emotion was that life was as precious as it was puzzling. It was
an ecstasy because it was an adventure; it was an adventure because
it was an opportunity. The goodness of the fairy tale was not
affected by the fact that there might be more dragons than princesses; it was good to be in a fairy tale. The test of all happiness is
gratitude; and I felt grateful, though I hardly knew to whom.
Children are grateful when Santa Claus puts in their stockings
gifts of toys or sweets. Could I not be grateful to Santa Claus when
he put in my stockings the gift of two miraculous legs? We thank
people for birthday presents of cigars and slippers. Can I thank no
one for the birthday present of birth?[7]

BUT I DEAL here with what ethic and philosophy come from being
fed on fairy tales. If I were describing them in detail I could note
many noble and healthy principles that arise from them. There is
the chivalrous lesson of "Jack the Giant Killer"; that giants should
be killed because they are gigantic. It is a manly mutiny against
pride as such. For the rebel is older than all the kingdoms, and the
Jacobin has more tradition than the Jacobite. There is the lesson of
"Cinderella," which is the same as that of the Magnificat—*exaltavit
humiles*. There is the great lesson of "Beauty and the Beast"; that a
thing must be loved *before* it is loveable. There is the terrible allegory of the "Sleeping Beauty," which tells how the human creature
was blessed with all birthday gifts, yet cursed with death; and how
death also may perhaps be softened to a sleep. But I am not concerned with any of the separate statutes of elfland, but with the

whole spirit of its law, which I learnt before I could speak, and shall retain when I cannot write. I am concerned with a certain way of looking at life, which was created in me by the fairy tales, but has since been meekly ratified by the mere facts.[8]

AT THE FOUR corners of a child's bed stand Perseus and Roland, Sigurd and St. George. If you withdraw the guard of heroes you are not making him rational; you are only leaving him to fight the devils alone.[9]

MY FIRST AND last philosophy, that which I believe in with unbroken certainty, I learnt in the nursery. I generally learnt it from a nurse; that is, from the solemn and star-appointed priestess at once of democracy and tradition. The things I believed most then, the things I believe most now, are the things called fairy tales. They seem to me to be the entirely reasonable things. They are not fantasies; compared with them other things are fantastic. Compared with them religion is abnormally right and rationalism abnormally wrong. Fairyland is nothing but the sunny country of common-sense. It is not earth that judges heaven, but heaven that judges earth; so for me at least it was not earth that criticised elfland, but elfland that criticised the earth.[10]

"CAN YOU NOT see," I said, "that fairy tales in their essence are quite solid and straightforward; but that this everlasting fiction about modern life is in its nature essentially incredible? Folk-lore means that the soul is sane, but that the universe is wild and full of marvels. Realism means that the world is dull and full of routine, but that the soul is sick and screaming. The problem of the fairy tale is—what will a healthy man do with a fantastic world? The problem of the modern novel is—what will a madman do with a dull world? In the fairy tales the cosmos goes mad; but the hero does not go mad. In the modern novels the hero is mad before the book begins, and suffers from the harsh steadiness and cruel sanity of the cosmos."[11]

THE POPULAR PREFERENCE for a story with "a happy ending" is not, or at least was not, a mere sweet-stuff optimism; it is the remains of the old idea of the triumph of the dragon-slayer, the ultimate apotheosis of the man beloved of heaven.[12]

WE ARE OF such stature as we will. But the elves grow small, not large, when they would mix with mortals.[13]

DAUGHTER OF MEN, if you would see a fairy as he truly is, look for his head above all the stars and his feet amid the floors of the sea. Old women have taught you that the fairies are too small to be seen. But I tell you the fairies are too mighty to be seen. For they are the elder gods before whom the giants were like pigmies. They are the Elemental Spirits, and any one of them is larger than the world. And you look for them in acorns and on toadstools and wonder that you never see them.[14]

FAITH

FAITH IS ALWAYS at a disadvantage; it is a perpetually defeated thing which survives all its conquerors.[15]

> DOCTOR. I should never call this woman weak-minded—no, by God, not even if she went to church.
>
> SMITH. Yet there are many as strong-minded who believe passionately in going to church.
>
> DOCTOR. Weren't there as many who believed passionately in Apollo?
>
> SMITH. And what harm came of believing in Apollo? And what a mass of harm may have come of not believing in

Apollo? Does it never strike you that doubt can be a madness, as well as faith? That asking questions may be a disease, as well as proclaiming doctrines? You talk of religious mania! Is there no such thing as irreligious mania? Is there no such thing in the house at this moment?[16]

Faith and reason

IT IS IDLE to talk always of the alternative of reason and faith. Reason is itself a matter of faith. It is an act of faith to assert that our thoughts have any relation to reality at all.[17]

False doctrines

LIFE IS FULL of a ceaseless shower of small coincidences; too small to be worth mentioning except for a special purpose, often too trifling even to be noticed, any more than we notice one snowflake falling on another. It is this that lends a frightful plausibility to all false doctrines and evil fads. There are always such props of accidental arguments upon anything. If I said suddenly that historical truth is generally told by red-haired men, I have no doubt that ten minutes' reflection (in which I decline to indulge) would provide me with a handsome list of instances in support of it.[18]

False humility

A MAN WAS meant to be doubtful about himself, but undoubting about the truth: this has been exactly reversed. Nowadays the part of a man that a man does assert is exactly the part he ought not to assert—himself. The part he doubts is exactly the part he ought not to doubt—the Divine Reason. Huxley preached a humility content to learn from Nature. But the new sceptic is so humble that he doubts if he can even learn.[19]

The family

IF WE WISH to preserve the family we must revolutionize the nation.[20]

THE INSTITUTION OF the family is to be commended for precisely the same reasons that the institution of the nation, or the institution of the city, are in this matter to be commended. It is a good thing for a man to live in a family for the same reason that it is a good thing for a man to be besieged in a city. It is a good thing for a man to live in a family in the same sense that it is a beautiful and delightful thing for a man to be snowed up in a street. They all force him to realise that life is not a thing from outside, but a thing from inside. Above all, they all insist upon the fact that life, if it be a truly stimulating and fascinating life, is a thing which, of its nature, exists in spite of ourselves.[21]

THE MODERN WRITERS who have suggested, in a more or less open manner, that the family is a bad institution, have generally confined themselves to suggesting, with much sharpness, bitterness, or pathos, that perhaps the family is not always very congenial. Of course the family is a good institution because it is uncongenial. It is wholesome precisely because it contains so many divergencies and varieties. It is, as the sentimentalists say, like a little kingdom, and, like most other little kingdoms, is generally in a state of something resembling anarchy.[22]

Farce

THE CASE OF farce, and its wilder embodiment in harlequinade, is especially important. That these high and legitimate forms of art, glorified by Aristophanes and Molière, have sunk into such contempt may be due to many causes: I myself have little doubt that it is due to the astonishing and ludicrous lack of belief in hope and hilarity which marks modern aesthetics.[23]

AND OF ALL the varied forms of the literature of joy, the form most truly worthy of moral reverence and artistic ambition is the form called "farce"—or its wilder shape in pantomime. To the quietest human being, seated in the quietest house, there will sometimes come a sudden and unmeaning hunger for the possibilities or impossibilities of things; he will abruptly wonder whether the teapot may not suddenly begin to pour out honey or sea-water, the clock to point to all hours of the day at once, the candle to burn green or crimson, the door to open upon a lake or a potato-field instead of a London street. Upon anyone who feels this nameless anarchism there rests for the time being the abiding spirit of pantomime.[24]

FATE

I DO NOT believe in a fate that falls on men however they act; but I do believe in a fate that falls on them unless they act.[25]

FATHER BROWN

THERE WAS A short railway official travelling up to the terminus, three fairly short market gardeners picked up two stations afterwards, one very short widow lady going up from a small Essex town, and a very short Roman Catholic priest [Father Brown] going up from a small Essex village. When it came to the last case, Valentin gave it up and almost laughed. The little priest was so much the essence of those Eastern flats; he had a face as round and dull as a Norfolk dumpling.[26]

THE DOOR OPENED inwards and there shambled into the room a shapeless little figure, which seemed to find its own hat and umbrella as unmanageable as a mass of luggage. The umbrella was a black and prosaic bundle long past repair, the hat was a broad-curved black hat, clerical but not common in England, the man was the very embodiment of all that is homely and helpless.[27]

THE FACE OF the little Catholic priest, which was commonly complacent and even comic, had suddenly become knotted with a curious frown. It was not the blank curiosity of his first innocence. It was rather that creative curiosity which comes when a man has the beginnings of an idea.[28]

"ONE IS NEVER thinking of the real sorrow," said the strange priest. "One can only be kind when it comes."[29]

FATHER BROWN LAID down his cigar and said carefully: "It isn't that they can't see the solution. It is that they can't see the problem."[30]

HE HAD THE notion that because I am a clergyman I should believe anything. Many people have little notions of that kind.[31]

THE FATHER OF FATHER BROWN
Chesterton as a Mystery Writer

On July 23, 1910, a mystery story appeared in the pages of the *Saturday Evening Post*—the widely popular periodical—which was, so its cover page proclaimed, founded by Benjamin Franklin in 1728.[1]

Sir Arthur Conan Doyle was still living at this time, but the mystery story published in the *Post* differed widely from any tale of Sherlock Holmes. One could even say that this new mystery story was highly unique. The master detective it introduced, a short, dumpling-faced cleric named Father Brown, was as wont to delve into matters of metaphysics as he was the minutia of forensic analysis. Self-deprecating humor and a searching, sympathetic knowledge of humanity were other distinguishing hallmarks of this story, as they were of all the stories of Father Brown that were to follow from the endlessly inventive pen of G. K. Chesterton. In all, he would write some fifty-two Father Brown stories.[2]

These stories met at once with a great and enduring popularity. They are, in fact, one of the reasons that Chesterton's name prompts a ready flicker of recognition today. Collected stories of Father Brown have continually remained in print and are avidly read. *The Penguin Complete Father Brown* appeared in 1984, and in 2005, the Modern Library published its collection entitled *Father Brown: The Essential Tales*. In the introduction to this edition, mystery novelist P. D. James wrote: "We read the Father Brown stories for a variety of pleasures, including their ingenuity, their wit and intelligence, and for the brilliance of the writing. But they provide more. Chesterton was concerned with the greatest of all problems, the vagaries of the human heart."

Chesterton's searching knowledge of the human heart, and the compelling ways in which it infused the character of Father Brown, had an unlikely result: it famously proved a catalyst for Sir Alec Guinness's embrace of Catholicism. While on location in Burgundy for the starring role in the 1954 British motion picture *Father Brown* (released later in America as *The Detective*), Guinness had a chance meeting that stirred him profoundly. It was a story he later recounted in his autobiography, *Blessings in Disguise*. Returning to his hotel one evening, still in wardrobe as Father Brown, Guinness met a young boy. As he recalled:

I hadn't gone far when I heard scampering footsteps and a piping voice calling, "Mon père!" My hand was seized by a boy of seven or eight, who clutched it tightly, swung it and kept up a non-stop prattle. He was full of excitement, hops, skips and jumps, but never let go of me. I didn't dare speak in case my excruciating French should scare him. Although I was a total stranger he obviously took me for a priest and so to be trusted. Suddenly with a "Bonsoir, Mon père," and a hurried sideways sort of bow, he disappeared through a hole in a hedge. He had had a happy, reassuring walk home, and I was left with an odd calm sense of elation. Continuing my walk I reflected that a Church which could inspire such a con-fidence in a child, making its priests, even when unknown, so easily approachable could not be as scheming and creepy as so often made out. I began to shake off my long-taught, long-absorbed prejudices.[3]

More recently, Father Brown stories in the public domain have begun to be read and recorded for Naxos Audio Books in brilliant performances by the acclaimed British actor David Timson (famous for his readings of the Sherlock Holmes mys-teries).[4] At this remove, one thing seems certain: the Father Brown mysteries have retained their perennial appeal and seem destined to live on for many years to come. And that, no doubt, would please their author immensely—a man who delved deeply into the mysteries of life, and the mysteries of the life to come.

FIELDING, HENRY

THE TWO HUNDREDTH anniversary of Henry Fielding is very justly celebrated, even if, as far as can be discovered, it is only cele-brated by the newspapers. It would be too much to expect that any such merely chronological incident should induce the people who write about Fielding to read him; this kind of neglect is only another name for glory. A great classic means a man whom one can praise without having read.[32]

Fighting what you fear

FIGHT THE THING that you fear. You remember the old tale of the English clergyman who gave the last rites to the brigand of Sicily, and how on his death-bed the great robber said, "I can give you no money, but I can give you advice for a lifetime: your thumb on the blade, and strike upwards."[33]

Finishing well

O well for him that loves the sun,
That sees the heaven-race ridden or run,
The splashing seas of sunset won,
And shouts for victory.[34]

Fireworks

IN THE FROSTY grey of winter twilight there comes a crackle and spurt of bluish fire; it is waved for an instant in a sort of weak excitement, and then fizzles out into darkness: and by the blue flash I can just see some little boys lurching by with a limp bolster and a loose flapping mask. They attempt to light another firework, but it emits only a kind of crackle; and then they fade away in the dark; while all around the frosted trees stand up indifferent and like candelabras of iron.[35]

SPEAKING OF CONFUCIANISM, I have heard it said that the whole art of fireworks came first from the land of Confucius. There is something not inappropriate in such an origin. The art of coloured glass can truly be called the most typically Christian of all arts or artifices. The art of coloured lights is as essentially Confucian as the art of coloured windows is Christian. Aesthetically, they produce somewhat the same impression on the fancy; the impression of something glowing and magical; something at once mysterious and transparent. But the difference between their substance and structure is the whole difference between the great western faith and the great eastern agnosticism. The Christian windows are solid and human, made of heavy lead, of hearty and characteristic colours; but behind them is the light. The colours of the fireworks are as festive and as varied; but behind them is the darkness. They themselves are their only illumination; even as in that stern philosophy, man is his own star. The rockets of ruby and sapphire fade away slowly upon the dome of hollowness and darkness. But the kings and saints in the old Gothic windows, dusky and opaque in this hour of midnight, still contain all their power of full flamboyance, and await the rising of the sun.[36]

First things

WE SHALL NEVER have a common peace in Europe till we have a common principle in Europe. People talk of "The United States of Europe"; but they forget that it needed the very doctrinal "Declaration of Independence" to make the United States of America. You cannot agree about nothing any more than you can quarrel about nothing.[37]

Foolishness

WHEN DICKENS DESCRIBED Mr. Chuckster, Dickens was, strictly speaking, making a fool of himself; for he was making a fool out of himself. And every kind of real lark, from acting a charade to making a pun, does consist in restraining one's nine hundred and ninety-nine serious selves and letting the fool loose.[38]

NOTHING HAS BEEN worse than the modern notion that a clever man can make a joke without taking part in it; without sharing in the general absurdity that such a situation creates. It is unpardonable conceit not to laugh at your own jokes. Joking is undignified; that is why it is so good for one's soul. Do not fancy you can be a detached wit and avoid being a buffoon; you cannot. If you are the Court Jester you must be the Court Fool.[39]

UNLESS A THING is dignified, it cannot be undignified. Why is it funny that a man should sit down suddenly in the street? There is only one possible or intelligent reason: that man is the image of God. It is not funny that anything else should fall down; only that a man should fall down. No one sees anything funny in a tree falling down. No one sees a delicate absurdity in a stone falling down. No man stops in the road and roars with laughter at the sight of the snow coming down. The fall of thunderbolts is treated with some gravity. The fall of roofs and high buildings is taken seriously. It is only when a man tumbles down that we laugh. Why do we laugh? Because it is a grave religious matter: it is the Fall of Man. Only man can be absurd: for only man can be dignified.[40]

THERE IS A certain solid use in fools. It is not so much that they rush in where angels fear to tread, but rather that they let out what devils intend to do. Some perversion of folly will float about nameless and pervade a whole society; then some lunatic gives it a name, and henceforth it is harmless.[41]

HIS SOUL WILL never starve for exploits and excitements who is wise enough to be made a fool of. He will make himself happy in the traps that have been laid for him; he will roll in their nets and sleep. All doors will fly open to him who has a mildness more defiant than mere courage. The whole is unerringly expressed in one fortunate phrase—he will be always "taken in." To be taken in everywhere is to see the inside of everything. It is the hospitality of circumstance. With torches and trumpets, like a guest, the greenhorn is taken in by Life. And the sceptic is cast out by it.[42]

FRANCE

THIS TOWN OF Belfort is famous for one of the most typical and powerful of the public monuments of France. From the café table at which I sit I can see the hill beyond the town on which hangs the high and flat-faced citadel, pierced with many windows, and warmed in the evening light. On the steep hill below it is a huge stone lion, itself as large as a hill. It is hacked out of the rock with a sort of gigantic impression. No trivial attempt has been made to make it like a common statue; no attempt to carve the mane into curls, or to distinguish the monster minutely from the earth out of which he rises, shaking the world. The face of the lion has something of the bold conventionality of Assyrian art. The mane of the lion is left like a shapeless cloud of tempest, as if it might literally be said of him that God had clothed his neck with thunder.[43]

FRANCIS OF ASSISI

FOR MOST PEOPLE there is a fascinating inconsistency in the position of St Francis. He expressed in loftier and bolder language than any earthly thinker the conception that laughter is as divine as tears. He called his monks the mountebanks of God. He never forgot to take pleasure in a bird as it flashed past him, or a drop of water as it fell from his finger: he was, perhaps, the happiest of the sons of men. Yet this man undoubtedly founded his whole polity on the negation of what we think the most imperious necessities; in his three vows of poverty, chastity, and obedience, he denied to himself and those he loved most, property, love, and liberty. Why was it that the most large-hearted and poetic spirits in that age found their most congenial atmosphere in these awful renunciations? Why did he who loved where all men were blind, seek to blind himself where all men loved? Why was he a monk, and not a troubadour? These questions are far too large to be answered fully here, but in any life of Francis they ought at least to have been asked; we have a suspicion that if they were answered we should suddenly find that much of the enigma of this sullen time of ours was answered also.[44]

IN THE RECORDS of the first majestic and yet fantastic developments of the foundation of St. Francis of Assisi is an account of a certain Blessed Brother Giles. I have forgotten most of it, but I remember one fact: that certain students of theology came to ask him whether he believed in free will, and, if so, how he could reconcile it with necessity. On hearing the question St. Francis's follower reflected a little while and then seized a fiddle and began capering and dancing about the garden, playing a wild tune and generally expressing a violent and invigorating indifference. The tune is not recorded, but it is the eternal chorus of mankind, that modifies all the arts and mocks all the individualisms, like the laughter and thunder of some distant sea.[45]

FREE LOVE

IT IS COMMON to meet nowadays men who talk of what they call Free Love as if it were something like Free Silver—a new and ingenious political scheme. They seem to forget that it is as easy to judge what it would be like as to judge of what legal marriage would be like. "Free Love" has been going on in every town and village since the beginning of the world; and the first fact that every man of the world knows about it is plain enough. It never does produce any of the wild purity and perfect freedom its friends attribute to it.[46]

FREE SPEECH

FREE SPEECH IS an idea which has at present all the unpopularity of a truism; so that we tend to forget that it was not so very long ago that it had the more practical unpopularity which attaches to a new truth. Ingratitude is surely the chief of the intellectual sins of man. He takes his political benefits for granted, just as he takes the skies and the seasons for granted.[47]

THE THEORY OF free speech, that truth is so much larger and stranger and more many-sided than we know of, that it is very much better at all costs to hear every one's account of it, is a theory which has been justified upon the whole by experiment, but which remains a very daring and even a very surprising theory.[48]

FREE THINKERS

NO, THE GREAT Free-thinker with his genuine ability does not in practice destroy Christianity, what he does destroy is the Free-thinker who went before.[49]

IT IS LARGELY because the free-thinkers, as a school, have hardly made up their minds whether they want to be more optimist or more pessimist than Christianity that their small but sincere movement has failed.[50]

FREE WILL

WHEN SOMEBODY DISCOVERED the Differential Calculus there was only one Differential Calculus he could discover. But when Shakespeare killed Romeo he might have married him to Juliet's old nurse if he had felt inclined. And Christendom has excelled in the narrative romance exactly because it has insisted on the theological free-will. It is a large matter and too much to one side of the road to be discussed adequately here; but this is the real objection to that torrent of modern talk about treating crime as disease, about making a prison merely a hygienic environment like a hospital, of healing sin by slow scientific methods. The fallacy of the whole thing is that evil is a matter of active choice, whereas disease is not.[51]

THERE WERE IN the French Revolution a class of people at whom everybody laughed, and at whom it was probably difficult, as a practical matter, to refrain from laughing. They attempted to erect, by means of huge wooden statues and brand-new festivals, the most extraordinary new religions. They adored the Goddess of Reason, who would appear, even when the fullest allowance has been made for their many virtues, to be the deity who had least smiled upon them.[52]

WIELDER OF THE FACILE PEN

Chesterton the Essayist

Few writers were ever as prolific as the knight-errant of Fleet Street whom the world remembers today as G. K. Chesterton. The sheer number of his essays alone suffices to make this point. He wrote thousands of them.[1]

The title of his best known collection of essays captured the essence of what his essays generally were: *Tremendous Trifles* (published in September 1909).

The essays within this book are not overlong (generally between six and eight pages), but they are by turns witty and whimsical, eloquent and profound. Chesterton, in his typical self-deprecating way, described this sampling of his essays as "no more than a sort of sporadic diary." They were in fact sketches originally published as part of an opinion column in a British periodical called the *Daily News*—a newspaper founded in the 1840s by Charles Dickens, who served as its first editor.[2] Chesterton doubtless took great pleasure in his duties as an opinion columnist, since he deeply admired Dickens's literary gifts, and was well aware of the paper's history.

But to return to Chesterton's essays. While *Tremendous Trifles* is perhaps the most popular collection of essays he published, it is also the most free ranging in terms of subject matter and (many would argue) the most successful. It could well be described as the "everything under the sun" book. But it is this very all-encompassing quality that imparts many of the collection's greatest merits. One glance through the table of contents attests Chesterton's omnivorous curiosity. Essay titles include "A Piece of Chalk," "The Advantages of Having One Leg," "On Lying in Bed," "The End of the World," and "How I Met the President."

As successful an essayist as Chesterton was, it has to be said that his performances were not always even. The reason for this is quickly evident: anyone who writes thousands of essays cannot always be in top form. Rush deadlines and frequency of publication sometimes yielded uneven craftsmanship and a tendency for Chesterton to repeat himself.

But then, these things are to be expected from a man who made his living primarily as a journalist. Working writers often fall victim to such venal shortcomings. One thing, however, is clear in almost every piece to issue from Chesterton's pen: he was a gifted essayist and this form of writing highly suited his vagabond curiosity and facile versatility.

T. S. Eliot is one of the more famous contemporaries to have weighed in on Chesterton the essayist. And while he readily conceded that Chesterton was at times spendthrift, he maintained: "some of his essays can be read again and again." This was high praise, albeit tempered by the mild censure that Chesterton wrote too much. Nonetheless Eliot concluded, "of his essay writing as a whole, one can only say that it is remarkable to have maintained such a high average with so large an output."[3]

Of Chesterton's collected essays that are strictly literary in nature, *Varied Types* (published in 1903) is perhaps the best. It falls within the especially fecund period (1903–8) that witnessed the greatest flowering of his literary gifts. As such his reflections on such writers as Charlotte Brontë, Sir Walter Scott, Tolstoy, and Robert Louis Stevenson remain valuable and rewarding well over one hundred years on. Such can be said more generally of the finest of Chesterton's essays—of which there are many indeed.

FUTURISTS

I FEEL [THIS same primary panic] also in our rush towards future visions of society. The modern mind is forced towards the future by a certain sense of fatigue, not unmixed with terror, with which it regards the past. It is propelled towards the coming time; it is, in the exact words of the popular phrase, knocked into the middle of next week. And the goad which drives it on thus eagerly is not an affectation for futurity. Futurity does not exist, because it is still future. Rather it is a fear of the past; a fear not merely of the evil in the past, but of the good in the past also. The brain breaks down under the unbearable virtue of mankind. There have been so many flaming faiths that we cannot hold; so many harsh heroisms that we cannot imitate; so many great efforts of monumental building or of military glory which seem to us at once sublime and pathetic. The future is a refuge from the fierce competition of our forefathers.[53]

THE LAST FEW decades have been marked by a special cultivation of the romance of the future. We seem to have made up our minds to misunderstand what has happened; and we turn, with a sort of relief, to stating what will happen—which is (apparently) much easier. . . .

But when full allowance has been made for this harmless element of poetry and pretty human perversity in the thing, I shall not hesitate to maintain here that this cult of the future is not only a weakness but a cowardice of the age.[54]

G

Gardens

I WAS WALKING the other day in a kitchen garden, which I find has somehow got attached to my premises, and I was wondering why I liked it. After a prolonged spiritual self-analysis I came to the conclusion that I like a kitchen garden because it contains things to eat. I do not mean that a kitchen garden is ugly; a kitchen garden is often very beautiful. The mixture of green and purple on some monstrous cabbage is much subtler and grander than the mere freakish and theatrical splashing of yellow and violet on a pansy. Few of the flowers merely meant for ornament are so ethereal as a potato. A kitchen garden is as beautiful as an orchard; but why is it that the word "orchard" sounds as beautiful as the word "flower-garden," and yet also sounds more satisfactory? I suggest again my extraordinarily dark and delicate discovery: that it contains things to eat.[1]

Gargoyles

IT IS NOT sufficient to have the obvious equilibrium of the Stoic. For mere resignation has neither the gigantic levity of pleasure nor the superb intolerance of pain. There is a vital objection to the advice merely to grin and bear it. The objection is that if you merely bear it, you do not grin. Greek heroes do not grin; but gargoyles do—because they are Christian. And when a Christian is pleased, he is (in the most exact sense) frightfully pleased; his pleasure is frightful. Christ prophesied the whole of Gothic architecture in that hour when nervous and respectable people (such people as now object to barrel organs) objected to the shouting of the gutter-snipes of Jerusalem. He said, "If these were silent, the very stones would cry out." Under the impulse of His spirit arose like a clamorous chorus the façades of the mediaeval cathedrals, thronged with shouting faces and open mouths. The prophecy has fulfilled itself: the very stones cry out.[2]

THE OLD GREEKS summoned godlike things to worship their god. The mediaeval Christians summoned all things to worship theirs, dwarfs and pelicans, monkeys and madmen. The modern realists summon all these million creatures to worship their god; and then have no god for them to worship. Paganism was in art a pure beauty; that was the dawn. Christianity was a beauty created by controlling a million monsters of ugliness; and that in my belief was the zenith and the noon. Modern art and science practically mean having the million monsters and being unable to control them; and I will venture to call that the disruption and the decay. The finest lengths of the Elgin marbles consist of splendid horses going to the temple of a virgin. Christianity, with its gargoyles and grotesques, really amounted to saying this: that a donkey could go before all the horses of the world when it was really going to the temple. Romance means a holy donkey going to the temple. Realism means a lost donkey going nowhere.[3]

GLASTONBURY

ONE SILVER MORNING I walked into a small grey town of stone, like twenty other grey western towns, which happened to be called Glastonbury; and saw the magic thorn of near two thousand years growing in the open air as casually as any bush in my garden.

In Glastonbury, as in all noble and humane things, the myth is more important than the history. One cannot say anything stronger of the strange old tale of St. Joseph and the Thorn than that it dwarfs St. Dunstan.[4]

BUT TO-DAY REAL agnosticism has declined along with real theology. People cannot leave a creed alone; though it is the essence of a creed to be clear. But neither can they leave a legend alone; though it is the essence of a legend to be vague. That sane half scepticism which was found in all rustics, in all ghost tales and fairy tales, seems to be a lost secret. Modern people must make scientifically certain that St. Joseph did or did not go to Glastonbury, despite the fact that it is now quite impossible to find out; and that it does not, in a religious sense, very much matter. But it is essential to feel that he may have gone to Glastonbury: all songs, arts, and dedications branching and blossoming like the thorn, are rooted in some such sacred doubt.[5]

A MAN NEVER knows what tiny thing will startle him to such ancestral and impersonal tears. Piles of superb masonry will often pass like a common panorama; and on this grey and silver morning the ruined towers of the cathedral stood about me somewhat vaguely like grey clouds. But down in a hollow where the local antiquaries are making a fruitful excavation, a magnificent old ruffian with a pickaxe (whom I believe to have been St. Joseph of Arimathea) showed me a fragment of the old vaulted roof which he had found in the earth; and on the whitish grey stone there was just a faint brush of gold. There seemed a piercing and swordlike pathos, an unexpected fragrance of all forgotten or desecrated things, in the bare survival of that poor little pigment upon the imperishable rock.[6]

TAKEN THUS, NOT heavily like a problem but lightly like an old tale, the [legend of St. Joseph and the thorns of Glastonbury] does lead one along the road of very strange realities, and the thorn is found growing in the heart of a very secret maze of the soul. Something is really present in the place; some closer contact with the thing which covers Europe but is still a secret. Somehow the grey town and the green bush touch across the world the strange small country of the garden and the grave; there is verily some communion between the thorn tree and the crown of thorns.[7]

GOD

THE RIDDLES OF God are more satisfying than the solutions of man.[8]

IT MAY BE that God makes every daisy separately, but has never got tired of making them. It may be that He has the eternal appetite of infancy; for we have sinned and grown old, and our Father is younger than we. The repetition in Nature may not be a mere recurrence; it may be a theatrical *encore*. Heaven may *encore* the bird who laid an egg. If the human being conceives and brings forth a human child instead of bringing forth a fish, or a bat, or a griffin, the reason may not be that we are fixed in an animal fate without life or purpose. It may be that our little tragedy has touched the gods, that they admire it from their starry galleries, and that at the end of every human drama man is called again and again before the curtain. Repetition may go on for millions of years, by mere choice, and at any instant it may stop. Man may stand on the earth generation after generation, and yet each birth be his positively last appearance.

This was my first conviction; made by the shock of my childish emotions meeting the modern creed in mid-career. I had always vaguely felt facts to be miracles in the sense that they are wonderful: now I began to think them miracles in the stricter sense that they were *wilful*. I mean that they were, or might be, repeated exercises of some will. In short, I had always believed that the world involved magic: now I thought that perhaps it involved a magician. And this pointed a profound emotion always present and sub-conscious; that this world of ours has some purpose; and if there is a purpose, there is a person. I had always felt life first as a story: and if there is a story there is a story-teller.[9]

GOD IS NOT a symbol of goodness. Goodness is a symbol of God.[10]

GOOD THINGS

AND THE MORE I considered Christianity, the more I found that while it had established a rule and order, the chief aim of that order was to give room for good things to run wild.[11]

ALL THINGS ARE from God; and above all, reason and imagination and the great gifts of the mind. They are good in themselves; and we must not altogether forget their origin even in their perversion.[12]

GOODNESS

THE HOMELESS SCEPTICISM of our time has reached a sub-conscious feeling that morality is somehow merely a matter of human taste—an accident of psychology. And if goodness only exists in certain human minds, a man wishing to praise goodness will naturally exaggerate the amount of it that there is in human minds or the number of human minds in which it is supreme. Every confession that man is vicious is a confession that virtue is visionary. Every book which admits that evil is real is felt in some vague way to be admitting that good is unreal. The modern instinct is that if the heart of man is evil, there is nothing that remains good. But the older feeling was that if the heart of man was ever so evil, there was something that remained good—goodness remained good.[13]

ONE CAN SOMETIMES do good by being the right person in the wrong place.[14]

GOTHIC ARCHITECTURE

ALONE AT SOME distance from the wasting walls of a disused abbey I found half sunken in the grass the grey and goggle-eyed visage of one of those graven monsters that made the ornamental water-spouts in the cathedrals of the Middle Ages. It lay there, scoured by ancient rains or striped by recent fungus, but still looking like the head of some huge dragon slain by a primeval hero. And as I looked at it, I thought of the meaning of the grotesque, and passed into some symbolic reverie of the three great stages of art.[15]

GOVERNMENT

ALL GOVERNMENT IS an ugly necessity.[16]

THIS IS THE first essential element in government, coercion; a necessary but not a noble element. I may remark in passing that when people say that government rests on force they give an admirable instance of the foggy and muddled cynicisms of modernity. Government does not rest on force. Government *is* force; it rests on consent or a conception of justice.[17]

IT IS SAID that modern government makes life safer; and the claim is very tenable. But at least it is certain that modern government makes life for the governing classes safer; and never before in the whole history of the world has it been so safe a business to govern.[18]

GRATITUDE

THE FACT IS that purification and austerity are even more necessary for the appreciation of life and laughter than for anything else. To let no bird fly past unnoticed, to spell patiently the stones and weeds, to have the mind a store-house of sunsets, requires a discipline in pleasure and an education in gratitude.[19]

GREATNESS

THERE IS A great man who makes every man feel small. But the real great man is the man who makes every man feel great.[20]

GREY

RICH COLOURS ACTUALLY look more luminous on a grey day, because they are seen against a sombre background and seem to be burning with a lustre of their own. Against a dark sky all flowers look like fireworks. There is something strange about them, at once vivid and secret, like flowers traced in fire.[21]

ON A GREY day the larkspur looks like fallen heaven; the red daisies are really the red lost eyes of day; and the sunflower is the vice-regent of the sun.[22]

THE LITTLE HAMLETS of the warm grey stone have a geniality which is not achieved by all the artistic scarlet of the suburbs; as if it were better to warm one's hands at the ashes of Glastonbury than at the painted flames of Croydon.[23]

LASTLY, THERE IS this value about the colour that men call colourless; that it suggests in some way the mixed and troubled average of existence, especially in its quality of strife and expectation and promise. Grey is a colour that always seems on the eve of changing to some other colour; of brightening into blue or blanching into white or bursting into green and gold. So we may be perpetually reminded of the indefinite hope that is in doubt itself; and when there is grey weather in our hills or grey hairs in our heads, perhaps they may still remind us of the morning.[24]

Growing older

The pale leaf falls in pallor, but the green leaf turns to gold;
We that have found it good to be young shall find it good to
 be old;
Life that bringeth the marriage-bell, the cradle and the grave.
Life that is mean to the mean of heart, and only brave to the
 brave.[25]

BETWEEN US, BY the peace of God, such truth can now be
 told;
Yea, there is strength in striking root and good in growing
 old.[26]

BUT THE POWER of hoping through everything, the knowledge that the soul survives its adventures, that great inspiration comes to the middle-aged; God has kept that good wine until now. It is from the backs of the elderly gentlemen that the wings of the butterfly should burst.[27]

H

Half-truths

THE THING FROM which England suffers just now more than from any other evil is not the assertion of falsehoods, but the endless and irrepressible repetition of half truths.[1]

Hardy, Thomas

THE SUBTLE AND sad change that was passing like twilight across the English brain at this time is very well expressed in the fact that men have come to mention the great name of [Owen] Meredith in the same breath as Mr. Thomas Hardy. Both writers, doubtless, disagreed with the orthodox religion of the ordinary English village. Most of us have disagreed with that religion until we made the simple discovery that it does not exist. But in any age where ideas could be even feebly disentangled from each other, it would have been evident at once that Meredith and Hardy were, intellectually speaking, mortal enemies. They were much more opposed to each other than Newman was to Kingsley; or than Abelard was to St. Bernard. But then they collided in a sceptical age, which is like colliding in a London fog. There can never be any clear controversy in a sceptical age.[2]

THE GOD OF Meredith is impersonal; but he is often more healthy and kindly than any of the persons. That of Thomas Hardy is almost made personal by the intense feeling that he is poisonous. Nature is always coming in to save Meredith's women; Nature is always coming in to betray and ruin Hardy's. It has been said that if God had not existed it would have been necessary to invent Him. But it is not often, as in Mr. Hardy's case, that it is necessary to invent Him in order to prove how unnecessary (and undesirable) He is. But Mr. Hardy is anthropomorphic out of sheer atheism. He personifies the universe in order to give it a piece of his mind. But the fight is unequal for the old philosophical reason: that the universe had already given Mr. Hardy a piece of its mind to fight with.[3]

IT MUST ALSO be remembered that it was long ago and during a pessimistic fashion that [Hardy] labelled himself a pessimist. There is much to show that he mellowed in later life and grew acquainted with more gracious moods. His own personality was always in the best sense gracious, being full not only of humanity but humility. Bitterly as he had quarrelled with a demon who did not exist—a demon whom he did not even believe to exist—he never quarrelled with the human beings who do exist, and are therefore so much more aggravating. And he seems himself to have come to doubt whether he had not wasted on the former quarrel a fire that should have been given entirely to the latter sympathy:

> "'You have not said what you meant to say,'
> Said my own voice speaking to me:
> 'That the greatest of things is charity.'"

Certainly there is no greater thing to say, and he often said it greatly. But his provincial traditions hid from him a larger meaning of the word, in the mouths of the older mystics who spoke of charity towards God.[4]

HERETICS

[THE MODERN MAN] says, with a conscious laugh, "I suppose I am very heretical," and looks round for applause. The word "heresy" not only means no longer being wrong; it practically means being clear-headed and courageous. The word "orthodoxy" not only no longer means being right; it practically means being wrong. All this can mean one thing, and one thing only. It means that people care less for whether they are philosophically right.[5]

IT IS FOOLISH, generally speaking, for a philosopher to set fire to another philosopher in Smithfield Market because they do not agree in their theory of the universe. That was done very frequently in the last decadence of the Middle Ages, and it failed altogether in its object. But there is one thing that is infinitely more absurd and unpractical than burning a man for his philosophy. This is the habit of saying that his philosophy does not matter. . . .

Mr. Bernard Shaw has put the view in a perfect epigram: "The golden rule is that there is no golden rule." We are more and more to discuss details in art, politics, literature. A man's opinion on tramcars matters; his opinion on Botticelli matters; his opinion on all things does not matter. He may turn over and explore a million objects, but he must not find that strange object, the universe; for if he does he will have a religion, and be lost.[6]

WHEN THE OLD Liberals removed the gags from all the heresies, their idea was that religious and philosophical discoveries might thus be made. Their view was that cosmic truth was so important that every one ought to bear independent testimony. The modern idea is that cosmic truth is so unimportant that it cannot matter what any one says. The former freed inquiry as men loose a noble hound; the latter frees inquiry as men fling back into the sea a fish unfit for eating. Never has there been so little discussion about the nature of men as now, when, for the first time, any one can discuss it. The old restriction meant that only the orthodox were allowed to discuss religion. Modern liberty means that nobody is allowed to discuss it.[7]

NOW, IN OUR time, philosophy or religion, our theory, that is, about ultimate things, has been driven out, more or less simultaneously, from two fields which it used to occupy. General ideals used to dominate literature. They have been driven out by the cry of "art for art's sake." General ideals used to dominate politics. They have been driven out by the cry of "efficiency," which may roughly be translated as "politics for politics' sake." Persistently for the last twenty years the ideals of order or liberty have dwindled in our books; the ambitions of wit and eloquence have dwindled in our parliaments. Literature has purposely become less political; politics have purposely become less literary. General theories of the relation of things have thus been extruded from both; and we are in a position to ask, "What have we gained or lost by this extrusion? Is literature better, is politics better, for having discarded the moralist and the philosopher?"

When everything about a people is for the time growing weak and ineffective, it begins to talk about efficiency. So it is that when a man's body is a wreck he begins, for the first time, to talk about health.[8]

NOW OUR AFFAIRS are hopelessly muddled by strong, silent men. And just as this repudiation of big words and big visions has brought forth a race of small men in politics, so it has brought forth a race of small men in the arts. Our modern politicians claim the colossal license of Caesar and the Superman, claim that they are too practical to be pure and too patriotic to be moral; but the upshot of it all is that a mediocrity is Chancellor of the Exchequer. Our new artistic philosophers call for the same moral license, for a freedom to wreck heaven and earth with their energy; but the upshot of it all is that a mediocrity is Poet Laureate.[9]

I AM NOT concerned with Mr. Bernard Shaw as one of the most brilliant and one of the most honest men alive; I am concerned with him as a Heretic—that is to say, a man whose philosophy is quite solid, quite coherent, and quite wrong.[10]

YOU HOLD THAT your heretics and sceptics have helped the world forward and handed on a lamp of progress. I deny it. Nothing is plainer from real history than that each of your heretics invented a complete cosmos of his own which the next heretic smashed entirely to pieces.[11]

HIGH PLACES AND VALLEYS

I WROTE SOME part of these rambling remarks on a high ridge of rock and turf overlooking a stretch of the central counties; the rise was slight enough in reality, but the immediate ascent had been so steep and sudden that one could not avoid the fancy that on reaching the summit one would look down at the stars. But one did not look down at the stars, but rather up at the cities; seeing as high in heaven the palace town of Alfred like a lit sunset cloud, and away in the void spaces, like a planet in eclipse, Salisbury. So, it may be hoped, until we die you and I will always look up rather than down at the labours and the habitations of our race; we will lift up our eyes to the valleys from whence cometh our help.[12]

THE HIGHEST TASK

IT MAY SOMETIMES happen that the highest task of a thinking citizen may be to do the exact opposite of the work which the Radicals had to do. It may be his highest duty to cling on to every scrap of the past that he can find, if he feels that the ground is giving way beneath him and sinking into mere savagery and forgetfulness of all human culture.[13]

HISTORY

HISTORY, AND EVEN archaeology, is intrinsically surprising; because it is the study of a story of surprises. For instance, a man looking at the round wheels of modern machinery, and delighted to see the wheels go round, may make a more or less mechanical calculation of what more wheels, or bigger wheels, might be used for doing in the future. But a man looking at the round arches of the old Roman and Norman architecture could not possibly have calculated from them that, a hundred years afterwards, the delicate energy of the Gothic would be piercing the sky with spires and pointed arches as if with spears and arrows.[14]

Holmes, Oliver Wendell

GENERAL AND FANTASTIC as was the characteristic writing of Oliver Wendell Holmes, there was at least one element in it which was really dominant and consistent, and that was the influence of his profession. A good doctor is by the nature of things a man who needs only the capricious gift of style to make him an amusing author. For a doctor is almost the only man who combines a very great degree of inevitable research and theoretic knowledge with a very great degree of opportunism. He unites, as it were, the exact virtues of a botanist with the wilder virtues of a commercial travel-ler. He is alone in combining those verbally similar but profoundly diverse things, a knowledge of the cosmos and a knowledge of the world.[15]

A CERTAIN QUAINT wisdom, a certain variegated experience and sudden synthesis . . . is pre-eminently characteristic of Holmes. This is pre-eminently characteristic of him, and it is characteristic of the one other man in literary history who bears a curious resem-blance to him. Sir Thomas Browne was also a physician, he was also a fantastic, he was also a humorist and a devout philosopher. In him also we have the same bewildering ingenuity of allusion and comparison, the same saturnalia of specialism, the same topsy-turvydom of learning. We have even a similarity between them in such other matters as a certain unmistakeable tinge of the aristocratic idea, the Cavalier tradition of manners and dignity, which is very noticeable in Holmes as compared with all other American writers. Holmes, again, has fully as much as Browne the notion that these scientific minutiae and these physical ingenuities with which he has become acquainted as a doctor, are very solemn symbols of a certain rude and awful benevolence in the nature of things, a Providence that speaks like a candid doctor. Across all the bound volumes to which Wendell Holmes put his name might be written the general title or description "Religio Medici."[16]

THIS SCIENTIFIC BASIS in Wendell Holmes has much to do with his most obviously characteristic quality, his power of startling and delightful simile. When he compares Shakespeare to an apple, and conversation to a garden hose, when he establishes his admirable parallel between natural poets and women with yellow hair, he is acting in a certain sense in the highest spirit of physical science. Physical science has everything in the world to do with fancy, though not perhaps much in the highest sense to do with imagination. Imagination as we have it in great poetry is concerned with the things that fall naturally into an harmonious picture; but fancy is concerned with things which conceal an intellectual affinity under a total pictorial difference. Imagination celebrates the stars and clouds together, but fancy and physical science alike see that a squib or a pipe-light, or perhaps even a humming-top, are more akin to the stars than a cloud is. The whole fascination of science lies in this disguised fraternity.[17]

THIS GENERAL CONSCIOUSNESS that the most perfect similarities exist in the most diverse examples is a thing that must have haunted the minds of hundreds of good-working physicians when they saw the same disease attacking an aspidestra in a fernery and an old gentleman in his arm-chair. But of all these silent and fanciful men one was born with the magic and almost non-human power of saying what he meant, the power of literature. He wrote the line that sums up the whole matter:

"The force that whirls the planet round
Delights in spinning tops."[18]

HE FOUND HIMSELF prominent both in the literary and scientific world at a time when science and the modern spirit were first making themselves felt to the modification of the ancient Puritanism of America. And he took, as will be seen from the pages of the *Autocrat*, a prominent and somewhat peculiar part in the fight. He was anything but a materialist, he was too much in love with a positive piety even to be described as an agnostic, yet he did not, like a large and growing part of the intellectual world of to-day, rise to a refuge in a luminous mysticism and cleanse deity of all materialistic notions, hanging it alone in the heaven of metaphysics. He took as his conception of God rather the happy father of the robust family of nature, a shrewd and benignant being, something between Jupiter and Æsculapius.[19]

THE ORTHODOX CHURCHES, doubtless formal and fatuous in many things, and deserving Holmes' humanitarian satire, were nevertheless founded on a certain grand metaphysical idea which Holmes never quite justly appreciated, the idea of the dignity and danger of the human soul, the pride and the peril of the *imago dei*. Doubtless this idea is transcendental, and in that sense unscientific in the orthodox creeds. But it is equally transcendental in the "Declaration of Independence."[20]

IT WAS IN *The Autocrat of the Breakfast-Table* that Holmes collected for the first time all this picturesque experience and frivolous wisdom, and embodied it in a form of which he rapidly became a dazzling master, the irregular monologue varied by conversations.

How rich and admirable are those conversations no one who has read them will ever forget. They blaze with wit, but not after the manner of a novel of the "smart set" in which the people are less important than their own trivial sayings, in which their vulgar souls are eclipsed by their own epigrams as their vulgar bodies are eclipsed by their own diamonds. At the breakfast table there is something more important even than the amazing cleverness which is lavished upon it. There is a human atmosphere which alone makes conversation possible.[21]

Holmes, Sherlock

WHEN ALL IS said and done, there have never been better detective stories than the old series of Sherlock Holmes; and though the name of that magnificent magician has been spread over the whole world, and is perhaps the one great popular legend made in the modern world, I do not think that Sir Arthur Conan Doyle has ever been thanked enough for them. As one of many millions, I offer my own mite of homage.[22]

Home

BUT AN ENGLISHMAN'S house is not only his castle; it is his fairy castle. Clouds and colours of every varied dawn and eve are perpetually touching and turning it from clay to gold, or from gold to ivory. There is a line of woodland beyond a corner of my garden which is literally different on every one of the three hundred and sixty-five days. Sometimes it seems as near as a hedge, and sometimes as far as a faint and fiery evening cloud.[23]

EVERY MAN, THOUGH he were born in the very belfry of Bow and spent his infancy climbing among chimneys, has waiting for him somewhere a country house which he has never seen; but which was built for him in the very shape of his soul. It stands patiently waiting to be found, knee-deep in orchards of Kent or mirrored in pools of Lincoln; and when the man sees it he remembers it, though he has never seen it before.[24]

FOR A PLAIN, hard-working man the home is not the one tame place in the world of adventure. It is the one wild place in the world of rules and set tasks. The home is the one place where he can put the carpet on the ceiling or the slates on the floor if he wants to.[25]

THE MAN WHO said that an Englishman's house is his castle said much more than he meant. The Englishman thinks of his house as something fortified, and provisioned, and his very surliness is at root romantic. And this sense would naturally be strongest on wild winter nights, when the lowered portcullis and the lifted draw-bridge do not merely bar people out but bar people in. The Englishman's house is most sacred, not merely when the King cannot enter it, but when the Englishman cannot get out of it.[26]

THE HONEST MAN

DIOGENES LOOKED FOR his honest man inside every crypt and cavern, but he never thought of looking for it inside the thief. And that is where the Founder of Christianity found the honest man; He found him on a gibbet and promised him Paradise. Just as Christianity looked for the honest man inside the thief, democracy looked for the wise man inside the fool.[27]

HOPE

But in this grey morn of man's life
Cometh sometime to the mind
A little light that leaps and flies,
Like a star blown on the wind.[28]

Human dignity

EVERYONE ON THIS earth should believe, amid whatever madness or moral failure, that your life and temperament have some object on earth. Believe that you have something to give the world which cannot otherwise be given.[29]

Human institutions

AN ALMOST UNNATURAL vigilance is really required of the citizen because of the horrible rapidity with which human institutions grow old. It is the custom in passing romance and journalism to talk of men suffering under old tyrannies. But, as a fact, men have almost always suffered under new tyrannies; under tyrannies that had been public liberties hardly twenty years before.[30]

Human nature

FOR HUMAN BEINGS, being children, have the childish wilfulness, the childish secrecy. And they never have from the beginning of the world done what the wise men have seen to be inevitable.[31]

AND AT THE end of my reflections I had really got no further than the sub-conscious feeling of my friend the bank-clerk—that there is something spiritually suffocating about our life; not about our laws merely, but about our life. Bank-clerks are without songs, not because they are poor, but because they are sad. . . . As I passed homewards I passed a little tin building of some religious sort, which was shaken with shouting as a trumpet is torn with its own tongue. *They* were singing anyhow; and I had for an instant a fancy I had often had before: that with us the super-human is the only place where you can find the human. Human nature is hunted and has fled into sanctuary.[32]

Humiliation

FOR WITH ANY recovery from morbidity there must go a certain healthy humiliation. There comes a certain point in such conditions when only three things are possible: first a perpetuation of Satanic pride, secondly tears, and third laughter.[33]

Humility

When all philosophies shall fail,
This word alone shall fit;
That a sage feels too small for life,
And a fool too large for it.[34]

THE MOST MARVELLOUS of those mystical cavaliers who wrote intricate and exquisite verse in England in the seventeenth century, I mean Henry Vaughan, put the matter in one line, intrinsically immortal and practically forgotten—

"Oh holy hope and high humility."

That adjective "high" is not only one of the sudden and stunning inspirations of literature; it is also one of the greatest and gravest definitions of moral science. However far aloft a man may go, he is still looking up, not only at God (which is obvious), but in a manner at men also: seeing more and more all that is towering and mysterious in the dignity and destiny of the lonely house of Adam.[35]

IN A VERY entertaining work, over which we have roared in childhood, it is stated that a point has no parts and no magnitude. Humility is the luxurious art of reducing ourselves to a point, not to a small thing or a large one, but to a thing with no size at all, so that to it all the cosmic things are what they really are—of immeasurable stature.[36]

Pride juggles with her toppling towers,
They strike the sun and cease,
But the firm feet of humility
They grip the ground like trees.[37]

Humour

MISERS GET UP early in the morning; and burglars, I am informed, get up the night before.[38]

ART, LIKE MORALITY, consists of drawing the line somewhere.[39]

I HAVE KNOWN some people of very modern views driven by their distress to the use of theological terms to which they attached no doctrinal significance, merely because a drawer was jammed tight and they could not pull it out. A friend of mine was particularly afflicted in this way. Every day his drawer was jammed, and every day in consequence it was something else that rhymes to it.[40]

SILVER IS SOMETIMES more valuable than gold . . . that is, in large quantities.[41]

WHEN LAST I saw an old gentleman running after his hat in Hyde Park, I told him that a heart so benevolent as his ought to be filled with peace and thanks at the thought of how much unaffected pleasure his every gesture and bodily attitude were at that moment giving to the crowd.[42]

ONE OF THE great disadvantages of hurry is that it takes such a long time.[43]

ALL THE JOKES about men sitting down on their hats are really theological jokes; they are concerned with the Dual Nature of

Man. They refer to the primary paradox that man is superior to all the things around him and yet is at their mercy.[44]

ALL THE BEST humour that exists in our language is Cockney humour. Chaucer was a Cockney; he had his house close to the Abbey. Dickens was a Cockney; he said he could not think without the London streets. The London taverns heard always the quaintest conversation, whether it was Ben Jonson's at the Mermaid or Sam Johnson's at the Cock.[45]

THE SECRET OF life lies in laughter and humility.[46]

HYPOCRISY

THE NEW HYPOCRITE [among modern statesmen] is one whose aims are really religious, while he pretends that they are worldly and practical.... It is a fight of creeds masquerading as policies.[47]

I

Ideals

POLITICIANS ARE NONE the worse for a few inconvenient ideals.[1]

HUMAN NATURE SIMPLY cannot subsist without a hope and aim of some kind; as the sanity of the Old Testament truly said, where there is no vision the people perish. . . . But it is precisely because an ideal is necessary to a man that the man without ideals is in permanent danger of fanaticism.[2]

IT IS A platitude, and none the less true for that, that we need to have an ideal in our minds with which to test all realities. But it is equally true, and less noted, that we need a reality with which to test ideals.[3]

BOTH ARISTOCRACY AND democracy are human ideals: the one saying that all men are valuable, the other that some men are more valuable. But nature does not say that cats are more valuable than mice; nature makes no remark on the subject. She does not even say that the cat is enviable or the mouse pitiable. We think the cat superior because we have (or most of us have) a particular philosophy to the effect that life is better than death. But if the mouse were a German pessimist mouse, he might not think that the cat had beaten him at all. He might think he had beaten the cat by getting to the grave first. Or he might feel that he had actually inflicted frightful punishment on the cat by keeping him alive. Just as a microbe might feel proud of spreading a pestilence, so the pessimistic mouse might exult to think that he was renewing in the cat the torture of conscious existence. It all depends on the philosophy of the mouse. You cannot even say that there is victory or superiority in nature unless you have some doctrine about what things are superior. You cannot even say that the cat scores unless there is a system of scoring. You cannot even say that the cat gets the best of it unless there is some best to be got.[4]

BUT THERE IS one feature in the past which more than all the rest defies and depresses the moderns and drives them towards this featureless future. I mean the presence in the past of huge ideals, unfulfilled and sometimes abandoned. The sight of these splendid failures is melancholy to a restless and rather morbid generation; and they maintain a strange silence about them—sometimes amounting to an unscrupulous silence. They keep them entirely out of their newspapers and almost entirely out of their history books.[5]

THE TASK OF modern idealists indeed is made much too easy for them by the fact that they are always taught that if a thing has been defeated it has been disproved. Logically, the case is quite clearly the other way. The lost causes are exactly those which might have saved the world. . . . Few people realize how many of the largest efforts, the facts that will fill history, were frustrated in their full design and come down to us as gigantic cripples.[6]

IDOLATRY

I HAVE ALWAYS noticed that people who begin by taking the intellect very seriously end up by having no intellects at all. The idolater worships wood and stone; and if he worships his own head it turns into wood and stone.[7]

Imago dei (the image of God)

THIS WORLD AND all our powers in it are far more awful and beautiful than even we know until some accident reminds us. If you wish to perceive that limitless felicity, limit yourself if only for a moment. If you wish to realise how fearfully and wonderfully God's image is made, stand on one leg. If you want to realise the splendid vision of all visible things—wink the other eye.[8]

Radio Dramatization

Mr. Welles and Mr. Chesterton

Few people in the history of cinema have earned as much critical acclaim as Orson Welles. His 1941 film, *Citizen Kane*, is generally considered the greatest motion picture ever made.

Far less well known is that in late December 1941, Welles paid a tribute to G. K. Chesterton through a reading of one of his poems. That poem was "The Truce of Christmas." Welles's dramatic reading of it was intended partly as a Christmas gift to his radio listening audience, and partly as a way to rally America—a nation reeling from the attack on Pearl Harbor just two weeks before.

"And now," Welles began, "because we want our [Christmas] greeting to be timely, and very beautiful too, here's the Chesterton poem I promised you."[1]

The Truce of Christmas

Passionate peace is in the sky—
And in the snow in silver sealed
The beasts are perfect in the field,

And men seem men so suddenly—
    (But take ten swords, and ten times ten
    And blow the bugle in praising men;
    For we are for all men under the sun,
    And they are against us every one;
    And misers haggle, and mad men clutch,
    And there is peril in praising much,
    And we have the terrible tongues uncurled
    That praise the world to the sons of the world.)
The idle humble hill and wood
Are bowed about the sacred birth,
And for one little while the earth
Is lazy with the love of good—
    (But ready are you, and ready am I,
    If the battle blow and the guns go by;
    For we are for all men under the sun,
    And they are against us every one;
    And the men that hate herd all together,
    To pride and gold, and the great white feather,
    And the thing is graven in star and stone
    That the men who love are all alone.)
Hunger is hard and time is tough,
But bless the beggars and kiss the kings,
For hope has broken the heart of things,
And nothing was ever praised enough.
    (But hold the shield for a sudden swing
    And point the sword when you praise a thing,
    For we are for all men under the sun,
    And they are against us every one;
    And mime and merchant, thane and thrall
    Hate us because we love them all;
    Only till Christmastide go by
    Passionate peace is in the sky.)[2]

Moving as the story surrounding Welles's reading of this poem is, it was not the first time he had paid tribute to Chesterton. Three years earlier, in 1938, he had staged a radio dramatization of Chesterton's novel *The Man Who Was Thursday* for the Mercury Radio Theatre (the acclaimed New York drama company he founded with John Housman).[3] It aired on both the CBS and Canadian CBC networks on September 5, 1938—a little less than two months before Welles's historic radio broadcast of H. G. Wells's *The War of the Worlds*.

There was something very fitting in this, since Chesterton and H. G. Wells had been cordial friends in life, however much they might have differed in how they saw the world. Both shared a love for toy theatres, for example, and they actually collaborated on several plays designed for them.[4] So for Orson Welles to have staged radio dramatizations of novels by both men was very much in keeping with the spirit of the friendship they shared—though Welles could not have known of the plays the two friends had written together.

Welles's dramatization of *The Man Who Was Thursday* was a *tour de force*, not least because he faced the daunting task of distilling Chesterton's novel into a program that would last just over fifty-seven minutes. But there is every reason to think that he looked on this challenge as a way to discharge a debt of gratitude. The acclaimed novelist Jorge Luis Borges is chief among those who have referenced Welles's long-standing interest in and admiration for Chesterton. In his review of *Citizen Kane*, Borges wrote: "In one of Chesterton's stories—'The Head of Caesar,' I think—the hero observes that nothing is so frightening as a labyrinth without a center. This film is precisely that labyrinth."[5]

For Borges to have linked Chesterton with Welles's cinematic masterpiece in this way is remarkable. Borges goes on to describe *Citizen Kane* as a metaphysical detective story—words that could be applied with equal justice to *The Man Who Was Thursday*, described as "a metaphysical thriller" by the literary critic Sir Kingsley Amis.[6]

All that has been said above about Orson Welles's appreciation for Chesterton attests the sheer diversity of ways in which Chesterton was a cultural influencer. Both instances where Welles drew on Chesterton's work took place after GKC's death in 1936—yet these instances allowed Chesterton's art to find an entirely new American audience in the widely popular medium of radio, as well as the increasingly important art form of film. Taken together, one thing is certain: not least among the artistic achievements of Chesterton is the fact that his writings so inspired the artistry of Orson Welles—as the introduction to his radio dramatisation of *The Man Who Was Thursday* so clearly reveals:

> G. K. C., Gilbert Keith Chesterton, great, greatly articulate Roman convert and liberal, has been dead now for two years. For a unique brand of common sense enthusiasm, for a singular gift of paradox, for a deep reverence and a high wit, and most of all for a free and shamelessly beautiful English prose, he will never be forgotten.[7]

Injustice

ALL INJUSTICE BEGINS in the mind.[9]

THE THINGS THAT happen here do not seem to mean anything; they mean something somewhere else. Somewhere else retribution will come on the real offender. Here it often seems to fall on the wrong person.[10]

Insanity

THE MAN WHO cannot believe his senses, and the man who cannot believe anything else, are both insane, but their insanity is proved not by any error in their argument, but by the manifest mistake of their whole lives. They have both locked themselves up in two boxes, painted inside with the sun and stars; they are both unable to get out, the one into the health and happiness of heaven, the other even into the health and happiness of the earth.[11]

Inspiration

IT IS STRANGE that men should see sublime inspiration in the ruins of an old church and see none in the ruins of a man.[12]

Intellect and morality

THE GREAT HUMAN dogma, then, is that the wind moves the trees. The great human heresy is that the trees move the wind. When people begin to say that the material circumstances have alone created the moral circumstances, then they have prevented all possibility of serious change. For if my circumstances have made me wholly stupid, how can I be certain even that I am right in altering those circumstances?

The man who represents all thought as an accident of environment is simply smashing and discrediting all his own thoughts—including that one. To treat the human mind as having an ultimate authority is necessary to any kind of thinking, even free thinking. And nothing will ever be reformed in this age or country unless we realise that the moral fact comes first.[13]

LIKE THE SUN at noonday, mysticism explains everything else by the blaze of its own victorious invisibility. Detached intellectualism is (in the exact sense of a popular phrase) all moonshine; for it is light without heat, and it is secondary light, reflected from a dead world. But the Greeks were right when they made Apollo the god both of imagination and of sanity; for he was both the patron of poetry and the patron of healing.[14]

"THE WORK OF the philosophical policeman," replied the man in blue, "is at once bolder and more subtle than that of the ordinary detective.... We have to trace the origin of those dreadful thoughts that drive men on at last to intellectual fanaticism and intellectual crime."[15]

J

JAMES, HENRY

HENRY JAMES ALWAYS stood, if ever a man did, for civilisation; for that ordered life in which it is possible to tolerate and to understand. His whole world is made out of sympathy; out of a whole network of sympathies. It is a world of wireless telegraphy for the soul; of a psychological brotherhood of men of which the communications could not be cut. Sometimes this sympathy is almost more terrible than antipathy; and his very delicacies produce a sort of promiscuity of minds. Silence becomes a rending revelation. Short spaces or short speeches become overweighted with the awful worth of human life. Minute unto minute uttereth speech, and instant unto instant showeth knowledge. It is only when we have realised how perfect is the poise of such great human art that we can also realise its peril, and know that any outer thing which cannot make it must of necessity destroy it.[1]

JINGOISM

WHAT WE REALLY need for the frustration and overthrow of a deaf and raucous Jingoism is a renascence of the love of the native land. When that comes, all shrill cries will cease suddenly. For the first of all the marks of love is seriousness: love will not accept sham bulletins or the empty victory of words. It will always esteem the most candid counsellor the best.[2]

"MY COUNTRY, RIGHT or wrong," is a thing that no patriot would think of saying except in a desperate case. It is like saying, "My mother, drunk or sober."[3]

JOAN OF ARC

I THOUGHT OF all that is noble in Tolstoy, the pleasure in plain things, especially in plain pity, the actualities of the earth, the reverence for the poor, the dignity of the bowed back. Joan of Arc had all that and with this great addition, that she endured poverty as well as admiring it; whereas Tolstoy is only a typical aristocrat trying to find out its secret. And then I thought of all that was brave and proud and pathetic in poor Nietzsche, and his mutiny against the emptiness and timidity of our time. I thought of his cry for the ecstatic equilibrium of danger, his hunger for the rush of great horses, his cry to arms. Well, Joan of Arc had all that, and again with this difference, that she did not praise fighting, but fought. We *know* that she was not afraid of an army, while Nietzsche, for all we know, was afraid of a cow. Tolstoy only praised the peasant; *she* was the peasant. Nietzsche only praised the warrior; *she* was the warrior. She beat them both at their own antagonistic ideals; she was more gentle than the one, more violent than the other. Yet she was a perfectly practical person who did something, while they are wild speculators who do nothing.[4]

JOHNSON, SAMUEL

THE DECAY OF taverns, which is but a part of the general decay of democracy, has undoubtedly weakened this masculine spirit of equality. I remember that a roomful of Socialists literally laughed when I told them that there were no two nobler words in all poetry than Public House. They thought it was a joke. Why they should think it a joke, since they want to make all houses public houses, I cannot imagine. But if anyone wishes to see the real rowdy egalitarianism which is necessary (to males, at least) he can find it as well as anywhere in the great old tavern disputes which come down to us in such books as Boswell's *Johnson*. It is worth while to mention that one name especially because the modern world in its morbidity has done it a strange injustice. The demeanor of Johnson, it is said, was "harsh and despotic." It was occasionally harsh, but it was never despotic. Johnson was not in the least a despot; Johnson was a demagogue, he shouted against a shouting crowd. The very fact that he wrangled with other people is proof that other people were allowed to wrangle with him. His very brutality was based on the idea of an equal scrimmage, like that of football. It is strictly true that he bawled and banged the table because he was a modest man. He was honestly afraid of being overwhelmed or even overlooked. Addison had exquisite manners and was the king of his company; he was polite to everybody; but superior to everybody; therefore he has been handed down forever in the immortal insult of Pope—

Like Cato, give his little Senate laws
     And sit attentive to his own applause.

Johnson, so far from being king of his company, was a sort of Irish Member in his own Parliament. Addison was a courteous superior and was hated. Johnson was an insolent equal and therefore was loved by all who knew him, and handed down in a marvelous book, which is one of the mere miracles of love.[5]

The Edwardian Dr. Johnson
Chesterton as a Man of Letters

If one were to look up the definition of a twentieth-century man of letters, Chesterton's picture would be waiting there.

"Perhaps no other writer of his time," the poet and literary scholar Bruce Murphy has written, "so deserved the title of man of letters as Gilbert Keith Chesterton. Author of literally scores of books and countless articles, he was a playwright, poet, journalist, novelist, mystery writer, and biographer, among other things."[1]

As a man of letters, Chesterton was much like Samuel Johnson, a writer whom he much admired and sometimes portrayed in costume. Of course, it has to be said straightaway that Johnson is "arguably the most distinguished man of letters in English history,"[2] and Chesterton's enduring influence does not begin to approach anything like Johnson's in the pantheon of British men of letters. Still, the two men were much alike, and in ways that are telling.

Johnson, as James Boswell showed in his *Life of Samuel Johnson*, was eminently quotable—wit vying with wisdom in lending pith to aphorisms and epigrams that are still remembered. Chesterton, for his part, often used the medium of paradox with great skill to refute an opponent's position in debate, or make a cogent point. Some potent examples include:

Pessimism says that life is so short that it gives nobody a chance; religion says that life is so short that it gives everybody his final chance.[3]

Stick to the man who looks out of the window and tries to understand the world. Keep clear of the man who looks in at the window and tries to understand you.[4]

A dead thing can go with the stream, but only a living thing can go against it.[5]

When it came to philosophy, Johnson had no formal training, but he "defended that discipline with his own humanistic wisdom."[6] Chesterton had no formal training in philosophy either, but few writers in the twentieth century have defended it publicly in a more stalwart or more colorful way—as in this instance: "What a man can believe depends upon his philosophy, not upon the clock or the century."[7] Three works, *Heretics*, *Orthodoxy*, and *The Everlasting Man*, most memorably display this aspect of Chesterton's literary legacy.

As poet Chesterton is still, like Johnson, anthologized and studied. And while it is true that Chesterton's poetry did not influence his era as Johnson's poetry shaped the Augustan age of English literature, he did in one respect surpass Johnson. Johnson never crafted an epic narrative poem of enduring influence and critical acclaim—Chesterton did. Since its publication in 1911, *The Ballad of the White Horse* has continually garnered praise from accomplished and influential writers, among them W. H. Auden, Graham Greene, C. S. Lewis, and Garry Wills— who has called Chesterton's poem a "neglected masterpiece in narrative verse."[8]

As a playwright, Johnson was also surpassed by Chesterton. Johnson's tragedy, *Irene*, was his only play and his greatest literary failure. Chesterton wrote two plays that have received critical praise and had an enduring influence. *Magic* (first staged in 1913) was a play admired by the acclaimed director Ingmar Bergman, who staged a production of it in the Göteborg City Theatre in March 1947.[9] Bergman later revisited themes suggested by Chesterton's play in his 1958 film *The Magician*. Of the second of Chesterton's plays, Garry Wills has called *The Surprise* (first published in 1952), "one dark joke of a playlet" that warrants inclusion among Chesterton's classic works. Dorothy L. Sayers wrote an introduction for this play when it first appeared in print.

Chesterton and Johnson were alike in crafting works of fiction. Chesterton wrote a classic novel, *The Man Who Was*

Thursday, while Johnson wrote a classic didactic romance, *Rasselas: The Prince of Abyssinia*. They were complementary as well in terms of their essay writing. Both were incredibly prolific, and wrote essays all of their adult lives. Both were spendthrift in writing so much, but then for many years both were working writers. Repetition and uneven craftsmanship are occupational hazards. Still, many of Johnson's essays are still in print and often cited.

Lastly, it can be said that there are many things to return to in Johnson. The same is true of Chesterton. This, perhaps, is the best measure of achievement when it comes to a man of letters. Garry Wills has written of this better than any critic has in recent memory:

> For the big things in [Chesterton] I still feel a kind of awe—for his lightning insights into the mysteries of the Christian faith (creation, the Trinity, the Incarnation). He is the best exponent of the ethos of democracy that I know. He presented this over and over in images that reveal the whole secret at a glance—as when he said that democracy is like blowing one's nose (one may not do it well, but one should do it oneself); that we do not cry out that a man with a high IQ is drowning, but that a *man* is drowning; that the essence of the jury system is a belief that every human is responsible for every other human being. He is the only one I know who has the gift of Samuel Johnson (a great hero of his)—that one wants to hear what he has to say on any subject. Even when he is wrong, he comes at a topic from such an individual viewpoint as to light up new scenery all around the topic. Yet this individuality is not, with either man, mere idiosyncrasy. The shock of the new comes from seeing how uncommon is real common sense. It is a shock that has never worn off for me.[10]

JOURNALISM

IF YOU ATTEMPT an actual argument with a modern paper of opposite politics, you will find that no medium is admitted between violence and evasion. You will have no answer except slanging or silence. A modern editor must not have that eager ear that goes with the honest tongue. He may be deaf and silent; and that is called dignity. Or he may be deaf and noisy; and that is called slashing journalism. In neither case is there any controversy; for the whole object of modern party combatants is to charge out of earshot.[6]

PEOPLE KNOW IN their hearts that journalism is a conventional art like any other, that it selects, heightens, and falsifies. Only its Nemesis is the same as that of other arts: if it loses all care for the truth it loses all form likewise.[7]

THE JOURNALIST, HAVING grown accustomed to talking down to the public, commonly talks too low at last, and becomes merely barbaric and unintelligible.[8]

MODERN WRITERS HAVE often made game of the old chronicles because they chiefly record accidents and prodigies; a church struck by lightning, or a calf with six legs. They do not seem to realise that this old barbaric history is the same as new democratic journalism. It is not that the savage chronicle has disappeared. It is merely that the savage chronicle now appears every morning.[9]

IT IS THE one great weakness of journalism as a picture of our modern existence, that it must be a picture made up entirely of exceptions. We announce on flaring posters that a man has fallen off a scaffolding. We do not announce on flaring posters that a man has not fallen off a scaffolding. Yet this latter fact is fundamentally more exciting, as indicating that that moving tower of terror and mystery, a man, is still abroad upon the earth. That the man has not fallen off a scaffolding is really more sensational; and it is also some thousand times more common. But journalism cannot reasonably be expected thus to insist upon the permanent miracles. Busy editors cannot be expected to put on their posters, "Mr. Wilkinson Still Safe," or "Mr. Jones, of Worthing, Not Dead Yet." They cannot announce the happiness of mankind at all. They cannot describe all the forks that are not stolen, or all the marriages that are not judiciously dissolved. Hence the complex picture they give of life is of necessity fallacious; they can only represent what is unusual. However democratic they may be, they are only concerned with the minority.[10]

AS IT IS, however, this misrepresentation of speeches is only a part of a vast journalistic misrepresentation of all life as it is. Journalism is popular, but it is popular mainly as fiction. Life is one world, and life seen in the newspapers another.[11]

OUR MODERN PRESS would rather appeal to physical arrogance, or to anything, rather than appeal to right and wrong.[12]

THE CURSE OF all journalism, but especially of that yellow journalism which is the shame of our profession, is that we think ourselves cleverer than the people for whom we write, whereas, in fact, we are generally even stupider.[13]

BUT THE MODERN editor regards himself far too much as a kind of original artist, who can select or suppress facts with the arbitrary ease of a poet or a caricaturist. . . . The old idea that he is simply a mode of expression of the public, an "organ" of opinion, seems to have entirely vanished from his mind. Today the editor is not only the organ, but the man who plays on the organ. For in all our modern movements we move away from Democracy.[14]

I WOULD MAKE a law, if there is none such at present, by which an editor, proved to have published false news without reasonable verification, should simply go to prison. This is not a question of influences or atmospheres; the thing could be carried out as easily and as practically as the punishment of thieves and murderers. Of course there would be the usual statement that the guilt was that of a subordinate. Let the accused editor have the right of proving this if he can; if he does, let the subordinate be tried and go to prison. Two or three good rich editors and proprietors properly locked up would take the sting out of the Yellow Press.[15]

ALWAYS A JOURNALIST, ALWAYS A JESTER
Chesterton the Journalist

For the entirety of his professional life, Chesterton was a practicing journalist. The articles he wrote numbered in the thousands, on almost every conceivable topic. But while it is tempting to dwell at length on the sheer breadth of his interests and articles, the best way to understand this facet of his writing is to ask the question: why did he do it?

"It is not I," Chesterton wrote in 1905, "it is not even a particular class of journalists or jesters who make jokes about the matters which are of most awful import; it is the whole human race."[1]

Why would he say this? Chesterton was proud to own himself a journalist because he discerned that it was a noble and necessary calling within a democratic society. But beyond this aspect of civic-mindedness (to which he attached great weight), there was a larger and kindred concern: one identified by Luke Timothy Johnson in a trenchant review of Garry Wills's excellent study *Chesterton*. Here, Johnson gets at the heart of why

Chesterton the lover of democracy was so ardently devoted to the journalist's calling:

> As Wills properly observes, the basis for Chesterton's deep democratic instincts is his metaphysical sensibility. If existence is equally existence in all its forms, then there is the most radical egalitarianism at the heart of things. A tree can reveal "the One who is" as well as a tabernacle. This is why Chesterton's apparently light essays on trivial topics like brown paper, telephone poles, or lying in bed were never truly light because, for him, such topics were never truly trivial. The shock of existence is equally shocking in things small as well as great. He matters for many of us, because, unlike most thinkers of the twentieth century, he identified himself not with the theories of the intellectual elite but with the common traditions tested by time.[2]

Seen in this light, Chesterton's calling as a journalist freed him to write about everything and anything. For a man of such vibrant intellectual curiosity, this was a God-send, and he reveled in it. His possible subject matter embraced nearly infinite variety, and it afforded him opportunities at the same time to affirm that trees as well as tabernacles could foster a sense of wonder. Or, to put it another way, each possessed the weight of glory. Seldom did Chesterton write better about this, than when he wrote:

> The very word "superficial" is founded on a fundamental mistake about life, the idea that second thoughts are best. The superficial impression of the world is by far the deepest. What we really feel, naturally and casually, about the look of skies and trees and the face of friends, that and that alone will almost certainly remain our vital philosophy to our dying day.[3]

Chesterton's reverence for "the common traditions tested by time" also meant that a journalist could speak a sober truth to his historical moment in the guise of a jest. Thus one of the most potent weapons in a journalist's arsenal was his wit. Chesterton's respect for this element of the journalist's art was never more in evidence than when he wrote the following about a man he much admired, Mark Twain:

> Wit requires an intellectual athleticism, because it is akin to logic. A wit must have something of the same running, working, and staying power as a mathematician or a metaphysician. Moreover, wit is a fighting thing and a working thing. A man may enjoy humour all by himself; he may see a joke when no one else sees it; he may see the point and avoid it. But wit is a sword; it is meant to make people feel the point as well as see it. All honest people saw the point of Mark Twain's wit. Not a few dishonest people felt it.[4]

Garry Wills, cited above, has rightly recognized that no matter what type of writing Chesterton turned his hand to— essays, literary criticism, poetry, plays, works of apologetics, or novels—his sense of first calling as a journalist was ever-present. Seen in this light, Chesterton's role as journalist takes on an overarching significance: it shaped everything he did. As Wills has written:

> Chesterton was always a journalist, no matter what he was writing, just as he was always a jester (two things he made almost synonymous in his role of commentator). . . . [J]ournalism was his entire career, and he refused ever to identify his work by another name.[5]

Joy and sorrow

THE TRUTH ABOUT life is that joy and sorrow are mingled in an almost rhythmical alternation like day and night.[16]

The joy of the Christian life

I HAVE BEGUN to realise that there are a good many people to whom my way of speaking about things appears like an indication that I am flippant or imperfectly insincere. Since, as a matter of fact, I am more certain of myself in this affair than I am of the existence of the moon, this naturally causes me some considerable regret; but I think I see the naturalness of the mistake, and how it arose in people so far removed from the Christian atmosphere. Christianity is itself so jolly a thing that it fills the possessor of it with a certain silly exuberance, which sad and high-minded rationalists might reasonably mistake for mere buffoonery and blasphemy; just as their prototypes, the sad-minded Stoics of old Rome did mistake the Christian joyousness for buffoonery and blasphemy. This difference holds good everywhere, in the old Pagan architecture and the grinning gargoyles of Christendom, in the preposterous motley of the Middle Ages and the dingy dress of this Rationalistic century.[17]

JOY, WHICH WAS the small publicity of the Pagan, is the gigantic secret of the Christian.[18]

MAN IS MORE himself, man is more manlike, when joy is the fundamental thing in him, and grief the superficial. Melancholy should be an innocent interlude, a tender and fugitive frame of mind; praise should be the permanent pulsation of the soul. Pessimism is at best an emotional half-holiday; joy is the uproarious labour by which all things live.[19]

"OUR ELEPHANT," SAID Syme, looking upwards, "has leapt into the sky like a grasshopper."

"And somehow," concluded Bull, "that's why I can't help liking old Sunday. No, it's not an admiration of force, or any silly thing like that. There is a kind of gaiety in the thing, as if he were bursting with some good news. Haven't you sometimes felt it on a spring day? You know Nature plays tricks, but somehow that day proves they are good-natured tricks. I never read the Bible myself, but that part they laugh at is literal truth, 'Why leap ye, ye high hills?' The hills do leap—at least, they try to. . . . Why do I like Sunday? . . . how can I tell you? . . . because he's such a Bounder."[20]

K

Knife

A KNIFE IS never bad except on such rare occasions as that in which it is neatly and scientifically planted in the middle of one's back.[1]

L

LAMPS

IT WAS ABOUT sunset, and the lamps were being lit. Auberon paused to look at them, for they were Chiffy's finest work, and his artistic eye never failed to feast on them. In memory of the Great Battle of the Lamps, each great iron lamp was surmounted by a veiled figure, sword in hand, holding over the flame an iron hood or extinguisher, as if ready to let it fall if the armies of the South and West should again show their flags in the city. Thus no child in Notting Hill could play about the streets without the very lamp-posts reminding him of the salvation of his country in the dreadful year.[1]

THE LAST IMPOSSIBILITY

DISTRIBUTE THE DIGNIFIED people and the capable people and the highly business-like people among all the situations which their ambition or their innate corruption may demand; but keep close to your heart, keep deep in your inner councils the absurd people; let the clever people pretend to govern you, let the un-impeachable people pretend to advise you, but let the fools alone influence you; let the laughable people whose faults you see and understand be the only people who are really inside your life, who really come near you or accompany you on your lonely march towards the last impossibility.[2]

Laws

THERE IS A great deal of difference between what laws define and what laws do.[3]

WE DO NOT need to get good laws to restrain bad people. We need to get good people to restrain bad laws.[4]

Lear, Edward

LEAR INTRODUCES HIS unmeaning words and his amorphous creatures not with the pomp of reason, but with the romantic prelude of rich hues and haunting rhythms.

> Far and few, far and few,
> Are the lands where the Jumblies live,

is an entirely different type of poetry to that exhibited in *Jabberwocky*. [Lewis] Carroll, with a sense of mathematical neatness, makes his whole poem a mosaic of new and mysterious words. But Edward Lear, with more subtle and placid effrontery, is always introducing scraps of his own elvish dialect into the middle of simple and rational statements, until we are almost stunned into admitting that we know what they mean. There is a genial ring of commonsense about such lines as,

> For his aunt Jobiska said "Every one knows
> That a Pobble is better without his toes,"

which is beyond the reach of Carroll. The poet seems so easy on the matter that we are almost driven to pretend that we see his meaning, that we know the peculiar difficulties of a Pobble, that we are as old travellers in the "Gromboolian Plain" as he is.[5]

Levity

MODERATE STRENGTH IS shown in violence, supreme strength is shown in levity.[6]

Liberals

NOW, I HAVE not lost my ideals in the least; my faith in fundamentals is exactly what it always was. What I have lost is my old childlike faith in practical politics. I am still as much concerned as ever about the Battle of Armageddon; but I am not so much concerned about the General Election. As a babe I leapt up on my mother's knee at the mere mention of it. No; the vision is always solid and reliable. The vision is always a fact. It is the reality that is often a fraud. As much as I ever did, more than I ever did, I believe in Liberalism. But there was a rosy time of innocence when I believed in Liberals.[7]

Liberty

MENTAL AND EMOTIONAL liberty are not so simple as they look. Really they require almost as careful a balance of laws and conditions as do social and political liberty. The ordinary aesthetic anarchist who sets out to feel everything freely gets knotted at last in a paradox that prevents him feeling at all. He breaks away from home limits to follow poetry. But in ceasing to feel home limits he has ceased to feel *The Odyssey*. He is free from national prejudices and outside patriotism. But being outside patriotism he is outside *Henry V*. Such a literary man is simply outside all literature: he is more of a prisoner than any bigot. For if there is a wall between you and the world, it makes little difference whether you describe yourself as locked in or as locked out.[8]

THERE CAN BE no liberty of thought unless it is ready to unsettle what has recently been settled, as well as what has long been settled. We are perpetually being told in the papers that what is wanted is a strong man who will do things. What is wanted is a strong man who will undo things; and that will be a real test of strength.[9]

LIFE

BUT LIFE IS a vale. Never forget at any moment of your existence to regard it in the light of a vale.[10]

THE FULL VALUE of this life can only be found by fighting; the violent take it by storm. And if we have accepted everything we have missed something—war. This life of ours is a very enjoyable fight, but a very miserable truce.[11]

I HAVE SAID that stories of magic alone can express my sense that life is not only a pleasure but a kind of eccentric privilege. I may express this other feeling of cosmic cosiness by allusion to another book always read in boyhood, "Robinson Crusoe," which I read about this time, and which owes its eternal vivacity to the fact that it celebrates the poetry of limits, nay, even the wild romance of prudence. Crusoe is a man on a small rock with a few comforts just snatched from the sea: the best thing in the book is simply the list of things saved from the wreck. The greatest of poems is an inventory. Every kitchen tool becomes ideal because Crusoe might have dropped it in the sea. It is a good exercise, in empty or ugly hours of the day, to look at anything, the coal-scuttle or the book-case, and think how happy one could be to have brought it out of the sinking ship on to the solitary island. But it is a better exercise still to remember how all things have had this hair-breadth escape: everything has been saved from a wreck. Every man has had one horrible adventure: as a hidden untimely birth he had not been, as infants that never see the light. Men spoke much in my boyhood of restricted or ruined men of genius: and it was common to say that many a man was a Great Might-Have-Been. To me it is a more solid and startling fact that any man in the street is a Great Might-Not-Have-Been.[12]

Literary greatness

IT IS UNTRUE to say that what matters is quality and not quantity. Most men have made one good joke in their lives; but to make jokes as Dickens made them is to be a great man. Many forgotten poets have let fall a lyric with one really perfect image; but when we open any play of Shakespeare, good or bad, at any page, important or unimportant, with the practical certainty of finding some imagery that at least arrests the eye and probably enriches the memory, we are putting our trust in a great man.[13]

Literature

EVERY GREAT LITERATURE has always been allegorical—allegorical of some view of the whole universe. *The Iliad* is only great because all life is a battle, *The Odyssey* because all life is a journey, *The Book of Job* because all life is a riddle.[14]

GREAT MEN LIKE Ariosto, Rabelais, and Shakespeare fall in foul places, flounder in violent but venial sin, sprawl for pages, exposing their gigantic weakness, are dirty, are indefensible; and then they struggle up again and can still speak with a convincing kindness and an unbroken honour of the best things in the world: Rabelais, of the instruction of ardent and austere youth; Ariosto, of holy chivalry; Shakespeare, of the splendid stillness of mercy.[15]

FOLK IN THE Middle Ages were not interested in a dragon or a glimpse of the devil because they thought that it was a beautiful prose idyll, but because they thought that it had really just been seen. It was not like so much artistic literature, a refuge indicating the dullness of the world: it was an incident pointedly illustrating the fecund poetry of the world.[16]

A WRITER'S TRUE CALLING
Chesterton the Literary Critic

Within the literary world, it is a truism that trends emerge and supplant one another almost constantly. Few writers and critics who once stood center stage remain there beyond their lifetimes. Literary reputations wax and wane, and are subject to continual debate. Yet amidst such a setting, Chesterton is justly famous for having revived the literary reputation of Charles Dickens.[1] No less an authority than T. S. Eliot held to this view, writing in 1927, "There is no better critic of Dickens living."[2]

Chesterton's study of Dickens is his most important work of criticism, and the most influential. When it was published in 1906, the literary fortunes of this preeminent Victorian novelist were at a low ebb. He seemed destined to remain among the rank of those novelists who were prolific and popular, but consigned to a second tier of literary artistry. Chesterton's study did more than any single book ever has to alter that perception.

More than one hundred years on, what Chesterton the critic was able to do for Dickens the writer remains singularly impressive. As scholar William Oddie has noted, Chesterton's study of Dickens

> was not simply a critical success: it led to a popular revival
> in interest in Dickens' writings, and to the publication of

the Everyman edition of his works from 1907 to 1911, with individual introductions to every novel by Chesterton himself (collected in 1911 in *Appreciations and Criticisms of the Works of Charles Dickens*).[3]

But it is not merely for his writings on Dickens that Chesterton is remembered. His first foray into the realm of literary criticism also met with considerable success, though not without a measure of criticism for its occasional misquotations and biographical inaccuracies. Chesterton the aspiring literary critic never shook free of the eccentricity (to his editors' collective dismay) of quoting from memory. Nevertheless, Browning scholar Iain Finlayson—while acknowledging these flaws—has written that Chesterton's study continues to be important "for consistently inspired and constantly inspiring psychological judgments about the poet and his work, which he gets right." Finlayson concluded that in this regard, Chesterton's book "has never been bettered."[4]

Robert Browning (published in May 1903) was a commissioned study of the poet written by Chesterton for Macmillan at the request of the distinguished editor John Morley. That Chesterton received this invitation in December 1901,[5] when he was only twenty-seven years old, was a high honor and a recognition of considerable literary gifts. Moreover, as Bernard Bergonzi has noted in his essay on Chesterton for *The Oxford Dictionary of National Biography*, this study not only contained "acute discussions of Browning's poetry," and revealed Chesterton to be "an excellent literary critic"—it also opened a window on Chesterton's intellectual and spiritual development. As Bergonzi has written:

> the book's real interest is the extent to which [Chesterton] identifies with his subject, and the clues it offers to his later

development. When he wrote it he was more than a young man embarking on a successful literary career. He was also engaged in a personal struggle to make sense of the world, a struggle which marked all his writing. He emphatically rejected the pessimism, positivism, and determinism which he saw as marking the late nineteenth century, and turned to those writers who were optimists and in love with life and the world, such as Whitman and Stevenson, and Browning, of whom he wrote, "In discussing anything, he must always fall back upon great speculative and eternal ideas" (*Robert Browning*, 1903, 118). This may or may not have been true of Browning, but it was entirely true of Chesterton. He saw Browning's love of nature and delight in human diversity as implying and resting on a belief in God.[6]

Two other literary studies by Chesterton also continue to be well regarded and oft cited, *William Blake* (published in November 1910) and *Chaucer* (published in April 1932). The former contains one of the most arresting passages regarding the primacy of faith in Blake's art. It stands testimony to the many moments of Chesterton's best writing as a critic:

The wise man will follow a star, low and large and fierce in the heavens, but the nearer he comes to it the smaller and smaller it will grow, till he finds it in the humble lantern over some little inn or stable. Not till we know the high things shall we know how lowly they are.[7]

Logic

YOU CAN ONLY find truth with logic if you have already found truth without it.[17]

Logicians

TO ACCEPT EVERYTHING is an exercise, to understand everything a strain. The poet only desires exaltations and expansion, a world to stretch himself in. The poet only asks to get his head into the heavens. It is the logician who seeks to get the heavens into his head. And it is his head that splits.[18]

A GREAT DEAL is said in these days about the value or valuelessness of logic. In the main, indeed, logic is not a productive tool so much as a weapon for defence. A man building up an intellectual system has to build like Nehemiah, with the sword in one hand and the trowel in the other. The imagination, the constructive quality, is the trowel, and argument is the sword. A wide experience of actual intellectual affairs will lead most people to the conclusion that logic is mainly valuable as a weapon wherewith to exterminate logicians.[19]

WHEN PEOPLE SAY that you can prove anything by logic, they are not using words in a fair sense. What they mean is that you can prove anything by bad logic.[20]

London

THE GREAT PALACES of pleasure which the rich build in London all have brazen and vulgar names. Their names are either snobbish, like the Hotel Cecil, or (worse still) cosmopolitan like the Hotel Metropole. But when I go in a third-class carriage from the nearest circle station to Battersea to the nearest circle station to the *Daily News*, the names of the stations are one long litany of solemn and saintly memories. Leaving Victoria I come to a park belonging especially to St. James the Apostle; thence I go to Westminster Bridge, whose very name alludes to the awful Abbey; Charing

Cross holds up the symbol of Christendom; the next station is called a Temple; and Blackfriars remembers the mediaeval dream of a Brotherhood.[21]

I HAVE FOUND the house where I was really born; the tall and quiet house from which I can see London afar off, as the miracle of man that it is.[22]

THE MORNING WAS wintry and dim, not misty, but darkened with that shadow of cloud or snow which steeps everything in a green or copper twilight. The light there is on such a day seems not so much to come from the clear heavens as to be a phosphorescence clinging to the shapes themselves. The load of heaven and the clouds is like a load of waters, and the men move like fishes, feeling that they are the floor of a sea. Everything in a London street completes the fantasy; the carriages and cabs themselves resemble deep-sea creatures with eyes of flame.[23]

LOVE

THE TRUTH WHICH the Brontës came to tell us is the truth that many waters cannot quench love.[24]

BUT SHAW HAD not learnt . . . what the rustic ballads of any country on earth would have taught him. He had not learnt, what universal common sense has put into all the folk-lore of the earth, that love cannot be thought of clearly for an instant except as monogamous. The old English ballads never sing the praises of "lovers." They always sing the praises of "true lovers," and that is the final philosophy of the question.[25]

> Lady, the stars are falling pale and small,
> Lady, we will not live if life be all,

Forgetting those good stars in heaven hung,
When all the world was young;
For more than gold was in a ring,
and love was not a little thing,
Between the trees in Ivywood,
when all the world was young.[26]

THE WAY TO love anything is to realise that it might be lost.[27]

THESE ESSAYS, FUTILE as they are considered as serious literature, are yet ethically sincere, since they seek to remind men that things must be loved first and improved afterwards.[28]

LOVE OF HUMANITY

LOVE OF HUMANITY is the commonest and most natural of the feelings of a fresh nature, and almost everyone has felt it alight capriciously upon him when looking at a crowded park or on a room full of dancers.[29]

LOYALTY

TO LOVE ANYTHING is to see it at once under lowering skies of danger. Loyalty implies loyalty in misfortune.[30]

LUNACY

I KNOW OF men who believe in themselves more colossally than Napoleon or Caesar. I know where flames the fixed star of certainty and success. I can guide you to the thrones of the Super-men. The men who really believe in themselves are all in lunatic asylums.[31]

THE LUNATIC IS the man who lives in a small world but thinks it is a large one; he is a man who lives in a tenth of the truth, and thinks it is the whole. The madman cannot conceive any cosmos outside a certain tale or conspiracy or vision.[32]

M

Macaulay, Thomas Babington

MACAULAY WAS CONCERNED to interpret the seventeenth century in terms of the triumph of the Whigs as champions of public rights; and he upheld this one-sidedly but not malignantly in a style of rounded and ringing sentences, which at its best is like steel.[1]

[MACAULAY'S] NOBLE ENDURING quality in our literature is this: that he truly had an abstract passion for history; a warm, poetic and sincere enthusiasm for great things as such; an ardour and appetite for great books, great battles, great cities, great men. He felt and used names like trumpets. The reader's greatest joy is in the writer's own joy, when he can let his last phrase fall like a hammer on some resounding name like Hildebrand or Charlemagne, on the eagles of Rome or the pillars of Hercules.[2]

MACAULAY TOOK IT for granted that common sense required some kind of theology, while Huxley took it for granted that common sense meant having none. Macaulay, it is said, never talked about his religion: but Huxley was always talking about the religion he hadn't got.[3]

MacDonald, George

THUS THERE WAS George MacDonald, a Scot of genius as genuine as Carlyle's; he could write fairy-tales that made all experience a fairy-tale. He could give the real sense that every one had the end of an elfin thread that must at last lead them into Paradise.[4]

BUT IN A certain rather special sense I for one can really testify to a book that has made a difference to my whole existence, which helped me to see things in a certain way from the start; a vision of things which even so real a revolution as a change of religious allegiance has substantially only crowned and confirmed. Of all the stories I ever read . . . it remains the most real, the most realistic, in the exact sense of the phrase the most like life. It is called *The Princess and the Goblin*, and is by George MacDonald.[5]

WHEN I READ [*The Princess and the Goblin*] as a child, I felt that the whole thing was happening inside a real human house, not essentially unlike the house I was living in, which also had staircases and rooms and cellars. This is where the fairy-tale differed from many other fairy-tales; above all, this is where the philosophy differed from many other philosophies.[6]

DR. GREVILLE MACDONALD, in his intensely interesting memoir of his father . . . has I think mentioned somewhere his sense of the strange symbolism of stairs. Another recurrent image in his romances was a great white horse; the father of the princess had one, and there was another in *The Back of the North Wind*. To this day I can never see a big white horse in the street without a sudden sense of indescribable things.[7]

AND THE PICTURE of life in this parable [*The Princess and the Goblin*] is not only truer than the image of a journey like that of *The Pilgrim's Progress*, it is even truer than the mere image of a siege like that of *The Holy War*. There is something not only imaginative but intimately true about the idea of the goblins being below the house and capable of besieging it from the cellars. When the evil things besieging us do appear, they do not appear outside but inside. Anyhow, that simple image of a house that is our home, that is rightly loved as our home, but of which we hardly know the best or the worst, and must always wait for the one and watch against the other, has always remained in my mind as something singularly solid and unanswerable; and was more corroborated than corrected when I came to give a more definite name to the lady watching over us from the turret, and perhaps to take a more practical view of the goblins under the floor.[8]

SINCE I FIRST read [*The Princess and the Goblin*] some five alternative philosophies of the universe have come to our colleges out of Germany, blowing through the world like the east wind. But for me that castle is still standing in the mountains and the light in its tower is not put out. All George MacDonald's other stories, interesting and suggestive in their several ways, seem to be illustrations and even disguises of that one.[9]

FOR THIS IS the very important difference between his sort of mystery and mere allegory. The commonplace allegory takes what it regards as the commonplaces or conventions necessary to ordinary men and women, and tries to make them pleasant or picturesque by dressing them up as princesses or goblins or good fairies. But George MacDonald did really believe that people were princesses and goblins and good fairies, and he dressed them up as ordinary men and women. The fairy-tale was the inside of the ordinary story and not the outside. One result of this is that all the inanimate objects that are the stage properties of the story retain that nameless glamour which they have in a literal fairy-tale.[10]

AND WHEN [MACDONALD] comes to be more carefully studied as a mystic, as I think he will be when people discover the possibility of collecting jewels scattered in a rather irregular setting, it will be found, I fancy, that he stands for a rather important turning point in the history of Christendom, as representing the particular Christian nation of the Scots. As protestants speak of the morning stars of the reformation, we may be allowed to note such names here and there as morning stars of the Reunion.[11]

THE PASSIONATE AND poetical Scots ought obviously, like the passionate and poetical Italians, to have had a religion which competed with the beauty and vividness of the passions, which did not let the devil have all the bright colours, which fought glory. . . .

There was only one who really represented what Scottish religion should have been, if it had continued the colour of the Scottish mediaeval poetry. In his particular type of literary work [MacDonald] did indeed realize the apparent paradox of a St. Francis of Aberdeen, seeing the same sort of halo round every flower and bird. It is not the same thing as any poet's appreciation of the beauty of the flower or bird. A heathen can feel that and remain heathen, or in other words remain sad. It is a certain special sense of significance, which the tradition that most values it calls sacramental. To have got back to it, or forward to it, at one bound of boyhood, out of the black Sabbath of a Calvinist town, was a miracle of imagination.[12]

A THOUGHTFUL MAN will now find more to think about in Vaughan or Crashaw than in Milton, but he will also find more to criticize; and nobody need deny that in the ordinary sense a casual reader may wish there was less of Blake and more of Keats. But even this allowance must not be exaggerated; and it is in exactly the same sense in which we pity a man who has missed the whole of Keats or Milton, that we can feel compassion for the critic who has not walked in the forest of [George MacDonald's] *Phantastes* or made the acquaintance of Mr. Cupples in the adventures of Alec Forbes.[13]

Madness

THE MADMAN IS not the man who has lost his reason. The madman is the man who has lost everything except his reason.[14]

"WHAT DOES IT all mean?" cried the other, with a gesture of passionate rationality. "Are you mad?"

"Not in the least," replied the King, pleasantly. "Madmen are always serious; they go mad from lack of humour."[15]

Magic

THE PROVOST OF Notting Hill seemed to have fallen into a kind of trance; in his eyes was an elvish light.

"I know of a magic wand, but it is a wand that only one or two may rightly use, and only seldom. It is a fairy wand of great fear, stronger than those who use it—often frightful, often wicked to use. But whatever is touched with it is never again wholly common; whatever is touched with it takes a magic from outside the world. If I touch, with this fairy wand, the railways and the roads of Notting Hill, men will love them, and be afraid of them for ever."

"What the devil are you talking about?" asked the King.

"It has made mean landscapes magnificent, and hovels outlast cathedrals," went on the madman. "Why should it not make lamp-posts fairer than Greek lamps; and an omnibus-ride like a painted ship? The touch of it is the finger of a strange perfection."

"What is your wand?" cried the King, impatiently.

"There it is," said Wayne; and pointed to the floor, where his sword lay flat and shining.[16]

DOCTOR. Well, it must be nice to be young and still see all those stars and sunsets. We old buffers won't be too strict with you if your view of things sometimes gets a bit—

mixed up, shall we say? If the stars get loose about the grass by mistake; or if, once or twice, the sunset gets into the east. We should only say, "Dream as much as you like. Dream for all mankind. Dream for us who can dream no longer. But do not quite forget the difference."

PATRICIA. What difference?

DOCTOR. The difference between the things that are beautiful and the things that are there. That red lamp over my door isn't beautiful; but it's there. You might even come to be glad it is there, when the stars of gold and silver have faded. I am an old man now, but some men are still glad to find my red star. I do not say they are the wise men.[17]

STRANGER. Have I committed a worse crime than thieving?

PATRICIA. You have committed the cruellest crime, I think, that there is.

STRANGER. And what is the cruellest crime?

PATRICIA. Stealing a child's toy.

STRANGER. And what have I stolen?

PATRICIA. A fairy tale.[18]

MAKING THINGS BETTER

BUT WHAT DO we mean by making things better? Most modern talk on this matter is a mere argument in a circle—that circle which we have already made the symbol of madness and of mere rationalism. Evolution is only good if it produces good; good is only good if it helps evolution. The elephant stands on the tortoise, and the tortoise on the elephant.

Obviously, it will not do to take our ideal from the principle in nature; for the simple reason that (except for some human or divine theory), there is no principle in nature. For instance, the cheap anti-democrat of to-day will tell you solemnly that there is no equality in nature. He is right, but he does not see the logical addendum. There is no equality in nature; also there is no inequality in nature. Inequality, as much as equality, implies a standard of value.[19]

Man

MAN IS AN uprooted tree. That is the only reason why unconscious nature has ever noticed him. That blind man who, after having the holy touch on his eyes, "saw men as trees walking" knew what he was talking about. It was a great renewal of youth and renovation of the fairy tale of fact. Men are trees walking. But it is only because they are uprooted trees that they can walk.[20]

IN SO FAR as I am Man I am the chief of creatures. In so far as I am a man I am the chief of sinners.[21]

[CHRISTIANITY] HAS MAINTAINED from the beginning that the danger was not in man's environment, but in man.[22]

THE HUMAN RACE, to which so many of my readers belong, has been playing at children's games from the beginning, and will probably do it till the end.[23]

MAN IS AN exception, whatever else he is. If he is not the image of God, then he is a disease of the dust. If it is not true that a divine being fell, then we can only say that one of the animals went entirely off its head.[24]

WE HAVE ALL read in scientific books, and, indeed, in all romances, the story of the man who has forgotten his name. This man walks about the streets and can see and appreciate everything; only he cannot remember who he is. Well, every man is that man in the story. Every man has forgotten who he is. One may understand the cosmos, but never the ego; the self is more distant than any star. Thou shalt love the Lord thy God; but thou shalt not know thyself. We are all under the same mental calamity; we have all forgotten our names. We have all forgotten what we really are. All that we call common-sense and rationality and practicality and positivism only means that for certain dead levels of our life we forget that we have forgotten. All that we call spirit and art and ecstasy only means that for one awful instant we remember that we forget.[25]

MAN IS MERELY man only when he is seen against the sky. If he is seen against any landscape, he is only a man of that land. If he is seen against any house, he is only a householder. Only where death and eternity are intensely present can human beings fully feel their fellowship. Once the divine darkness against which we stand is really dismissed from the mind (as it was very nearly dismissed in the Victorian time) the differences between human beings become overpoweringly plain; whether they are expressed in the high caricatures of Dickens or the low lunacies of Zola.

This can be seen in a sort of picture in the Prologue of *The Canterbury Tales*; which is already pregnant with the promise of the English novel. The characters there are at once graphically and delicately differentiated; the Doctor with his rich cloak, his careful meals, his coldness to religion; the Franklin, whose white beard was so fresh that it recalled the daisies, and in whose house it snowed meat and drink; the Summoner, from whose fearful face, like a red cherub's, the children fled, and who wore a garland like a hoop; the Miller with his short red hair and bagpipes and brutal head, with which he could break down a door; the Lover who was as sleepless as a nightingale.[26]

IT IS THE simple truth that man does differ from the brutes in kind and not in degree; and the proof of it is here; that it sounds like a truism to say that the most primitive man drew a picture of a monkey and that it sounds like a joke to say that the most intelligent monkey drew a picture of a man. Something of division and disproportion has appeared; and it is unique. Art is the signature of man.[27]

MAN HAS ALWAYS lost his way. He has been a tramp ever since Eden; but he always knew, or thought he knew, what he was looking for. Every man has a house somewhere in the elaborate cosmos; his house waits for him waist deep in slow Norfolk rivers or sunning itself upon Sussex downs. Man has always been looking for that home which is the subject matter of this book. But in the bleak and blinding hail of skepticism to which he has been now so long subjected, he has begun for the first time to be chilled, not merely in his hopes, but in his desires. For the first time in history he begins really to doubt the object of his wanderings on the earth. He has always lost his way; but now he has lost his address.[28]

ALL THE HUMAN things are more dangerous than anything that affects the beasts—sex, poetry, property, religion.... Man is always something worse or something better than an animal; and a mere argument from animal perfection never touches him at all.... [N]o animal is either chivalrous or obscene.[29]

FOG FOR US is the chief form of that outward pressure which compresses mere luxury into real comfort. It makes the world small, in the same spirit as in that common and happy cry that the world is small, meaning that it is full of friends. The first man that emerges out of the mist with a light is for us Prometheus, a saviour bringing fire to men, greater than the heroes, better than the saints, Man Friday. Every rumble of a cart, every cry in the distance, marks the heart of humanity beating undaunted in the darkness. It is wholly human; man toiling in his cloud. If real darkness is like the embrace of God, this is the dark embrace of man.[30]

Mankind's best friend

IN OUR FRIENDS the richness of life is proved to us by what we have gained; in the faces in the street the richness of life is proved to us by the hint of what we have lost. And this feeling for strange faces and strange lives, when it is felt keenly by a young man, almost always expresses itself in a desire after a kind of vagabond beneficence, a desire to go through the world scattering goodness like a capricious god. It is desired that mankind should hunt in vain for its best friend as it would hunt for a criminal; that he should be an anonymous Saviour, an unrecorded Christ.[31]

Marriage

THE PRINCIPLE EXPRESSED in the Prayer Book in the words "for better, for worse" . . . is the principle that all noble things have to be paid for, even if you only pay for them with a promise.[32]

THE MODERN WORLD (intent on anarchy in everything, even in Government) refuses to perceive the permanent element of tragic constancy which inheres in all passion, and which is the origin of marriage. Marriage rests on the fact that you cannot have your cake and eat it; that you cannot lose your heart and have it.[33]

Marxists

WE HAVE PEOPLE who represent that all great historic motives were economic, and then have to howl at the top of their voices in order to induce the modern democracy to act on economic motives. The extreme Marxian politicians in England exhibit themselves as a small, heroic minority, trying vainly to induce the world to do what, according to their theory, the world always does.

The truth is, of course, that there will be a social revolution the moment the thing has ceased to be purely economic. You can never have a revolution in order to establish a democracy. You must have a democracy in order to have a revolution.[34]

MATERIALISM

NOW IT IS the charge against the main deductions of the materialist that, right or wrong, they gradually destroy his humanity; I do not mean only kindness, I mean hope, courage, poetry, initiative, all that is human. For instance, when materialism leads men to complete fatalism (as it generally does), it is quite idle to pretend that it is in any sense a liberating force. It is absurd to say that you are especially advancing freedom when you only use free thought to destroy free will. The determinists come to bind, not to loose. They may well call their law the "chain" of causation. It is the worst chain that ever fettered a human being.[35]

THE CHRISTIAN IS quite free to believe that there is a considerable amount of settled order and an inevitable development in the universe. But the materialist is not allowed to admit into his spotless machine the slightest speck of spiritualism or miracle.[36]

OUR MATERIALISTIC MASTERS could, and probably will, put Birth Control into an immediate practical programme while we are all discussing the dreadful danger of somebody else putting it into a distant Utopia.[37]

THE SANE MAN knows that he has a touch of the beast, a touch of the devil, a touch of the saint, a touch of the citizen. Nay, the really sane man knows that he has a touch of the madman. But the materialist's world is quite simple and solid, just as the madman is quite sure he is sane.[38]

THIS IS THE most enormous and at the same time the most secret of the modern tyrannies of materialism. In theory the thing ought to be simple enough. A really human human being would always put the spiritual things first. A walking and speaking statue of God finds himself at one particular moment employed as a shop assistant. He has in himself a power of terrible love, a promise of paternity, a thirst for some loyalty that shall unify life, and in the ordinary course of things he asks himself, "How far do the existing conditions of those assisting in shops fit in with my evident and epic destiny in the matter of love and marriage?" But here, as I have said, comes in the quiet and crushing power of modern materialism. It prevents him rising in rebellion, as he would otherwise do. By perpetually talking about environment and visible things, by perpetually talking about economics and physical necessity, painting and keeping repainted a perpetual picture of iron machinery and merciless engines, of rails of steel, and of towers of stone, modern materialism at last produces this tremendous impression in which the truth is stated upside down.[39]

MEMORY

IT IS VERY unfortunate that we so often know a thing that is past only by its tail end. We remember yesterday only by its sunsets.[40]

I FANCY THAT Shakespeare and Balzac, if moved to prayers, might not ask to be remembered, but to be forgotten . . . for if they were forgotten they would be everlastingly re-discovered and re-read. It is a monotonous memory which keeps us in the main from seeing things as splendid as they are.[41]

MERE SPIRITUALITY

WHEN SCIENTIFIC EVOLUTION was announced, some feared that it would encourage mere animality. It did worse: it encouraged mere spirituality. It taught men to think that so long as they were passing from the ape they were going to the angel. But you can pass from the ape and go to the devil.[42]

THE MIDDLE AGES

THE EDEN OF the Middle Ages was really a garden, where each of God's flowers—truth and beauty and reason—flourished for its own sake, and with its own name. The Eden of modern progress is a kitchen garden.[43]

MANKIND HAS NOT passed through the Middle Ages. Rather mankind has retreated from the Middle Ages in reaction and rout. The Christian ideal has not been tried and found wanting. It has been found difficult; and left untried.[44]

THE GREAT GREEKS preferred to carve their gods and heroes doing nothing. Splendid and philosophic as their composure is there is always about it something that marks the master of many slaves. But if there was one thing the early mediaevals liked it was representing people doing something—hunting or hawking, or rowing boats, or treading grapes, or making shoes, or cooking something in a pot. "Quicquid agunt homines, votum, timor, ira voluptas."[45] (I quote from memory.) The Middle Ages is full of that spirit in all its monuments and manuscripts. Chaucer retains it in his jolly insistence on everybody's type of trade and toil. It was the earliest and youngest resurrection of Europe, the time when social order was strengthening, but had not yet become oppressive; the time when religious faiths were strong, but had not yet been exasperated.

For this reason the whole effect of Greek and Gothic carving is different. The figures in the Elgin marbles, though often reining their steeds for an instant in the air, seem frozen for ever at that perfect instant. But a mass of mediaeval carving seems actually a sort of bustle or hubbub in stone. Sometimes one cannot help feeling that the groups actually move and mix, and the whole front of a great cathedral has the hum of a huge hive.[46]

The middle classes

IT IS THE custom in our little epoch to sneer at the middle classes. Cockney artists profess to find the bourgeoisie dull; as if artists had any business to find anything dull. Decadents talk contemptuously of its conventions and its set tasks; it never occurs to them that conventions and set tasks are the very way to keep that greenness in the grass and that redness in the roses—which they have lost for ever.[47]

The mind that precedes matter

IF WE WANT to uproot inherent cruelties or lift up lost populations we cannot do it with the scientific theory that matter precedes mind; we can do it with the supernatural theory that mind precedes matter.[48]

Miracles

BUT IN TRUTH this notion that it is "free" to deny miracles has nothing to do with the evidence for or against them. It is a lifeless verbal prejudice of which the original life and beginning was not in the freedom of thought, but simply in the dogma of materialism. The man of the nineteenth century did not disbelieve in the Resurrection because his liberal Christianity allowed him to doubt it. He disbelieved in it because his very strict materialism did not allow him to believe it. Tennyson, a very typical nineteenth-century man, uttered one of the instinctive truisms of his contemporaries when he said that there was faith in their honest doubt. There was indeed. Those words have a profound and even a horrible truth. In their doubt of miracles there was a faith in a fixed and godless fate; a deep and sincere faith in the incurable routine of the cosmos.[49]

THE ASSUMPTION THAT there is something in the doubt of miracles akin to liberality or reform is literally the opposite of the truth. If a man cannot believe in miracles there is an end of the matter; he is not particularly liberal, but he is perfectly honourable and logical, which are much better things. But if he can believe in miracles, he is certainly the more liberal for doing so; because they mean first, the freedom of the soul, and secondly, its control over the tyranny of circumstance.

Sometimes this truth is ignored in a singularly naive way, even by the ablest men. For instance, Mr. Bernard Shaw speaks with a hearty old-fashioned contempt for the idea of miracles, as if they were a sort of breach of faith on the part of nature: he seems strangely unconscious that miracles are only the final flowers of his own favourite tree, the doctrine of the omnipotence of will. Just in the same way he calls the desire for immortality a paltry selfishness, forgetting that he has just called the desire for life a healthy and heroic selfishness. How can it be noble to wish to make one's life infinite and yet mean to wish to make it immortal?[50]

WHAT MATTERS ABOUT a religion is not whether it can work marvels like any ragged Indian conjurer, but whether it has a true philosophy of the Universe. The Romans were quite willing to admit that Christ was a God. What they denied was that He was *the* God—the highest truth of the cosmos. And this is the only point worth discussing about Christianity.[51]

THE MOST INCREDIBLE thing about miracles is that they happen.[52]

Modern art

THIS USE OF the chorus to humanise and dilute a dark story is strongly opposed to the modern view of art. Modern art has to be what is called "intense." It is not easy to define being intense; but, roughly speaking, it means saying only one thing at a time, and saying it wrong. Modern tragic writers have to write short stories; if they wrote long stories (as the man said of philosophy) cheerfulness would creep in. Such stories are like stings; brief, but purely painful. And doubtless they bore some resemblance to some lives lived under our successful scientific civilisation; lives which tend in any case to be painful, and in many cases to be brief.[53]

Modern books

IN FRONT OF me, as I close this page, is a pile of modern books that I have been turning over . . . a pile of ingenuity, a pile of futility. . . . I can see the inevitable smash of the philosophies of Schopenhauer and Tolstoy, Nietzsche and Shaw, as clearly as an inevitable railway smash could be seen from a balloon. They are all on the road to the emptiness of the asylum. For madness may be defined as using mental activity so as to reach mental helplessness; and they have nearly reached it.[54]

Modern criticism

MODERN CRITICISM, LIKE all weak things, is overloaded with words. In a healthy condition of language a man finds it very difficult to say the right thing, but at last says it. In this empire of journalese a man finds it so very easy to say the wrong thing that he never thinks of saying anything else. False or meaningless phrases lie so ready to his hand that it is easier to use them than not to use them.

These wrong terms picked up through idleness are retained through habit, and so the man has begun to think wrong almost before he has begun to think at all.[55]

Modern European free-thinkers

IN ACTUAL MODERN Europe a free-thinker does not mean a man who thinks for himself. It means a man who, having thought for himself, has come to one particular class of conclusions, the material origin of phenomena, the impossibility of miracles, the improbability of personal immortality and so on.[56]

Modern humanitarianism

I AM HERE only following the outlines of [the modern humanitarians'] argument, which consists in maintaining that man has been progressively more lenient, first to citizens, then to slaves, then to animals, and then (presumably) to plants. I think it wrong to sit on a man. Soon, I shall think it wrong to sit on a horse. Eventually (I suppose) I shall think it wrong to sit on a chair. That is the drive of the argument. And for this argument it can be said that it is possible to talk of it in terms of evolution or inevitable progress. A perpetual tendency to touch fewer and fewer things might, one feels, be a mere brute unconscious tendency, like that of a species to produce fewer and fewer children. This drift may be really evolutionary, because it is stupid.[57]

THE MODERN HUMANITARIAN can love all opinions, but he cannot love all men; he seems sometimes, in the ecstasy of his humanitarianism, even to hate them all. He can love all opinions, including the opinion that men are unlovable.[58]

"YOU WILL SHED blood for that!" he cried. "For a cursed point of view—"

"Oh, you kings, you kings!" cried out Adam, in a burst of scorn. "How humane you are, how tender, how considerate! You will make war for a frontier, or the imports of a foreign harbour; you will shed blood for the precise duty on lace, or the salute to an admiral. But for the things that make life itself worthy or miserable—how humane you are!"[59]

MODERN KINGS

THERE IS NO fear that a modern king will attempt to override the constitution; it is more likely that he will ignore the constitution and work behind its back.[60]

THE MODERN MIND

NOW IN HISTORY there is no Revolution that is not a Restoration. Among the many things that leave me doubtful about the modern habit of fixing eyes on the future, none is stronger than this: that all the men in history who have really done anything with the future have had their eyes fixed upon the past. I need not mention the Renaissance, the very word proves my case. The originality of Michael Angelo and Shakespeare began with the digging up of old vases and manuscripts.[61]

THE MODERN MIND is not a donkey that wants kicking to make it go on. The modern mind is more like a motor-car on a lonely road which two amateur motorists have been just clever enough to take to pieces, but are not quite clever enough to put together again.[62]

I ESCAPED, HOWEVER, and as I leapt on an omnibus I saw again the enormous emblem of the Marble Arch. I saw that massive symbol of the modern mind: a door with no house to it; the gigantic gate of Nowhere.[63]

BRAVE MEN ARE vertebrates; they have their softness on the surface and their toughness in the middle. But these modern cowards are all crustaceans; their hardness is all on the cover and their softness is inside.[64]

THIS IS, FIRST and foremost, what I mean by the narrowness of the new ideas, the limiting effect of the future. Our modern prophetic idealism is narrow because it has undergone a persistent process of elimination. We must ask for new things because we are not allowed to ask for old things. The whole position is based on this idea that we have got all the good that can be got out of the ideas of the past. But we have not got all the good out of them, perhaps at this moment not any of the good out of them. And the need here is a need of complete freedom for restoration as well as revolution.[65]

BUT THE MODERNS have invented a much subtler and more poisonous kind of eulogy. The modern method is to take the prince or rich man, to give a credible picture of his type of personality, as that he is business-like, or a sportsman, or fond of art, or convivial, or reserved; and then enormously exaggerate the value and importance of these natural qualities. Those who praise Mr. Carnegie do not say that he is as wise as Solomon and as brave as Mars; I wish they did. It would be the next most honest thing to giving their real reason for praising him, which is simply that he has money. The journalists who write about Mr. Pierpont Morgan do not say that he is as beautiful as Apollo; I wish they did. What they do is to take the rich man's superficial life and manner, clothes, hobbies, love of cats, dislike of doctors, or what not; and then with the assistance of this realism make the man out to be a prophet and a saviour of his kind.[66]

THE MODERN MIND is forced towards the future by a certain sense of fatigue, not unmixed with terror, with which it regards the past.[67]

THE MODERN NOTION of impressing the public by a mere demonstration of unpopularity, by being thrown out of meetings or thrown into jail is largely a mistake. It rests on a fallacy touching the true popular value of martyrdom. . . . The assumption is that if you show your ordinary sincerity (or even your political ambition) by being a nuisance to yourself as well as to other people, you will have the strength of the great saints who passed through the fire. Any one who can be hustled in a hall for five minutes, or put in a cell for five days, has achieved what was meant by martyrdom, and has a halo.[68]

Modern nations

THE MORE MODERN nations detest each other the more meekly they follow each other; for all competition is in its nature only a furious plagiarism.[69]

Modern philosophy

A NEW PHILOSOPHY generally means in practice the praise of some old vice.[70]

THE WHOLE MEANING of literature is simply to cut a long story short; that is why our modern books of philosophy are never literature.[71]

The modern statesman

THE MODERN STATESMAN is utterly ignorant of democracy (or of aristocracy, for that matter); but he is not ignorant of his own trade. His trade is the trade of a conjurer. It is not so honourable as that of a conjurer, because the conjurer only wishes his fraud to last for an instant.[72]

COMPROMISE USED TO mean that half a loaf was better than no bread. Among modern statesmen it really seems to mean that half a loaf is better than a whole loaf.[73]

THE MODERN WORLD

THE MODERN WORLD seems to have no notion of preserving different things side by side, of allowing its proper and proportionate place to each, of saving the whole varied heritage of culture. It has no notion except that of simplifying something by destroying nearly everything.[74]

IN THE MODERN world we are primarily confronted with the extraordinary spectacle of people turning to new ideals because they have not tried the old. Men have not got tired of Christianity; they have never found enough Christianity to get tired of. Men have never wearied of political justice; they have wearied of waiting for it.[75]

THE MODERN WORLD is filled with men who hold dogmas so strongly that they do not even know that they are dogmas.[76]

IF THE MODERN world will not insist on having some sharp and definite moral law, capable of resisting the counter-attractions of art and humour, the modern world will simply be given over as a spoil to anybody who can manage to do a nasty thing in a nice way. Every murderer who can murder entertainingly will be allowed to murder. Every burglar who burgles in really humorous attitudes will burgle as much as he likes.[77]

THE WHOLE MODERN world, or at any rate the whole modern Press, has a perpetual and consuming terror of plain morals. Men always attempt to avoid condemning a thing upon merely moral grounds. If I beat my grandmother to death to-morrow in the middle of Battersea Park, you may be perfectly certain that people will say everything about it except the simple and fairly obvious fact that it is wrong.[78]

THE MODERN WORLD is not evil; in some ways the modern world is far too good. It is full of wild and wasted virtues. When a religious scheme is shattered (as Christianity was shattered at the Reformation), it is not merely the vices that are let loose. The vices are, indeed, let loose, and they wander and do damage. But the virtues are let loose also; and the virtues wander more wildly, and the virtues do more terrible damage. The modern world is full of the old Christian virtues gone mad. The virtues have gone mad because they have been isolated from each other and are wandering alone. Thus some scientists care for truth; and their truth is pitiless. Thus some humanitarians only care for pity; and their pity (I am sorry to say) is often untruthful.[79]

MODERNISM

THESE PAGES CONTAIN a sort of recurring protest against the boast of certain writers that they are merely recent. They brag that their philosophy of the universe is the last philosophy or the new philosophy, or the advanced and progressive philosophy. I have said much against a mere modernism. . . . It is incomprehensible to me that any thinker can calmly call himself a modernist; he might as well call himself a Thursdayite.[80]

BUT I NEVER succeeded in saying the quite clear and obvious thing that is really the matter with modernism. The real objection to modernism is simply that it is a form of snobbishness. It is an attempt to crush a rational opponent not by reason, but by some mystery of superiority, by hinting that one is specially up to date or particularly "in the know." To flaunt the fact that we have had all the last books from Germany is simply vulgar; like flaunting the fact that we have had all the last bonnets from Paris. To introduce into philosophical discussions a sneer at a creed's antiquity is like introducing a sneer at a lady's age. It is caddish because it is irrelevant. The pure modernist is merely a snob; he cannot bear to be a month behind the fashion.[81]

The modernist church

ALMOST EVERY CONTEMPORARY proposal to bring freedom into the church is simply a proposal to bring tyranny into the world. For freeing the church now does not even mean freeing it in all directions. It means freeing that peculiar set of dogmas loosely called scientific, dogmas of monism, of pantheism, or of Arianism, or of necessity. And every one of these . . . can be shown to be the natural ally of oppression.[82]

Modernity

"BUT I DO not think," continued Wayne, "that this horrible silence of modernity will last, though I think for the present it will increase. What a farce is this modern liberality! Freedom of speech means practically, in our modern civilisation, that we must only talk about unimportant things. We must not talk about religion, for that is illiberal; we must not talk about bread and cheese, for that is talking shop; we must not talk about death, for that is depressing; we must not talk about birth, for that is indelicate. It cannot last. Something must break this strange indifference, this strange dreamy egoism, this strange loneliness of millions in a crowd. Something must break it. Why should it not be you and I?"[83]

"TERRIBLY QUIET; THAT is in two words the spirit of this age, as I have felt it from my cradle. I sometimes wondered how many other people felt the oppression of this union between quietude and terror. I see blank well-ordered streets and men in black moving about inoffensively, sullenly. It goes on day after day, day after day, and nothing happens; but to me it is like a dream from which I might wake screaming."[84]

IT IS CUSTOMARY to complain of the bustle and strenuousness of our epoch. But in truth the chief mark of our epoch is a profound laziness and fatigue. . . . Scientific phrases are used like scientific wheels and piston-rods to make swifter and smoother yet the path of the comfortable. Long words go rattling by us like long railway trains. We know they are carrying thousands who are too tired or too indolent to walk and think for themselves.[85]

EVERYTHING THAT IS done in a hurry is certain to be antiquated; that is why modern industrial civilisation bears so curious a resemblance to barbarism.[86]

Moderns

MODERNS HAVE NOT the moral courage, as a rule, to avow the sincere spiritual bias behind their fads; they become insincere even about their sincerity.[87]

Modesty

MODESTY IS TOO fierce and elemental a thing for the modern pedants to understand. I had almost said too savage a thing. It has in it the joy of escape, and the ancient shyness of freedom.[88]

Monogamy

ALL THE THINGS that make monogamy a success are, in their nature, un-dramatic things: the silent growth of an instinctive confidence, the common wounds and victories, the accumulation of customs, the rich maturing of old jokes.[89]

Monsters

IN ONE OF Stevenson's letters there is a characteristically humorous remark about the appalling impression produced on him in childhood by the beasts with many eyes in the Book of Revelation: "If that was heaven, what in the name of Davy Jones was hell like?" Now in sober truth there is a magnificent idea in these monsters of the Apocalypse. It is, I suppose, the idea that beings really more beautiful or more universal than we are might appear to us frightful and even confused. Especially they might seem to have senses at once more multiplex and more staring; an idea very imaginatively seized in the multitude of eyes. I like those monsters beneath the throne very much. But I like them beneath the throne. It is when one of them goes wandering in deserts and finds a throne for himself that evil faiths begin, and there is (literally) the devil to pay.[90]

Morality

MORALITY DID NOT begin by one man saying to another, "I will not hit you if you do not hit me"; there is no trace of such a transaction. There *is* a trace of both men having said, "We must not hit each other in the holy place." They gained their morality by guarding their religion.[91]

WE OFTEN HEAR it said, for instance, "What is right in one age is wrong in another." This is quite reasonable, if it means that there is a fixed aim, and that certain methods attain at certain times and not at other times.[92]

Motor-cars

BUT ABOUT MOTORING there is something magical, like going to the moon; and I say the thing should be kept exceptional and felt as something breathless and bizarre. My ideal hero would own his horse, but would have the moral courage to hire his motor. Fairy tales are the only sound guide-books to life; I like the Fairy Prince to ride on a white pony out of his father's stables, which are of ivory and gold. But if in the course of his adventures he finds it necessary to travel on a flaming dragon, I think he ought to give the dragon back to the witch at the end of the story. It is a mistake to have dragons about the place.[93]

Mountains

IF THERE BE any value in scaling the mountains, it is only that from them one can behold the plains.[94]

Movements

THE MODERN WORLD is full of lawless little men and mad little movements.[95]

Music

MUSIC IS MERE beauty; it is beauty in the abstract, beauty in solution. It is a shapeless and liquid element of beauty.[96]

Mystery

TO THE MAN who sees the marvellousness of all things, the surface of life is fully as strange and magical as its interior; clearness and plainness of life is fully as mysterious as its mysteries.[97]

IT IS COMPLETE error to suppose that because a thing is vulgar therefore it is not refined; that is, subtle and hard to define. A drawing-room song of my youth which began "In the gloaming, O, my darling," was vulgar enough as a song; but the connection between human passion and the twilight is none the less an exquisite and even inscrutable thing.[98]

I FOUND MY way back to the city, and some time afterwards I actually saw in the street my two men talking, no doubt still saying, one that Science had changed all in Humanity, and the other that Humanity was now pushing the wings of the purely intellectual. But for me Humanity was hooked on to an accidental picture. I thought of a low and lonely house in the flats, behind a veil or film of slight trees, a man breaking the ground as men have broken from the first morning, and a huge grey horse champing his food within a foot of a child's head, as in the stable where Christ was born.[99]

I WAS ALONE in the flat fields out of sight of the city. On one side of the road was one of those small, thin woods which are common in all countries, but of which, by a coincidence, the mystical painters of Flanders were very fond. The night was closing in with cloudy purple and grey; there was one ribbon of silver, the last rag of the sunset. Through the wood went one little path, and somehow it suggested that it might lead to some sign of life—there was no other sign of life on the horizon. I went along it, and soon sank into a sort of dancing twilight of all those tiny trees. There is something subtle and bewildering about that sort of frail and fantastic wood. A forest of big trees seems like a bodily barrier; but somehow that mist of thin lines seems like a spiritual barrier. It is as if one were caught in a fairy cloud or could not pass a phantom. When I had well lost the last gleam of the high road a curious and definite feeling came upon me. Now I suddenly felt something much more practical and extraordinary—the absence of humanity: inhuman loneliness. Of course, there was nothing really lost in my state; but the mood may hit one anywhere. I wanted men—any men; and I felt our awful alliance over all the globe. And at last, when I had walked for what seemed a long time, I saw a light too near the earth to mean anything except the image of God.[100]

AS THEY RACED along to the gate out of which the elephant had vanished, Syme felt a glaring panorama of the strange animals in the cages which they passed. Afterwards he thought it queer that he should have seen them so clearly. He remembered especially seeing pelicans, with their preposterous, pendant throats. He wondered why the pelican was the symbol of charity, except it was that it wanted a good deal of charity to admire a pelican. He remembered a hornbill, which was simply a huge yellow beak with a small bird tied on behind it. The whole gave him a sensation, the vividness of which he could not explain, that Nature was always making quite mysterious jokes. Sunday had told them that they would understand him when they had understood the stars. He wondered whether even the archangels understood the hornbill.[101]

"LISTEN TO ME," cried Syme with extraordinary emphasis. "Shall I tell you the secret of the whole world? It is that we have only known the back of the world. We see everything from behind, and it looks brutal. That is not a tree, but the back of a tree. That is not a cloud, but the back of a cloud. Cannot you see that every-thing is stooping and hiding a face? If we could only get round in front—"[102]

"AND YOU," said Syme, leaning forward, "what are you?"

"I? What am I?" roared the President, and he rose slowly to an incredible height, like some enormous wave about to arch above them and break. "You want to know what I am, do you? Bull, you are a man of science. Grub in the roots of those trees and find out the truth about them. Syme, you are a poet. Stare at those morning clouds. But I tell you this, that you will have found out the truth of the last tree and the top-most cloud before the truth about me. You will understand the sea, and I shall be still a riddle; you shall know what the stars are, and not know what I am. Since the beginning of the world all men have hunted me like a wolf—kings and sages, and poets and lawgivers, all the churches, and all the philosophies. But I have never been caught yet, and the skies will fall in the time I turn to bay. I have given them a good run for their money, and I will now."[103]

IT WILL BE said that a rational person accepts the world as mixed of good and evil with a decent satisfaction and a decent endurance. But this is exactly the attitude which I maintain to be defective. It is, I know, very common in this age; it was perfectly put in those quiet lines of Matthew Arnold which are more piercingly blasphemous than the shrieks of Schopenhauer—

> "Enough we live:—and if a life,
> With large results so little rife,
> Though bearable, seem hardly worth
> This pomp of worlds, this pain of birth."

I know this feeling fills our epoch, and I think it freezes our epoch. For our Titanic purposes of faith and revolution, what we need is not the cold acceptance of the world as a compromise, but some way in which we can heartily hate and heartily love it. We do not want joy and anger to neutralize each other and produce a surly contentment; we want a fiercer delight and a fiercer discontent. We have to feel the universe at once as an ogre's castle, to be stormed, and yet as our own cottage, to which we can return at evening.[104]

N

Natural beauty

A SUNSET OF copper and gold had just broken down and gone to pieces in the west, and grey colours were crawling over everything in earth and heaven; also a wind was growing, a wind that laid a cold finger upon flesh and spirit. The bushes at the back of my garden began to whisper like conspirators; and then to wave like wild hands in signal.[1]

IT WAS ONE of those days which more than once this year broke the retreat of winter; a winter day that began too late to be spring. We were already clear of the obstructing crowds and quickening our pace through a borderland of market gardens and isolated public-houses, when the grey showed golden patches and a good light began to glitter on everything. The cab went quicker and quicker. The open land whirled wider and wider; but I did not lose my sense of being battled with and thwarted that I had felt in the thronged slums. Rather the feeling increased, because of the great difficulty of space and time. The faster went the car, the fiercer and thicker I felt the fight.

The whole landscape seemed charging at me—and just missing me. The tall, shining grass went by like showers of arrows; the very trees seemed like lances hurled at my heart, and shaving it by a hair's breadth. Across some vast, smooth valley I saw a beech-tree by the white road stand up little and defiant. It grew bigger and bigger with blinding rapidity. It charged me like a tilting knight, seemed to hack at my head, and pass by. Sometimes when we went round a curve of road, the effect was yet more awful. It seemed as if some tree or windmill swung round to smite like a boomerang. The sun by this time was a blazing fact; and I saw that all Nature is chivalrous and militant. We do wrong to seek peace in Nature; we should rather seek the nobler sort of war; and see all the trees as green banners.[2]

AS I SEE the corn grow green all about my neighbourhood, there rushes on me for no reason in particular a memory of the winter. I say "rushes," for that is the very word for the old sweeping lines of the ploughed fields. From some accidental turn of a train journey or a walking tour, I saw suddenly the fierce rush of the furrows. The furrows are like arrows; they fly along an arc of sky. They are like leaping animals; they vault an inviolable hill and roll down the other side. They are like battering battalions; they rush over a hill with flying squadrons and carry it with a cavalry charge. They have all the air of Arabs sweeping a desert, of rockets sweeping the sky, of torrents sweeping a watercourse. Nothing ever seemed so living as those brown lines as they shot sheer from the height of a ridge down to their still whirl of the valley.[3]

THIS PARTICULAR EVENING, if it is remembered for nothing else, will be remembered in that place for its strange sunset. It looked like the end of the world. All the heaven seemed covered with a quite vivid and palpable plumage; you could only say that the sky was full of feathers, and of feathers that almost brushed the face. Across the great part of the dome they were grey, with the strangest tints of violet and mauve and an unnatural pink or pale green; but towards the west the whole grew past description, transparent and passionate, and the last red-hot plumes of it covered up the sun like something too good to be seen. The whole was so close about the earth, as to express nothing but a violent secrecy.[4]

VERY GRADUALLY AND very vaguely he realised into what rich roads the carriage was carrying him. He saw that they passed the stone gates of what might have been a park, that they began gradually to climb a hill which, while wooded on both sides, was somewhat more orderly than a forest. Then there began to grow upon him, as upon a man slowly waking from a healthy sleep, a pleasure in everything. He felt that the hedges were what hedges should be, living walls; that a hedge is like a human army, disciplined, but all the more alive. He saw high elms behind the hedges, and vaguely thought how happy boys would be climbing there. Then his carriage took a turn of the path, and he saw suddenly and quietly, like a long, low, sunset cloud, a long, low house, mellow in the mild light of sunset. All the six friends compared notes afterwards and quarrelled; but they all agreed that in some unaccountable way the place reminded them of their boyhood. It was either this elm-top or that crooked path, it was either this scrap of orchard or that shape of a window; but each man of them declared that he could remember this place.[5]

THE FIRE FADED, and the slow, strong stars came out. And the seven strange men were left alone, like seven stone statues on their chairs of stone. Not one of them had spoken a word.

They seemed in no haste to do so, but heard in silence the hum of insects and the distant song of one bird. Then Sunday spoke, but so dreamily that he might have been continuing a conversation rather than beginning one.

"We will eat and drink later," he said. "Let us remain together a little, we who have loved each other so sadly, and have fought so long. I seem to remember only centuries of heroic war, in which you were always heroes—epic on epic, iliad on iliad, and you always brothers in arms."[6]

NATURE

"DO YOU KNOW, Hump," he said, "I think modern people have somehow got their minds all wrong about human life. They seem to expect what Nature has never promised; and then try to ruin all that Nature has really given."[7]

THE ESSENCE OF all pantheism, evolutionism, and modern cosmic religion is really in this proposition: that Nature is our mother. Unfortunately, if you regard Nature as a mother, you discover that she is a step-mother. The main point of Christianity was this: that Nature is not our mother: Nature is our sister. We can be proud of her beauty, since we have the same father; but she has no authority over us.[8]

BUT NATURE CANNOT be making a careful picture made of many picked colours, unless Nature is personal. If the end of the world were mere darkness or mere light it might come as slowly and inevitably as dusk or dawn. But if the end of the world is to be a piece of elaborate and artistic chiaroscuro, then there must be design in it, either human or divine. The world, through mere time, might grow black like an old picture, or white like an old coat; but if it is turned into a particular piece of black and white art—then there is an artist.[9]

WAS NOT EVERYTHING, after all, like this bewildering woodland, this dance of dark and light? Everything only a glimpse, the glimpse always unforeseen, and always forgotten. For Gabriel Syme had found in the heart of that sun-splashed wood what many modern painters had found there. He had found the thing which the modern people call Impressionism, which is another name for that final scepticism which can find no floor to the universe.[10]

NATURE AND THE ARTIFICIAL

TO THIS MAN, at any rate, the inconceivable had happened. The artificial city had become to him nature, and he felt the curbstones and gas-lamps as things as ancient as the sky.[11]

The new theology

CERTAIN NEW THEOLOGIANS dispute original sin, which is the only part of Christian theology which can really be proved.[12]

NOW LET US take in order the innovations that are the notes of the new theology or the modernist church. . . .

I take the most obvious instance first, the case of miracles. For some extraordinary reason, there is a fixed notion that it is more liberal to disbelieve in miracles than to believe in them. Why, I cannot imagine, nor can anybody tell me. For some inconceivable cause a "broad" or "liberal" clergyman always means a man who wishes at least to diminish the number of miracles; it never means a man who wishes to increase that number. It always means a man who is free to disbelieve that Christ came out of His grave; it never means a man who is free to believe that his own aunt came out of her grave. It is common to find trouble in a parish because the parish priest cannot admit that St. Peter walked on water; yet how rarely do we find trouble in a parish because the clergyman says that his father walked on the Serpentine? And this is not because (as the swift secularist debater would immediately retort) miracles cannot be believed in our experience. It is not because "miracles do not happen," as in the dogma which Matthew Arnold recited with simple faith. More supernatural things are *alleged* to have happened in our time than would have been possible eighty years ago. Men of science believe in such marvels much more than they did: the most perplexing, and even horrible, prodigies of mind and spirit are always being unveiled in modern psychology. Things that the old science at least would frankly have rejected as miracles are hourly being asserted by the new science. The only thing which is still old-fashioned enough to reject miracles is the New Theology.[13]

BUT ALWAYS HIS triumphs are the triumphs of a highly sensitive man: a man must feel insults before he can so insultingly and splendidly avenge them. He is a naked man, who carries a naked sword. The quality of his literary style is so successful that it succeeds in escaping definition. The quality of his logic is that of a long but passionate patience, which waits until he has fixed all corners of an iron trap. But the quality of his moral comment on the age remains what I have said: a protest of the rationality of religion as against the increasing irrationality of mere Victorian comfort and compromise.[14]

SO FAR AS the present purpose is concerned, his protest died with him: he left few imitators and (it may easily be conceived) no successful imitators. The suggestion of him lingers on in the exquisite Elizabethan perversity of Coventry Patmore; and has later flamed out from the shy volcano of Francis Thompson.[15]

Newspapers

WE HAVE ALMOST up to the last instant trusted the newspapers as organs of public opinion. Just recently some of us have seen (not slowly, but with a start) that they are obviously nothing of the kind. They are, by the nature of the case, the hobbies of a few rich men.[16]

Nietzsche, Friedrich

THE MOST BRILLIANT exponent of the egoistic school, Nietzsche, with deadly and honourable logic, admitted that the philosophy of self-satisfaction led to looking down upon the weak, the cowardly, and the ignorant. Looking down on things may be a delightful experience, only there is nothing, from a mountain to a cabbage, that is really *seen* when it is seen from a balloon. The philosopher of the ego sees everything, no doubt, from a high and rarified heaven; only he sees everything foreshortened or deformed.[17]

THIS, INCIDENTALLY, IS almost the whole weakness of Nietzsche, whom some are representing as a bold and strong thinker. No one will deny that he was a poetical and suggestive thinker; but he was quite the reverse of strong. He was not at all bold. He never put his own meaning before himself in bald abstract words: as did Aristotle and Calvin, and even Karl Marx, the hard, fearless men of thought. Nietzsche always escaped a question by a physical metaphor, like a cheery minor poet. He said, "beyond good and evil," because he had not the courage to say, "more good than good and evil," or, "more evil than good and evil." Had he faced his thought without metaphors, he would have seen that it was nonsense. So, when he describes his hero, he does not dare to say, "the purer man," or "the happier man," or "the sadder man," for all these are ideas; and ideas are alarming. He says "the upper man," or "over man," a physical metaphor from acrobats or alpine climbers. Nietzsche is truly a very timid thinker. He does not really know in the least what sort of man he wants evolution to produce. And if he does not know, certainly the ordinary evolutionists, who talk about things being "higher," do not know either.[18]

NIETZSCHE SCALES STAGGERING mountains, but he turns up ultimately in Tibet. He sits down beside Tolstoy in the land of nothing and Nirvana. They are both helpless—one because he must not grasp anything, and the other because he must not let go of anything. The Tolstoian's will is frozen by a Buddhistic instinct that all special actions are evil. But the Nietzscheite's will is quite equally frozen by his view that all special actions are good; for if all special actions are good, none of them are special. They stand at the cross roads, and one hates all the roads and the other likes all the roads. The result is—well, some things are not hard to calculate. They stand at the cross roads.[19]

MAN, THE CENTRAL pillar of the world, must be upright and straight; around him all the trees and beasts and elements and devils may crook and curl like smoke if they choose. All really imaginative literature is only the contrast between the weird curves of Nature and the straightness of the soul. Man may behold what ugliness he likes if he is sure that he will not worship it; but there are some so weak that they will worship a thing only because it is ugly. These must be chained to the beautiful. It is not always wrong even to go, like Dante, to the brink of the lowest promontory and look down at hell. It is when you look up at hell that a serious miscalculation has probably been made.

Therefore I see no wrong in riding with the Nightmare tonight; she whinnies to me from the rocking tree-tops and the roaring wind; I will catch her and ride her through the awful air. Woods and weeds are alike tugging at the roots in the rising tempest, as if all wished to fly with us over the moon, like that wild amorous cow whose child was the Moon-Calf. We will rise to that mad infinite where there is neither up nor down, the high topsy-turveydom of the heavens. I will answer the call of chaos and old night. I will ride on the Nightmare; but she shall not ride on me.[20]

Noble passions

THE RIDICULOUS THEORY that men should have no noble passions or sentiments in public may have been designed to make private life holy and undefiled, but it has had very little actual effect except to make public life cynical and preposterously unmeaning.[21]

Nonsense

THERE ARE TWO ways of dealing with nonsense in this world. One way is to put nonsense in the right place; as when people put nonsense into nursery rhymes. The other is to put nonsense in the wrong place; as when they put it into educational addresses, psychological criticisms, and complaints against nursery rhymes or other normal amusements of mankind.[22]

NOVELS

A GOOD NOVEL tells us the truth about its hero; but a bad novel tells us the truth about its author.[23]

IN [THE NOVEL'S] development women played a peculiar part, English women especially, and Victorian women most of all.[24]

WHEN I SAY "novel," I mean a fictitious narrative (almost invariably, but not necessarily, in prose) of which the essential is that the story is not told for the sake of its naked pointedness as an anecdote, or for the sake of the irrelevant landscapes and visions that can be caught up in it, but for the sake of some study of the difference between human beings.[25]

THE TRUTH IS, I think, that the modern novel is a new thing; not new in its essence (for that is a philosophy for fools), but new in the sense that it lets loose many of the things that are old.[26]

UNCONVENTIONAL
Chesterton the Novelist

It is a riddle, wrapped in a mystery, inside an enigma." These words of Winston Churchill, were they ever to have been applied to Chesterton's most highly regarded novel, *The Man Who Was Thursday*, would have pleased him greatly. It is the kind of phrase that was his stock in trade.

This sentiment was a pervasive theme in all but one of the six novels Chesterton published during his lifetime.[1] They are, in sequence: *The Napoleon of Notting Hill* (1904); *The Ball and the Cross* (serialized from 1905–6);[2] *The Man Who Was Thursday* (1907);[3] *Manalive* (1912); *The Flying Inn* (1914) and *The Return of Don Quixote* (1927).

The Man Who Was Thursday attracted the attention of some of the best writers of the last century. T. S. Eliot, W. H. Auden, J. R. R. Tolkien, C. S. Lewis, Jorge Luis Borges, and Frederick Buechner are but some of those who have confessed their admiration for this work.[4] Subtitled "a nightmare," the story pitted anarchy against order—an exploration, by turns fantastic and sobering, of why men ought to love light more than darkness.

The Napoleon of Notting Hill imagined an England where medieval mores and valor supplanted a tired and lifeless modernity years in the future. Both novels, highly original and innovative, were admired by T. S. Eliot, who stated in 1936 that Chesterton "reached a high imaginative level with *The Napoleon of Notting Hill*, and higher with *The Man Who Was Thursday*, romances in which he turned the Stevensonian fantasy to more serious purpose."[5]

The Ball and the Cross, for its part, was a fictional clash between theism and atheism. It was described by literary critic L. Wardlaw Miles as "a mixture of wild adventure, roaring farce, and religious symbolism." It was, Miles noted perceptively, a recasting of "favorite ideas" present in *The Man Who Was Thursday*.[6]

A review in the *Times Literary Supplement* described *Manalive*—a farcical whodunit—as a "metaphysical extravaganza"—a work marked by "keen wit and a strange intermittent beauty."[7]

The Flying Inn, meanwhile, was a more straightforward affair—a satiric exploration of what a future England would be like should Prohibition be implemented. Lastly, *The Return of Don Quixote* marked a return to what one reviewer called "Mr. Chesterton's utopian romances."[8] Borrowing essential elements from Cervantes's seventeenth-century novel, it introduced a twentieth-century Don Quixote to England. This book garnered significant critical praise, the reviewer for the *Sunday Times* declaring it "a triumph of fine satire, wise and witty and wholly delightful; just possibly, too, the most brilliant of the author's romantic experiments."[9]

About all of these novels, there hung an unmistakable air of mystery—a pervasive sense of otherness. That was as Chesterton meant it to be. For his novels are, at heart, potent combinations of mysticism and romance in the best and highest sense of those words. In his acclaimed study of William Blake—a kindred artistic spirit—Chesterton came as close, perhaps, as he ever did to explaining what he was on about in his novels, and what he wanted people to understand:

> Mysticism is generally felt vaguely to be itself vague—a thing of clouds and curtains, of darkness or concealing vapours, of bewildering conspiracies or impenetrable symbols. Some quacks have indeed dealt in such things: but no true mystic ever loved darkness rather than light. No pure mystic ever loved mere mystery. The mystic does not bring doubts or riddles: the doubts and riddles exist already. We all feel the riddle of the earth without anyone to point it out. The mystery of life is the plainest part of it. The clouds and curtains of darkness, the confounding vapours, these are the daily weather of this world.[10]

O

Obscurity

THERE IS SOMETHING psychologically Christian about the idea of seeking for the opinion of the obscure rather than taking the obvious course of accepting the opinion of the prominent.[1]

Oddities

ODDITIES ONLY STRIKE ordinary people. Oddities do not strike odd people. This is why ordinary people have a much more exciting time; while odd people are always complaining of the dullness of life.[2]

The Old Testament

THE CENTRAL IDEA of the great part of the Old Testament may be called the idea of the loneliness of God. God is not the only chief character of the Old Testament; God is properly the only character in the Old Testament.[3]

THE PRESENT IMPORTANCE of the book of Job cannot be expressed adequately even by saying that it is the most interesting of ancient books. We may almost say of the book of Job that it is the most interesting of modern books. In truth, of course, neither of the two phrases covers the matter, because fundamental human religion and fundamental human irreligion are both at once old and new; philosophy is either eternal or it is not philosophy.[4]

THE FIRST OF the intellectual beauties of the book of Job is that it is all concerned with this desire to know the actuality; the desire to know what is, and not merely what seems.[5]

[IN THE BOOK of Job,] when God is speaking of snow and hail in the mere catalogue of the physical cosmos, He speaks of them as a treasury that He has laid up against the day of battle—a hint of some huge Armageddon in which evil shall be at last over-thrown.

Nothing could be better, artistically speaking, than this opti-mism breaking though agnosticism like fiery gold round the edges of a black cloud.[6]

THE BOOK OF Job is chiefly remarkable, as I have insisted through-out, for the fact that it does not end in a way that is conventionally satisfactory. Job is not told that his misfortunes were due to his sins or a part of any plan for his improvement. But in the prologue we see Job tormented not because he was the worst of men, but because he was the best. It is the lesson of the whole work that man is most comforted by paradoxes.[7]

THE WRITERS OF the Book of Genesis had no theory of gravita-tion, which to the normal person will appear a fact of as much importance as that they had no umbrellas. But the theory of gravi-tation has a curiously Hebrew sentiment in it—a sentiment of combined dependence and certainty, a sense of grappling unity, by which all things hang upon one thread. "Thou hast hanged the world upon nothing," said the author of the Book of Job, and in that sentence wrote the whole appalling poetry of modern astron-omy. The sense of the preciousness and fragility of the universe, the sense of being in the hollow of a hand, is one which the round and rolling earth gives in its most thrilling form.[8]

Old things

AND IN THE darkest of the books of God there is written a truth that is also a riddle. It is of the new things that men tire—of fashions and proposals and improvements and change. It is the old things that startle and intoxicate. It is the old things that are young. There is no sceptic who does not feel that many have doubted before. There is no rich and fickle man who does not feel that all his novelties are ancient. There is no worshipper of change who does not feel upon his neck the vast weight of the weariness of the universe. But we who do the old things are fed by nature with a perpetual infancy.[9]

THERE IS NO new ideal imaginable by the madness of modern sophists, which will be anything like so startling as fulfilling any one of the old ones. On the day that any copybook maxim is carried out there will be something like an earthquake on the earth. There is only one thing new that can be done under the sun; and that is to look at the sun. If you attempt it on a blue day in June, you will know why men do not look straight at their ideals. There is only one really startling thing to be done with the ideal, and that is to do it. It is to face the flaming logical fact, and its frightful consequences. Christ knew that it would be a more stunning thunderbolt to fulfil the law than to destroy it.[10]

Oligarchies

A FRESH AND fierce philosophy of oligarchy and the wise few is spreading . . . all over the world. We have a logical answer to that philosophy. . . . We have a basic defence of democracy. . . . Our answer is "There are no wise few; for in all men rages the folly of the Fall. Take your strongest, happiest, handsomest, best born, best bred, best instructed men on earth and give them special power for half an hour and because they are men they will begin to [perform] badly."[11]

Omnibus, riding an

THE KING, MEANWHILE, was rattling along on the top of his blue omnibus. The traffic of London as a whole had not, of course, been greatly disturbed by these events, for the affair was treated as a Notting Hill riot, and that area was marked off as if it had been in the hands of a gang of recognised rioters. The blue omnibuses simply went round as they would have done if a road were being mended, and the omnibus on which the correspondent of the *Court Journal* was sitting swept round the corner of Queen's Road, Bayswater.

The King was alone on the top of the vehicle, and was enjoying the speed at which it was going.

"Forward, my beauty, my Arab," he said, patting the omnibus encouragingly, "fleetest of all thy bounding tribe. Are thy relations with thy driver, I wonder, those of the Bedouin and his steed? Does he sleep side by side with thee—"[12]

Optimism and pessimism

UPON THE WHOLE, I came to the conclusion that the optimist thought everything good except the pessimist, and that the pessimist thought everything bad, except himself. It would be unfair to omit altogether from the list the mysterious but suggestive definition said to have been given by a little girl, "An optimist is a man who looks after your eyes, and a pessimist is a man who looks after your feet." I am not sure that this is not the best definition of all.

There is even a sort of allegorical truth in it. For there might, perhaps, be a profitable distinction drawn between that more dreary thinker who thinks merely of our contact with the earth from moment to moment, and that happier thinker who considers rather our primary power of vision and of choice of road.[13]

SORROW AND PESSIMISM are indeed, in a sense, opposite things, since sorrow is founded on the value of something and pessimism upon the value of nothing. And in practice we find that those poets or political leaders who come from the people, and whose experiences have really been searching and cruel, are the most sanguine people in the world. These men out of the old agony are always optimists; they are sometimes offensive optimists.[14]

ORIGINAL SIN

CARLYLE SAID THAT men were mostly fools. Christianity with a surer and more reverent realism, says they are all fools. This doctrine is sometimes called the doctrine of original sin. It may also be described as the doctrine of the equality of men.[15]

ORTHODOXY

ONE SEARCHES FOR truth, but it may be that one pursues instinctively the more extraordinary truths.[16]

IT IS THE purpose of the writer to attempt an explanation, not of whether the Christian Faith can be believed, but of how he personally has come to believe it. The book is therefore arranged upon the positive principle of a riddle and its answer. It deals first with all the writer's own solitary and sincere speculations and then with all the startling style in which they were all suddenly satisfied by the Christian Theology.[17]

WHEN THE WORD "orthodoxy" is used here it means the Apostles' Creed, as understood by everybody calling himself Christian until a very short time ago and the general historic conduct of those who held such a creed.[18]

THIS IS THE thrilling romance of Orthodoxy. People have fallen into a foolish habit of speaking of orthodoxy as something heavy, humdrum, and safe. There never was anything so perilous or so exciting as orthodoxy. It was sanity: and to be sane is more dramatic than to be mad. . . . It is always easy to let the age have its head; the difficult thing is to keep one's own. It is always easy to be a modernist; as it is easy to be a snob. To have fallen into any of those open traps of error and exaggeration which fashion after fashion and sect after sect set along the historic path of Christendom—that would indeed have been simple. It is always simple to fall; there are an infinity of angles at which one falls, only one at which one stands. To have fallen into any one of the fads from Gnosticism to Christian Science would indeed have been obvious and tame. But to have avoided them all has been one whirling adventure; and in my vision the heavenly chariot flies thundering through the ages, the dull heresies sprawling and prostrate, the wild truth reeling but erect.[19]

P

PANTHEISM

THERE IS NO real possibility of getting out of pantheism any special impulse to moral action. For pantheism implies in its nature that one thing is as good as another; whereas action implies in its nature that one thing is greatly preferable to another.[1]

PARADOX

"THERE ARE DEGREES of seriousness," replied Syme. "I have never doubted that you were perfectly sincere in this sense, that you thought what you said well worth saying, that you thought a paradox might wake men up to a neglected truth."[2]

"YOU ARE NOT sufficiently democratic," answered the policeman, "but you were right when you said just now that our ordinary treatment of the poor criminal was a pretty brutal business. I tell you I am sometimes sick of my trade when I see how perpetually it means merely a war upon the ignorant and the desperate. But this new movement of ours is a very different affair. We deny the snobbish English assumption that the uneducated are the dangerous criminals. We remember the Roman Emperors. We remember the great poisoning princes of the Renaissance. We say that the dangerous criminal is the educated criminal. We say that the most dangerous criminal now is the entirely lawless modern philosopher. Compared to him, burglars and bigamists are essentially moral men; my heart goes out to them. They accept the essential ideal of man; they merely seek it wrongly. Thieves respect property. They merely wish the property to become their property that they may more perfectly respect it. But philosophers dislike property as property; they wish to destroy the very idea of personal possession. Bigamists respect marriage, or they would not go through the highly ceremonial and even ritualistic formality of bigamy. But philosophers despise marriage as marriage. Murderers respect human life; they merely wish to attain a greater fulness of human life in themselves by the sacrifice of what seems to them to be lesser lives. But philosophers hate life itself, their own as much as other people's."[3]

"WHEN I FIRST saw Sunday," said Syme slowly, "I only saw his back; and when I saw his back, I knew he was the worst man in the world. His neck and shoulders were brutal, like those of some apish god. His head had a stoop that was hardly human, like the stoop of an ox. In fact, I had at once the revolting fancy that this was not a man at all, but a beast dressed up in men's clothes."

"Get on," said Dr. Bull.

"And then the queer thing happened. I had seen his back from the street, as he sat in the balcony. Then I entered the hotel, and coming round the other side of him, saw his face in the sunlight. His face frightened me, as it did everyone; but not because it was brutal, not because it was evil. On the contrary, it frightened me because it was so beautiful, because it was so good."

"Syme," exclaimed the Secretary, "are you ill?"

"It was like the face of some ancient archangel, judging justly after heroic wars. There was laughter in the eyes, and in the mouth honour and sorrow."[4]

TROUBLE AND EXULTATION go on in a design larger than any of ours, neither vanishing at all. Beyond our greatest happiness there lie dangers, and after our greatest dangers there remaineth a rest.[5]

Pathos

HIS PATHOS WAS natural, almost casual. The Stoics, ancient and modern, were proud, proud of concealing their tears. [Christ] never concealed His tears; He showed them plainly on His open face at any daily sight, such as the far sight of His native city.[6]

Patriotism

ADAM WAYNE, AS a boy, had for his dull streets in Notting Hill the ultimate and ancient sentiment that went out to Athens or Jerusalem. He knew the secret of the passion, those secrets which make real old national songs sound so strange to our civilisation. He knew that real patriotism tends to sing about sorrows and forlorn hopes much more than about victory. He knew that in proper names themselves is half the poetry of all national poems.[7]

Peacemakers

THERE ARE TWO kinds of peacemakers in the modern world; and they are both, though in various ways, a nuisance. The first peacemaker is the man who goes about saying that he agrees with everybody. He confuses everybody. The second peacemaker is the man who goes about saying that everybody agrees with him. He enrages everybody. Between the two of them they produce a hundred times more disputes and distractions than we poor pugnacious people would ever have thought of in our lives.[8]

I HAVE A simple, melodramatic mind; there is nothing lofty or peace-loving about me; and I thoroughly enjoy seeing people knocked down on the stage. I should have no objection to seeing them knocked down in real life, if the people were wisely and thoughtfully selected.[9]

SYME STIRRED SHARPLY in his seat, but otherwise there was silence, and the incomprehensible went on.

"But you were men. You did not forget your secret honour, though the whole cosmos turned an engine of torture to tear it out of you. I knew how near you were to hell. I know how you, Thursday, crossed swords with King Satan, and how you, Wednesday, named me in the hour without hope."

There was complete silence in the starlit garden, and then the black-browed Secretary, implacable, turned in his chair towards Sunday, and said in a harsh voice—

"Who and what are you?"

"I am the Sabbath," said the other without moving. "I am the peace of God."[10]

PERSPECTIVE

I SOMETIMES THINK it is a pity that people travel in foreign countries; it narrows their minds so much.[11]

THE TELESCOPE MAKES the world smaller; it is only the microscope that makes it larger. Before long the world will be cloven with a war between the telescopists and the microscopists. The first study large things and live in a small world; the second study small things and live in a large world.[12]

I THINK THAT we must always conceive of that which is the goal of all our endeavours as something which is in some strange way near. Science boasts of the distance of its stars; of the terrific remoteness of the things of which it has to speak. But poetry and religion always insist upon the proximity, the almost menacing closeness of the things with which they are concerned. Always the Kingdom of Heaven is "At Hand"; and Looking-glass Land is only through the looking-glass. So I for one should never be astonished if the next twist of a street led me to the heart of that maze in which all the mystics are lost. I should not be at all surprised if I turned one corner in Fleet Street and saw a yet queerer-looking lamp; I should not be surprised if I turned a third corner and found myself in Elfland.[13]

PESSIMISTS

THE PESSIMISTS WHO attack the universe are always under this disadvantage. They have an exhilarating consciousness that they could make the sun and moon better; but they also have the depressing consciousness that they could not make the sun and moon at all. A man looking at a hippopotamus may sometimes be tempted to regard a hippopotamus as an enormous mistake; but he is also bound to confess that a fortunate inferiority prevents him personally from making such mistakes.[14]

PHILOSOPHERS

IT IS A good rule of philosophy when regarding an end to refer to the beginning.[15]

A PHILOSOPHER CANNOT talk about any single thing down to a pumpkin, without showing whether he is wise or foolish; but he can easily talk about everything without anyone having any views about him beyond gloomy suspicions.[16]

BUCK LOOKED AT his map with knitted brows.

"Was that Portobello Road?" he asked.

"Yes," said Barker—"yes; Portobello Road. I saw it afterwards; but, my God, what a place it was! Buck, have you ever stood and let a six foot of man lash and lash at your head with six feet of pole with six pounds of steel at the end? Because, when you have had that experience, as Walt Whitman says, 'you re-examine philosophies and religions.'"[17]

A Lover of Wisdom
Chesterton the Philosopher

In its most basic and literal sense, a philosopher is defined as a "lover of wisdom." G. K. Chesterton was certainly that, but was he a philosopher in the more formal sense of the word—one who systematically investigates and propounds theories as to the ultimate meaning of things?

The Pulitzer Prize–winning author and historian Garry Wills contends that he was not, and in so doing makes an important distinction. "Chesterton was not a philosopher," he wrote, "nor did he want to be. He was a defender of philosophy, which is quite another thing."[1]

Thus it was as a defender of philosophy, in the pages of his book *Heretics*, that Chesterton wrote some of his most resonant and powerful lines. He commenced this book by speaking directly to his own historical moment—the world of the early twentieth century—and stating that "philosophy or religion, our theory, that is, about ultimate things, has been driven out, more or less simultaneously, from two fields that it used to occupy."[2] These two fields were literature and politics, and he mourned that they were now bereft of that which had formerly imbued them with strength, meaning, and beauty. "General theories of the relation of things have been extruded from both," he observed, "and we are in a position to ask, 'What have we gained or lost by this extrusion? Is literature better, is politics better, for having discarded the moralist and the philosopher?'"[3] This was a recipe for disaster, a prescription for a society in which things continually fall apart. He wished to do what he could to keep the world that he knew from coming to ruin.

To illustrate the poverty (and the danger) of a world in which the moralist and the philosopher have been banished, Chesterton told a parable. "I revert," he began, to the doctrinal methods of the thirteenth century, inspired by the general hope of getting something done.

Suppose that a great commotion arises in the street about something, let us say a lamp-post, which many influential persons desire to pull down. A grey-clad monk, who is the spirit of the Middle Ages, is approached upon the matter, and begins to say, in the arid manner of the Schoolmen, "Let us first of all consider, my brethren, the value of Light. If Light be in itself good."

At this point he is somewhat excusably knocked down. All the people make a rush for the lamp-post, the lamp-post is down in ten minutes, and they go about congratulating each other on their unmediaeval practicality. But as things go on they do not work out so easily. Some people have pulled the lamp-post down because they wanted the electric light; some because they wanted old iron; some because they wanted darkness, because their deeds were evil. Some thought it not enough of a lamp-post, some too much; some acted because they wanted to smash municipal machinery; some because they wanted to smash something. And there is war in the night, no man knowing whom he strikes.

So, gradually and inevitably, to-day, to-morrow, or the next day, there comes back the conviction that the monk was right after all, and that all depends on what is the philosophy of Light. Only what we might have discussed under the gas-lamp, we now must discuss in the dark.[4]

Such was the state of a world in which anti-Christian ideas ran amok or were in the ascendant. But in one respect the anti-Christian writers of Chesterton's day had done believers like him a great service: they had shown what a world could be like should such ideas attain anything like a cultural currency. "We who are Christians," he wrote, "never knew the great philosophic common sense which inheres in that mystery until the anti-Christian writers pointed it out to us."[5]

Therefore Chesterton issued a call for cultural renewal by means of something he had personally experienced: a re-acquaintance with Christianity, the source of all that was best and good regarding First Things and their right relation to one another. Only then could people truly begin to know each other as they should, and understand the world in which they lived. Only then could they unriddle the ultimate meaning of things.

His was a clarion call for Christians to defend and commend the faith to a world that would be fatally impoverished without it. In the closing lines of *Heretics* he sought to rally the faithful in words that still stir the soul:

> We shall be left defending not only the incredible virtues and sanities of human life, but something more incredible still, this huge impossible universe which stares us in the face. We shall fight for visible prodigies as if they were invisible. We shall look on the impossible grass and skies with a strange courage. We shall be of those who have seen and believed.[6]

THE PILGRIM'S PROGRESS

THE PILGRIM'S PROGRESS certainly exhibits all the marks of such a revival of primitive power and mystery. . . . Nowhere, perhaps, except in Homer, is there such a perfect description conveyed by the use of merely plain words. The description in Bunyan of how Moses came like a wind up the road, and was but a word and a blow; or how Apollyon straddled quite over the breadth of the way and swore by his infernal den—these are things which can only be paralleled in sudden and splendid phrases out of Homer or the Bible, such as the phrase about the monstrous and man-killing hands of Achilles, or the war-horse who laughs at the shaking of the spear.[18]

THERE MAY BE some—I do not know if there are—who will be so much alienated by the seventeenth century apparatus of the great story ... so weary of old texts, so scornful of old doctrines, that they will fancy that this ancient Puritan poetry of danger is interesting only from a literary and not at all from a philosophical or religious point of view. For such people there is, I suppose, still waiting untried that inevitable mood in which a man may stand amid a field of flowers in the quiet sunlight and realise suddenly that of all conceivable things the most acutely dangerous thing is to be alive.[19]

BEFORE THE PURITANS were swept off the scene for ever, they had done two extraordinary things. They had broken to pieces in plain battle on an English meadow the chivalry of a great nation, bred from its youth to arms. And they had brought forth from their agony a small book, called *The Pilgrim's Progress*, which was greater literature than the whole contemporary culture of the great Renaissance, founded on three generations of the worship of learning and art.

The Pilgrim's Progress certainly exhibits all the marks of such a revival of primitive power and mystery. Its resemblance to the Bible is not a mere imitation of style; it is also a coincidence of mood. Bunyan, who was a soldier in Cromwell's army, had himself been thrown into a world almost as ferocious and obscure as that of Gideon, or the Maccabees, and he was really under the influence of the same kind of emotion. This was simply because, as I have said, Puritanism was a thing barbaric, and therefore eternal.[20]

THE PECULIAR FRAME of mind of Puritanism was a sense of the deadly danger of existence. ... It is this general and acute sense of danger that is the soul of Puritanism, and the soul of *The Pilgrim's Progress*. There are an innumerable company of good and picturesque figures in *The Pilgrim's Progress*. There is the dark man clad in bright vesture (that admirable person), there is Mr. Worldly-wiseman, whose conversation is indistinguishable from that of a modern philanthropist. There is Apollyon, whose eloquence is like the noblest eloquence of the seventeenth century. There is the Giant Despair, who needs no introduction to the modern enlightened world. But no figure in the whole story quite seizes on the imagination, at once pictorial and spiritual, like the figure with which the whole graphic parable begins. The wild figure of the Pilgrim himself, with the burden on his back, and his fingers in his ears, running like mad out of the clamorous and scornful and derisive city, which is called the City of Destruction—this certainly is the embodiment of the actual literary energy of Bunyan.[21]

Pleasure, refusal of

NOW SHUTTING OUT things is all very well, but it has one simple corollary: that from everything we shut out, we are ourselves shut out.[22]

> PATRICIA. We can't turn life into a pleasure. But we can choose such pleasures as are worthy of us and our immortal souls.[23]

Plutocracy

THE KEY FACT in the new development of plutocracy is that it will use its own blunder as an excuse for further crimes. Everywhere the very completeness of the impoverishment will be made a reason for the enslavement; though the men who impoverished were the same who enslaved.[24]

Poetry

THE CENTRAL IDEA of poetry is the idea of guessing right, like a child.[25]

To have known the things that from the weak are furled,
Perilous ancient passions, strange and high;
It is something to be wiser than the world.[26]

In a time of sceptic moths and cynic rusts,
And fattened lives that of their sweetness tire
In a world of flying loves and fading lusts,
It is something to be sure of a desire.
Lo, blessed are our ears for they have heard.[27]

It is something to have wept as we have wept,
It is something to have done as we have done,
It is something to have watched when all men slept,
And seen the stars which never see the sun.[28]

I know the bright baptismal rains,
I love your tender troubled skies,
I know your little climbing lanes,
Are peering into Paradise,
From open hearth to orchard cool,
How bountiful and beautiful.[29]

When God to all His paladins
By His own splendour swore
To make a fairer face than heaven
Of dust and nothing more.[30]

POETRY DEALS ENTIRELY with those great eternal and mainly forgotten wishes which are the ultimate despots of existence. Poetry presents things as they are to our emotions, not as they are to any theory, however plausible, or any argument, however conclusive. If love is in truth a glorious vision, poetry will say that it is a glorious vision, and no philosophers will persuade poetry to say that it is the exaggeration of the instinct of sex. If bereavement is a bitter and continually aching thing, poetry will say that it is so, and no philosophers will persuade poetry to say that it is an evolutionary stage of great biological value. And here comes in the whole value and object of poetry, that it is perpetually challenging all systems with the test of a terrible sincerity.[31]

ONLY POETRY CAN realise motives, because motives are all pictures of happiness. And the supreme and most practical value of poetry is this, that in poetry, as in music, a note is struck which expresses beyond the power of rational statement a condition of mind, and all actions arise from a condition of mind. Prose can only use a large and clumsy notation; it can only say that a man is miserable, or that a man is happy; it is forced to ignore that there are a million diverse kinds of misery and a million diverse kinds of happiness. Poetry alone, with the first throb of its metre, can tell us whether the depression is the kind of depression that drives a man to suicide, or the kind of depression that drives him to the Tivoli. Poetry can tell us whether the happiness is the happiness that sends a man to a restaurant, or the much richer and fuller happiness that sends him to church.[32]

THERE IS IN life an element of elfin coincidence which people reckoning on the prosaic may perpetually miss. As it has been well expressed in the paradox of Poe, wisdom should reckon on the unforeseen.[33]

POETS

THERE IS A notion adrift everywhere that imagination, especially mystical imagination, is dangerous to man's mental balance. Poets are commonly spoken of as psychologically unreliable; and generally there is a vague association between wreathing laurels in your hair and sticking straws in it. Facts and history utterly contradict this view. Most of the very great poets have been not only sane, but extremely business-like; and if Shakespeare ever really held horses, it was because he was much the safest man to hold them.[34]

THE POETS ARE those who rise above the people by understanding them. Of course, most of the Poets wrote in prose—Rabelais, for instance, and Dickens.[35]

THE CHARM OF children is very subtle; it is even complex, to the extent of being almost contradictory. It is, at its very plainest, mingled of a regard for hilarity and a regard for helplessness. The sentiment of twilight, in the vulgarest drawing-room song or the coarsest pair of sweethearts, is, so far as it goes, a subtle sentiment. It is strangely balanced between pain and pleasure; it might also be called pleasure tempting pain. The plunge of impatient chivalry by which we all admire a man fighting odds is not at all easy to define separately; it means many things, pity, dramatic surprise, a desire for justice, a delight in experiment and the indeterminate. . . .

Poets are those who share these popular sentiments, but can so express them that they prove themselves the strange and delicate things that they really are.[36]

THE SINGER OF THE WHITE HORSE
Chesterton the Poet

Chesterton, though not always a great performer as a poet, was nonetheless a greatly gifted one. Often anthologized during his lifetime, he is anthologized still—three poems ("The Secret People," "The Rolling English Road," and "Gold Leaves") appearing in the critically acclaimed *Oxford Book of Twentieth-Century English Verse*, edited by Philip Larkin.

In America, *Modern British Poetry*, published in 1920 and edited by Robert Frost's great friend Louis Untermeyer, contained three poems by Chesterton: "Lepanto," "A Prayer in Darkness," and "The Donkey." The last of these, "The Donkey," was also included in *The Oxford Book of English Verse* (1939), edited by Arthur Quiller-Couch, the celebrated "Q" so often referenced in the book and film *84 Charing Cross Road*.

"The Donkey" is representative of the best short poems that Chesterton wrote. It reads, in part:

> *The tattered outlaw of the earth,*
> *Of ancient crooked will;*
> *Starve, scourge, deride me: I am dumb,*
> *I keep my secret still.*
> *Fools! For I also had my hour;*
> *One far fierce hour and sweet:*
> *There was a shout about my ears,*
> *And palms before my feet.*[1]

But while it is interesting to note the poems still anthologized today (or those anthologized during Chesterton's lifetime), they are not the best indicator of the finest lines he wrote. Some of the dedicatory verse he wrote for his novels is of a high order as well, such as these lines from the opening pages of *The Man Who Was Thursday*—which pay tribute to Walt Whitman and Robert Louis Stevenson, and allude to John Bunyan's *Holy War*:

> *Not all unhelped we held the fort, our tiny flags unfurled;*
> *Some giants laboured in that cloud to lift it from the world.*
> *I find again the book we found, I feel the hour that flings*
> *Far out of fish-shaped Paumanok some cry of cleaner things;*
> *And the Green Carnation withered, as in forest fires that pass,*
> *Roared in the wind of all the world ten million leaves of grass;*
> *Or sane and sweet and sudden as a bird sings in the rain—*
> *Truth out of Tusitala spoke and pleasure out of pain.*
> *Yea, cool and clear and sudden as a bird sings in the grey,*
> *Dunedin to Samoa spoke, and darkness unto day.*
> *But we were young; we lived to see God break their bitter charms,*
> *God and the good Republic come riding back in arms:*

We have seen the City of Mansoul, even as it rocked, relieved—
Blessed are they who did not see, but being blind, believed.[2]

Frederick Buechner, in an essay for the book *Speak What We Feel*, while noting the indebtedness of Chesterton the poet to these writers, also commends the following unpublished manuscript lines, which possess straightforward virtues all their own:

You say grace before meals.
All right.
But I say grace before the play and the opera,
And grace before the concert and the pantomime,
And grace before I open a book,
And grace before sketching, painting,
Swimming, fencing, boxing, walking, playing, dancing;
And grace before I dip the pen in the ink.[3]

At the other end of the poetic spectrum, it was W. H. Auden who declared Chesterton a worthy rival to the great writer of nonsense verse, Edward Lear. In discussing Chesterton's book *Greybeards at Play*, Auden wrote: "I have no hesitation in saying that it contains some of the best pure nonsense verse in English.... By natural gift, Chesterton was, I think, essentially a comic poet."[4]

Auden may well be right in saying that Chesterton was by natural gift a comic poet, but Garry Wills has offered one important and telling qualification to that view. Wills believes that when Chesterton wrote *The Ballad of the White Horse*, he penned a "neglected masterpiece in narrative verse."[5]

Nor is Wills alone in singling out this epic poem for high praise. C. S. Lewis, according to his biographer and friend George Sayer, knew much of the *Ballad* by heart. He thought it "marvelous stuff," and said to Sayer in 1934: "Don't you like the way Chesterton takes hold of you in that poem, shakes you, and makes you want to cry? . . . Here and there it achieves the heroic, the rarest quality in modern literature."[6] Elsewhere, Lewis described the *Ballad* as "permanent and dateless,"[7] and then offered this considered assessment:

> Does not the central theme of the *Ballad*—the highly paradoxical message which Alfred receives from the Virgin—embody the feeling, and the only possible feeling, with which in any age almost defeated men take up such arms as are left them and win?[8]

Auden also admired *The Ballad of the White Horse*, saying that it was, perhaps, Chesterton's "greatest 'serious' poem."[9] Nor did he think, as some critics did, that the poem was overlong. "I do not, however, I am happy to say, find the length excessive. When, for example, Elf the Minstrel, Earl Ogier, and Guthrum express in turns their conceptions of the Human Condition, what they sing could not be further condensed without loss."[10]

The Ballad of the White Horse was a poem unlike any other in the Chesterton canon. It was, as Wills has written, his "most serious artistic endeavor" as a poet—one that took four years to complete—and called forth his most extended labor and care in composition.[11]

Novelist Graham Greene may well have voiced the most generous praise of the *Ballad* ever to appear in print. In an interview with the *Observer* in March 1978, he called Chesterton an "underestimated poet," and in support of this claim stated: "Put *The Ballad of the White Horse* against [T. S. Eliot's] *The Waste Land*. If I had to lose one of them, I'm not sure that . . . well, anyhow, let's just say I re-read *The Ballad* more often!"[12]

Chesterton's narrative epic "describes a desperate but ultimately victorious battle fought by the Christian King Alfred against the pagan Danish invaders."[13] It clearly reflects, as

Wills has noted, the influence of Chesterton's early reading of Sir Walter Scott and Lord Macaulay. But a poem to which it has often been compared is Coleridge's *Rime of the Ancient Mariner*.[14] Perhaps the best thing to say in this regard is that it moves in the tradition of epic poems written by all three men.

In summary, it seems very safe to say that those who delve deeply into Chesterton's best verse have much to discover and savor. His gifts as a poet were not least among the many literary gifts he possessed. The best poems to issue from his pen offer a rich and promising field of study—to say nothing of rewarding the reader who, like C. S. Lewis, richly enjoyed poems that "take hold of you."

POETS AND PROFESSORS

ROUGHLY SPEAKING, THERE are three kinds of people in this world. The first kind of people are People; they are the largest and probably the most valuable class. We owe to this class the chairs we sit down on, the clothes we wear, the houses we live in; and, indeed (when we come to think of it), we probably belong to this class ourselves. The second class may be called for convenience the Poets; they are often a nuisance to their families, but, generally speaking, a blessing to mankind. The third class is that of the Professors or Intellectuals; sometimes described as the thoughtful people; and these are a blight and a desolation both to their families and also to mankind. Of course, the classification sometimes overlaps, like all classification. Some good people are almost poets and some bad poets are almost professors.[37]

POLITICAL THEORY

THAT IS MY political theory: that we should make England worth copying instead of telling everybody to copy her.[38]

Politics

IT IS TERRIBLE to contemplate how few politicians are hanged.[39]

RESPONSIBILITY, A HEAVY and cautious responsibility of speech, is the easiest thing in the world; anybody can do it. That is why so many tired, elderly, and wealthy men go in for politics.[40]

FOR FEAR OF the newspapers politicians are dull, and at last they are too dull even for the newspapers. The speeches in our time are more careful and elaborate, because they are meant to be read, and not to be heard. And exactly because they are more careful and elaborate, they are not so likely to be worthy of a careful and elaborate report. They are not interesting enough. So the moral cowardice of modern politicians has, after all, some punishment attached to it by the silent anger of heaven.[41]

THE WHOLE MODERN world has divided itself into Conservatives and Progressives. The business of Progressives is to go on making mistakes. The business of the Conservatives is to prevent the mistakes from being corrected.[42]

TOWARDS THE END of the nineteenth century there appeared . . . two incredible figures; they were the pure Conservative and the pure Progressive; two figures which would have been overwhelmed with laughter by any other intellectual commonwealth of history. There was hardly a human generation which could not have seen the folly of merely going forward or merely standing still; of mere progressing or mere conserving. In the coarsest Greek Comedy we might have a joke about a man who wanted to keep what he had, whether it was yellow gold or yellow fever. In the dullest mediæval morality we might have a joke about a progressive gentleman who, having passed heaven and come to purgatory, decided to go further and fare worse. The twelfth and thirteenth centuries were an age of quite impetuous progress; men made in one rush, roads, trades, synthetic philosophies, parliaments, university settlements, a law that could cover the world and such spires as had never struck the sky. But they would not have said that they wanted progress, but that they wanted the road, the parliaments, and the spires.[43]

Popular philosophy

"BOSH," ANSWERED GRANT. "I never said a word against eminent men of science. What I complain of is a vague popular philosophy, which supposes itself to be scientific when it is really nothing but a sort of new religion and an uncommonly nasty one."[44]

Popular systems (and oppression)

THIS STARTLING SWIFTNESS with which popular systems turn oppressive is the third fact for which we shall ask our perfect theory of progress to allow. It must always be on the look out for every privilege being abused, for every working right becoming a wrong. In this matter I am entirely on the side of the revolutionists. They are really right to be always suspecting human institutions; they are right not to put their trust in princes nor in any child of man. The chieftain chosen to be the friend of the people becomes the enemy of the people; the newspaper started to tell the truth now exists to prevent the truth being told. Here, I say, I felt that I was really at last on the side of the revolutionary. And then I caught my breath again: for I remembered that I was once again on the side of the orthodox.

Christianity spoke again and said: "I have always maintained that men were naturally backsliders; that human virtue tended of its own nature to rust or to rot; I have always said that human beings as such go wrong, especially happy human beings, especially proud and prosperous human beings. This eternal revolution, this suspicion sustained through centuries, you (being a vague modern) call the doctrine of progress. If you were a philosopher you would call it, as I do, the doctrine of original sin."[45]

POUSSIN, NICOLAS

WHEN PAGANISM WAS re-throned at the Renaissance, it proved itself for the first time a religion by the sign that only its own worshippers could slay it. It has taken them three centuries, but they have thrashed it threadbare. Just as poets invoked Mars and Venus, for every trivial flirtation, so Poussin and his school multiplied nymphs and satyrs with the recurrence of an endless wall-paper, till a bacchanal has become as respectable as a bishop and the god of love is too vulgar for a valentine.... This is the root of the strange feeling of sadness evoked by the groups and landscapes of Poussin. We are looking at one of the dead loves of the world. Never were men born so much out of the time as the modern neo-pagans. For this is the second death of the gods—a death after resurrection. And when a ghost dies, it dies eternally.[46]

POWER

THERE IS, AS a ruling element in modern life, in all life, this blind and asinine appetite for mere power.[47]

PRIDE

SELF IS THE Gorgon. Vanity sees it in the mirror of other men and lives. Pride studies it for itself and is turned to stone.[48]

PRIDE IS THE downward drag of all things into an easy solemnity.[49]

SURELY THE VILEST point of human vanity is exactly that; to ask to be admired for admiring what your admirers do not admire.[50]

ALL THAT IS the matter with the proud is that they will not admit that they are vain.[51]

PRIVATE LIVES

PRIVATE LIVES ARE more important than public reputations.[52]

PROGRESS

BUT IF THE beatification of the world is not a work of nature but a work of art, then it involves an artist. And here again my contemplation was cloven by the ancient voice which said, "I could have told you all this a long time ago. If there is any certain progress it can only be my kind of progress, the progress towards a complete city of virtues and dominations where righteousness and peace contrive to kiss each other. An impersonal force might be leading you to a wilderness of perfect flatness or a peak of perfect height. But only a personal God can possibly be leading you (if, indeed, you are being led) to a city with just streets and architectural proportions, a city in which each of you can contribute exactly the right amount of your own colour to the many-coloured coat of Joseph."[53]

THIS IS THE whole weakness of certain schools of progress and moral evolution. They suggest that there has been a slow movement towards morality, with an imperceptible ethical change in every year or at every instant. There is only one great disadvantage in this theory. It talks of a slow movement towards justice; but it does not permit a swift movement. A man is not allowed to leap up and declare a certain state of things to be intrinsically intolerable.[54]

I HAVE ALWAYS felt a certain insufficiency about the ideal of Progress, even of the best sort which is a Pilgrim's Progress. It hardly suggests how near both the best and the worst things are to us from the first; even perhaps especially at the first.[55]

NOW HERE COMES in the whole collapse and huge blunder of our age. We have mixed up two different things, two opposite things. Progress should mean that we are always changing the world to suit the vision. Progress does mean (just now) that we are always changing the vision. It should mean that we are slow but sure in bringing justice and mercy among men: it does mean that we are very swift in doubting the desirability of justice and mercy.[56]

PROGRESS SHOULD MEAN that we are always walking towards the New Jerusalem. It does mean that the New Jerusalem is always walking away from us. We are not altering the real to suit the ideal. We are altering the ideal: it is easier.[57]

IT HAS APPEARED to me that progress should be something else besides a continual parricide; therefore I have investigated the dust-heaps of humanity, and found a treasure in all of them. I have found that humanity is not incidentally engaged, but eternally and systematically engaged, in throwing gold into the gutter and diamonds into the sea. I have found that every man is disposed to call the green leaf of the tree a little less green than it is, and the snow of Christmas a little less white than it is; therefore I have imagined that the main business of a man, however humble, is defence.[58]

THE SIMPLE KEY to the power of our upper classes is this: that they have always kept carefully on the side of what is called Progress. . . . Novelty is to them a luxury verging on a necessity. They, above all, are so bored with the past and with the present, that they gape, with a horrible hunger, for the future.[59]

PROGRESSIVES

EACH SECESSION IN turn must be right because it is recent, and progress must progress by growing smaller and smaller. That is the progressive theory, the legacy of seventeenth-century sectarianism, the dogma implied in much modern politics, and the evident enemy of democracy. Democracy is reproached with saying that the majority is always right. But progress says that the minority is always right. Progressives are prophets; and fortunately not all the people are prophets. Thus in the atmosphere of this slowly dying sectarianism anybody who chooses to prophesy and prohibit can tyrannise over the people.[60]

PROPERTY

FOR THE MASS of men the idea of artistic creation can only be expressed by an idea unpopular in present discussions—the idea of property. The average man cannot cut clay into the shape of a man; but he can cut earth into the shape of a garden; and though he arranges it with red geraniums and blue potatoes in alternate straight lines, he is still an artist; because he has chosen. The average man cannot paint the sunset whose colors he admires; but he can paint his own house with what color he chooses, and though he paints it pea green with pink spots, he is still an artist; because that is his choice. Property is merely the art of the democracy. It means that every man should have something that he can shape in his own image, as he is shaped in the image of heaven.[61]

PROPHETS

WE ARE NOT, as a matter of fact, mere examples of those who stone the prophets and leave it to their posterity to build their sepulchres. If the world would only produce our perfect prophet, solemn, searching, universal, nothing would give us keener pleasure than to build his sepulchre. In our eagerness we might even bury him alive.[62]

Public houses ("pubs")

I know where Men can still be found,
Anger and clamorous accord,
And virtues growing from the ground,
And fellowship of beer and board,
And song, that is a sturdy chord,
And hope, that is a hardy shrub,
And goodness, that is God's last word—
Will someone take me to a pub?[63]

Public opinion

PUBLIC OPINION CAN be a prairie fire. It eats up everything that opposes it.[64]

IT SEEMS STRANGELY forgotten that the indifference of a nation is sacred as well as its differences. Even public apathy is a kind of public opinion—and in many cases a very sensible kind. If I ask everybody to vote about Mineral Meals and do not get a single ballot-paper returned, I may say that the citizens have not voted. But they have.[65]

Public puppets

MANY OF US live publicly with featureless public puppets, images of the small public abstractions. It is when we pass our own private gate, and open our own secret door, that we step into the land of giants.[66]

Public schools

THE ONE THING that is never taught by any chance in the atmosphere of public schools is exactly that—there is a whole truth of things, and that in knowing it and speaking it we are happy.[67]

R

REAL LOVE

ALL MODERN PHILOSOPHIES are chains which connect and fetter; Christianity is a sword which separates and sets free. No other philosophy makes God actually rejoice in the separation of the universe into living souls. But according to orthodox Christianity this separation between God and man is sacred, because this is eternal. That a man may love God it is necessary that there should be not only a God to be loved, but a man to love him. All those vague theosophical minds for whom the universe is an immense melting-pot are exactly the minds which shrink instinctively from that earthquake saying of our Gospels, which declare that the Son of God came not with peace but with a sundering sword. The saying rings entirely true even considered as what it obviously is; the statement that any man who preaches real love is bound to beget hate. . . . Sham love ends in compromise and common philosophy; but real love has always ended in bloodshed.[1]

REALISTS

THE OLD RELIGIONISTS tortured men physically for a moral truth. The new realists torture men morally for a physical truth.[2]

REASON

REASON AND JUSTICE grip the remotest and loneliest star.[3]

Reasons for writing

THE LAST INDICTMENT against this book is the worst of all. It is simply this: that if all goes well this book will be unintelligible gibberish. For it is mostly concerned with attacking attitudes which are in their nature accidental and incapable of enduring. Brief as is the career of such a book as this, it may last just twenty minutes longer than most of the philosophies that it attacks. In the end it will not matter to us whether we wrote well or ill; whether we fought with flails or reeds. It will matter to us greatly on what side we fought.[4]

Reasons to believe

I FELT IN my bones; first, that this world does not explain itself. It may be a miracle with a supernatural explanation; it may be a conjuring trick, with a natural explanation. But the explanation of the conjuring trick, if it is to satisfy me, will have to be better than the natural explanations I have heard. The thing is magic, true or false. Second, I came to feel as if magic must have a meaning; and meaning must have someone to mean it. There was something personal in the world, as in a work of art; whatever it meant it meant violently. Third, I thought this purpose beautiful in its old design, in spite of its defects, such as dragons. Fourth, that the proper form of thanks to it is some form of humility and restraint: we should thank God for beer and Burgundy by not drinking too much of them. We owed, also, an obedience to whatever made us. And last, and strangest, there had come into my mind a vague and vast impression that in some way all good was a remnant to be stored and held sacred out of some primordial ruin. Man had saved his good as Crusoe saved his goods: he had saved them from a wreck. All this I felt and the age gave me no encouragement to feel it. And all this time I had not even thought of Christian theology.[5]

Red

RED IS THE most joyful and dreadful thing in the physical universe; it is the fiercest note, it is the highest light, it is the place where the walls of this world of ours wear thinnest and something beyond burns through. It glows in the blood which sustains and in the fire which destroys us, in the roses of our romance and in the awful cup of our religion. It stands for all passionate happiness, as in faith or in first love.[6]

PAINTING THE TOWN red is a delightful thing until it is done. It would be splendid to see the cross of St. Paul's as red as the cross of St. George, and the gallons of red paint running down the dome or dripping from the Nelson Column. But when it is done, when you have painted the town red, an extraordinary thing happens. You cannot see any red at all. I can see, as in a sort of vision, the successful artist standing in the midst of that frightful city, hung on all sides with the scarlet of his shame. And then, when everything is red, he will long for a red rose in a green hedge and long in vain; he will dream of a red leaf and be unable even to imagine it. He has desecrated the divine colour, and he can no longer see it, though it is all around. I see him, a single black figure against the red-hot hell that he has kindled, where spires and turrets stand up like immobile flames: he is stiffened in a sort of agony of prayer. Then the mercy of Heaven is loosened, and I see one or two flakes of snow very slowly begin to fall.[7]

Reform

WE NEED NOT debate about the mere words evolution or progress: personally I prefer to call it reform. For reform implies form. It implies that we are trying to shape the world in a particular image; to make it something that we see already in our minds. Evolution is a metaphor from mere automatic unrolling. Progress is a metaphor from merely walking along a road—very likely the wrong road. But reform is a metaphor for reasonable and determined men: it means that we see a certain thing out of shape and we mean to put it into shape. And we know what shape.[8]

RELIGION

AND IT DID for one wild moment cross my mind that, perhaps, those might not be the very best judges of the relation of religion to happiness who, by their own account, had neither one nor the other.[9]

IT HAS OFTEN been said, very truly, that religion is the thing that makes the ordinary man feel extraordinary; it is an equally important truth that religion is the thing that makes the extraordinary man feel ordinary.[10]

RELIGION, FOR INSTANCE, is too often in our days dismissed as irrelevant. Even if we think religion insoluble, we cannot think it irrelevant. Even if we ourselves have no view of the ultimate verities, we must feel that wherever such a view exists in a man it must be more important than anything else in him.[11]

RELIGION, THE IMMORTAL maiden, has been a maid-of-all-work as well as a servant of mankind. She provided men at once with the theoretic laws of an unalterable cosmos; and also with the practical rules of the rapid and thrilling game of morality. She taught logic to the student and told fairy tales to the children; it was her business to confront the nameless gods whose fear is on all flesh, and also to see the streets were spotted with silver and scarlet, that there was a day for wearing ribbons or an hour for ringing bells.[12]

THE MOTHER CAN bring up a child without choosing a religion for him, but not without choosing an environment for him. If she chooses to leave out the religion, she is choosing the environment— and an infernally dismal, unnatural environment too. The mother can bring up the child alone on a solitary island in the middle of a large lake, lest the child should be influenced by superstitions and social conditions. But the mother is choosing the island and the lake and the loneliness.[13]

RELIGIOUS LIBERTY

RELIGIOUS LIBERTY MIGHT be supposed to mean that everybody is free to discuss religion. In practice it means that hardly anybody is allowed to mention it.[14]

RELIGIOUS PERSECUTION

RELIGIOUS PERSECUTION DOES not consist in thumbscrews or fires of Smithfield; the essence of religious persecution is this: that the man who happens to have material power in the State, either by wealth or by official position, should govern his fellow-citizens not according to their religion or philosophy, but according to his own.[15]

REPENTANCE

THE HEART OF the true Middle Ages might be found far better, for instance, in the noble tale of Tannhauser, in which the dead staff broke into leaf and flower to rebuke the pontiff who had declared even one human being beyond the strength of sorrow and pardon.[16]

RESEARCH

RESEARCH IS THE search of people who don't know what they want.[17]

Responsibility

MOST MODERN FREEDOM is at root fear. It is not so much that we are too bold to endure rules; it is rather that we are too timid to endure responsibilities.[18]

Revolt

THERE ARE CROWDS who do not care to revolt; but there are no crowds who do not like someone else to do it for them; a fact which the safest oligarchs may be wise to learn.[19]

[SYME] CAME OF a family of cranks, in which all the oldest people had all the newest notions. One of his uncles always walked about without a hat, and another had made an unsuccessful attempt to walk about with a hat and nothing else. His father cultivated art and self-realisation; his mother went in for simplicity and hygiene. Hence the child, during his tenderer years, was wholly un-acquainted with any drink between the extremes of absinth and cocoa, of both of which he had a healthy dislike. The more his mother preached a more than Puritan abstinence the more did his father expand into a more than pagan latitude; and by the time the former had come to enforcing vegetarianism, the latter had pretty well reached the point of defending cannibalism.

Being surrounded with every conceivable kind of revolt from infancy, Gabriel had to revolt into something, so he revolted into the only thing left—sanity. But there was just enough in him of the blood of these fanatics to make even his protest for common sense a little too fierce to be sensible. His hatred of modern lawlessness had been crowned also by an accident. It happened that he was walking in a side street at the instant of a dynamite outrage. He had been blind and deaf for a moment, and then seen, the smoke clearing, the broken windows and the bleeding faces. After that he went about as usual—quiet, courteous, rather gentle; but there was a spot on his mind that was not sane. He did not regard anarchists, as most of us do, as a handful of morbid men, combining ignorance with intellectualism. He regarded them as a huge and pitiless peril.[20]

Rich and poor

"THAT WHICH IS large enough for the rich to covet," said Wayne, drawing up his head, "is large enough for the poor to defend."[21]

Riddles

THERE ARE VITAL riddles in life.[22]

Romanticism

PEOPLE WELCOMED THE return of adventurous novels about alien places and times, the trenchant and swordlike stories of Stevenson. But I am not narrowly on the side of the romantics. I think that glimpses of the gloom of our civilisation ought to be recorded. I think that the bewilderments of the solitary and sceptical soul ought to be preserved, if it be only for the pity (yes, and the admiration) of the happier time.[23]

ROMANCE, INDEED, DOES not consist by any means so much in experiencing adventures as in being ready for them. How little the actual boy cares for incidents in comparison to tools and weapons may be tested by the fact that the most popular story of adventure is concerned with a man who lived for years on a desert island with two guns and a sword, which he never had to use on an enemy.[24]

NO GENUINE CRITICISM of romance will ever arise until we have grasped the fact that romance lies not upon the outside of life but absolutely in the centre of it.[25]

Ruskin, John

AS AN ARTIST in prose he is one of the most miraculous products of the extremely poetical genius of England. The length of a Ruskin sentence is like that length in the long arrow that was boasted of by the drawers of the long bow. He draws, not a cloth-yard shaft but a long lance to his ear: he shoots a spear. But the whole goes light as a bird and straight as a bullet. There is no Victorian writer before him to whom he even suggests a comparison, technically considered, except perhaps De Quincey; who also employed the long rich rolling sentence that, like a rocket, bursts into stars at the end.[26]

S

SANITY

OF A SANE man there is only one safe definition. He is a man who can have tragedy in his heart and comedy in his head.[1]

SATAN

THE DEVIL PLOTTED since the world was young with alchemies of fire and witches' oils and magic. But he never made a man.[2]

SAVONAROLA

SAVONAROLA ADDRESSED HIMSELF to the hardest of all earthly tasks, that of making men turn back and wonder at the simplicities they had learnt to ignore. It is strange that the most unpopular of all doctrines is the doctrine which declares the common life divine. Democracy, of which Savonarola was so fiery an exponent, is the hardest of gospels; there is nothing that so terrifies men as the decree that they are all kings. Christianity, in Savonarola's mind, identical with democracy, is the hardest of gospels; there is nothing that so strikes men with fear as the saying that they are all the sons of God.[3]

SCEPTICS

THERE IS A sceptic far more terrible than he who believes that everything began in matter. It is possible to meet the sceptic who believes that everything began in himself.[4]

THE HUMAN INTELLECT is free to destroy itself. Just as one generation could prevent the very existence of the next generation, by all entering a monastery or jumping into the sea, so one set of thinkers can in some degree prevent further thinking by teaching the next generation that there is no validity in any human thought. It is idle to talk always of the alternative of reason and faith. Reason is itself a matter of faith. It is an act of faith to assert that our thoughts have any relation to reality at all. If you are merely a sceptic, you must sooner or later ask yourself the question, "Why should *anything* go right; even observation and deduction?"[5]

WE ARE ON the road to producing a race of men too mentally modest to believe in the multiplication table. We are in danger of seeing philosophers who doubt the law of gravity as being a mere fancy of their own. Scoffers of old time were too proud to be convinced; but these are too humble to be convinced. The meek do inherit the earth; but the modern sceptics are too meek even to claim their inheritance. It is exactly this intellectual helplessness which is our second problem.[6]

THE YOUNG SCEPTIC says, "I have a right to think for myself." But the old sceptic, the complete sceptic, says, "I have no right to think for myself. I have no right to think at all."[7]

SCIENCE

WHEN MEN OF science (or, more often, men who talk about science) speak of studying history or human society scientifically they always forget that there are two quite distinct questions involved. It may be that certain facts of the body go with certain facts of the soul, but it by no means follows that a grasp of such facts of the body goes with a grasp of the things of the soul.[8]

WHAT CAN PEOPLE mean when they say that science has disturbed their view of sin? What sort of view of sin can they have had before science disturbed it? Did they think that it was something to eat? When people say that science has shaken their faith in immortality, what do they mean? Did they think that immortality was a gas?

Of course the real truth is that science has introduced no new principle into the matter at all. A man can be a Christian to the end of the world, for the simple reason that a man could have been an Atheist from the beginning of it. The materialism of things is on the face of things; it does not require any science to find it out. A man who has lived and loved falls down dead and the worms eat him. That is Materialism if you like. That is Atheism if you like. If mankind has believed in spite of that, it can believe in spite of anything. But why our human lot is made any more hopeless because we know the names of all the worms who eat him, or the names of all the parts of him that they eat, is to a thoughtful mind somewhat difficult to discover. My chief objection to these semi-scientific revolutionists is that they are not at all revolutionary. They are the party of platitude. They do not shake religion: rather religion seems to shake them. They can only answer the great paradox by repeating the truism.[9]

WHATEVER ELSE THE worst doctrine of depravity may have been, it was a product of spiritual conviction; it had nothing to do with remote physical origins. Men thought mankind wicked because they felt wicked themselves. If a man feels wicked, I cannot see why he should suddenly feel good because somebody tells him that his ancestors once had tails.[10]

PHYSICAL SCIENCE IS like simple addition: it is either infallible or it is false. To mix science up with philosophy is only to produce a philosophy that has lost all its ideal value and a science that has lost all its practical value.[11]

I AM HONESTLY bewildered as to the meaning of such passages as [the type] in which the advanced person writes that because geologists know nothing about the Fall, therefore any doctrine of depravity is untrue. Because science has not found something which obviously it could not find, therefore something entirely different—the psychological sense of evil—is untrue. You might sum up this writer's argument abruptly, but accurately, in some way like this—"We have not dug up the bones of the Archangel Gabriel, who presumably had none, therefore little boys, left to themselves, will not be selfish." To me it is all wild and whirling; as if a man said—"The plumber can find nothing wrong with our piano; so I suppose that my wife does love me."[12]

SCOTLAND

THE SPIRITUAL COLOUR of Scotland, like the local colour of so many Scottish moors, is a purple that in some lights can look like grey. The national character is in reality intensely romantic and passionate—indeed, excessively and dangerously romantic and passionate. Its emotional torrent has only too often been turned towards revenge, or lust, or cruelty, or witchcraft. There is no drunkenness like Scotch drunkenness; it has in it the ancient shriek and the wild shrillness of the Maenads on the mountains.[13]

SCOTT, SIR WALTER

AN APPRECIATION OF Scott might be made almost a test of decadence. If ever we lose touch with this one most reckless and defective writer, it will be a proof to us that we have erected round ourselves a false cosmos, a world of lying and horrible perfection, leaving outside of it Walter Scott and that strange old world which is as confused and as indefensible and as inspiring and as healthy as he.[14]

IT IS SAID that Scott is neglected by modern readers; if so, the matter could be more appropriately described by saying that modern readers are neglected by Providence. The ground of this neglect, in so far as it exists, must be found, I suppose, in the general sentiment that, like the beard of Polonius, he is too long. Yet it is surely a peculiar thing that in literature alone a house should be despised because it is too large, or a host impugned because he is too generous. If romance be really a pleasure, it is difficult to understand the modern reader's consuming desire to get it over, and if it be not a pleasure, it is difficult to understand his desire to have it at all.[15]

The sea

FOR THE EDGE of the sea is like the edge of a sword; it is sharp, military, and decisive; it really looks like a bolt or bar, and not like a mere expansion. It hangs in heaven, grey, or green, or blue, changing in colour, but changeless in form, behind all the slippery contours of the land and all the savage softness of the forests, like the scales of God held even.[16]

CONSIDER, FOR INSTANCE, what wastes of wordy imitation and ambiguity the ordinary educated person in the big towns could pour out on the subject of the sea. A country girl I know in the county of Buckingham had never seen the sea in her life until the other day. When she was asked what she thought of it she said it was like cauliflowers. Now that is a piece of pure literature—vivid, entirely independent and original, and perfectly true.[17]

FOR THREE DAYS and three nights the sea had charged England as Napoleon charged her at Waterloo. The phrase is instinctive, because away to the last grey line of the sea there was only the look of galloping squadrons, impetuous, but with a common purpose.

The sea came on like cavalry, and when it touched the shore it opened the blazing eyes and deafening tongues of the artillery. I saw the worst assault at night on a seaside parade where the sea smote on the doors of England with the hammers of earthquake, and a white smoke went up into the black heavens. There one could thoroughly realise what an awful thing a wave really is. I talk like other people about the rushing swiftness of a wave. But the horrible thing about a wave is its hideous slowness. It lifts its load of water laboriously: in that style at once slow and slippery in which a Titan might lift a load of rock and then let it slip at last to be shattered into shock of dust. In front of me that night the waves were not like water: they were like falling city walls. The breaker rose first as if it did not wish to attack the earth; it wished only to attack the stars. For a time it stood up in the air as naturally as a tower; then it went a little wrong in its outline, like a tower that might some day fall. When it fell it was as if a powder magazine blew up.[18]

Sects

FROM TIME TO time, as we all know, a sect appears in our midst announcing that the world will very soon come to an end. Generally, by some slight confusion or miscalculation, it is the sect that comes to an end.[19]

Secular progressivism

ONCE ABOLISH THE God, and the government becomes the God.[20]

Secularists

NOT ONLY IS the faith the mother of all worldly energies, but its foes are the fathers of all worldly confusion. The secularists have not wrecked divine things; but the secularists have wrecked secular things, if that is any comfort to them. The Titans did not scale heaven; but they laid waste the world.[21]

THE SECULARISTS LABORIOUSLY explain that martyrdoms do not prove a faith to be true, as if anybody was ever such a fool as to suppose that they did. What they did prove, or, rather, strongly suggest, was that something had entered human psychology which was stronger than strong pain.[22]

I HAVE KNOWN people who protested against religious education with arguments against any education, saying that the child's mind must grow freely or that the old must not teach the young. I have known people who showed that there could be no divine judgment by showing that there can be no human judgment, even for practical purposes. They burned their own corn to set fire to the church; they smashed their own tools to smash it; any stick was good enough to beat it with, though it were the last stick of their own dismembered furniture. We do not admire, we hardly excuse, the fanatic who wrecks this world for love of the other. But what are we to say to the fanatic who wrecks this world out of hatred of the other? He sacrifices the very existence of humanity to the non-existence of God. He offers his victims not to the altar, but merely to assert the idleness of the altar and the emptiness of the throne. He is ready to ruin even that primary ethic by which all things live, for his strange and eternal vengeance upon someone who never lived at all.[23]

SEEING

NOW, THERE IS a law written in the darkest of the Books of Life, and it is this: If you look at a thing nine-hundred and ninety-nine times, you are perfectly safe; if you look at it the thousandth time, you are in frightful danger of seeing it for the first time.[24]

Self-deprecation

I CANNOT UNDERSTAND the people who take literature seriously;
but I can love them, and I do. Out of my love I warn them to keep
clear of this book. It is a collection of crude and shapeless papers
upon current or rather flying subjects; and they must be published pretty much as they stand. They were written, as a rule, at
the last moment; they were handed in the moment before it was
too late.[25]

Sentimentalists

WE HEAR OF the stark sentimentalist, who talks as if there were no
problem at all: as if physical kindness would cure everything: as if
one need only pat Nero and stroke Ivan the Terrible. This mere
belief in bodily humanitarianism is not sentimental; it is simply
snobbish. For if comfort gives men virtue, the comfortable classes
ought to be virtuous—which is absurd.[26]

THIS IS THE essence of the Sentimentalist; that he seeks to enjoy
every idea without its sequence, and every pleasure without its
consequence.[27]

Seriousness

SERIOUSNESS IS NOT a virtue. It would be a heresy, but a much
more sensible heresy, to say that seriousness is a vice. It is really a
natural trend or lapse into taking one's-self gravely, because it is the
easiest thing to do. It is much easier to write a good *Times* leading
article, than a good joke in *Punch*. For solemnity flows out of men
naturally, but laughter is a leap. It is easy to be heavy: hard to be
light. Satan fell by the force of gravity.[28]

THE FIRST OF all the difficulties that I have in controverting Mr. Blatchford is simply this, that I shall be very largely going over his own ground. My favourite text-book of theology is [his book] *God and my Neighbour*, but I cannot repeat it in detail. If I gave each of my reasons for being a Christian, a vast number of them would be Mr. Blatchford's reasons for not being one.

For instance, Mr. Blatchford and his school point out that there are many myths parallel to the Christian story; that there were Pagan Christs, and Red Indian Incarnations, and Patagonian Crucifixions, for all I know or care. But does not Mr. Blatchford see the other side of this fact? If the Christian God really made the human race, would not the human race tend to rumours and per-versions of the Christian God? If the centre of our life is a certain fact, would not people far from the centre have a muddled version of that fact? If we are so made that a Son of God must deliver us, is it odd that Patagonians should dream of a Son of God?

The Blatchfordian position really amounts to this—that because a certain thing has impressed millions of different people as likely or necessary, therefore it cannot be true. And then this bashful being, veiling his own talents, convicts the wretched G.K.C. of paradox! I like paradox, but I am not prepared to dance and dazzle to the extent of [Mr. Blatchford], who points to humanity crying out to a thing, and pointing to it from immemorial ages, as a proof that it cannot be there.[29]

SMITH. May I say a word? I have a great dislike of a quarrel, for a reason quite beyond my duty to my cloth.

MORRIS. And what is that?

SMITH. I object to a quarrel because it always interrupts an argument. May I bring you back for a moment to the argument? You were saying that these modern conjuring tricks are simply the old miracles when they have once been found out. But surely another view is possible. When we speak of things being sham, we generally mean that they are imitations of things that are genuine. Take that Reynolds over there of the Duke's great-grandfather. [*Points to a picture on the wall.*] If I were to say it was a copy . . .

MORRIS. Wal, the Duke's real amiable; but I reckon you'd find what you call the interruption of an argument.

SMITH. Well, suppose I did say so, you wouldn't take it as meaning that Sir Joshua Reynolds never lived. Why should sham miracles prove to us that real Saints and Prophets never lived. There may be sham magic and real magic also.[30]

SHAKESPEARE, WILLIAM

WHEN A THING of the intellect is settled it is not dead: rather it is immortal. The multiplication table is immortal, and so is the fame of Shakespeare. But the fame of Zola is not dead or not immortal; it is at its crisis, it is in the balance; and may be found wanting. The French, therefore, are quite right in considering it a living question. It is still living as a question, because it is not yet solved. But Shakespeare is not a living question: he is a living answer.[31]

FOR MY PART, therefore, I think the French Zola controversy much more practical and exciting than the English Shakespeare one. The admission of Zola to the Pantheon may be regarded as defining Zola's position. But nobody could say that a statue of Shakespeare, even fifty feet high, on the top of St. Paul's Cathedral, could define Shakespeare's position. It only defines our position towards Shakespeare. It is he who is fixed; it is we who are unstable.[32]

WE CAN ONLY say of [Shakespeare] what we can say of Dickens.

We can only say that he came from nowhere and that he went everywhere.[33]

SHAKESPEARE IS QUITE himself; it is only some of his critics who have discovered that he was somebody else.[34]

ONE OF HIS hobbies was to wait for the American Shakespeare—a hobby more patient than angling.[35]

SHAW, GEORGE BERNARD

MOST PEOPLE EITHER say that they agree with Bernard Shaw or that they do not understand him. I am the only person who understands him, and I do not agree with him.[36]

SHAW IS LIKE the Venus of Milo; all that there is of him is admirable.[37]

IT IS NOT easy to dispute violently with a man for twenty years, about sex, about sin, about sacraments, about personal points of honour, about all the most sacred or delicate essentials of existence, without sometimes being irritated or feeling that he hits unfair blows or employs discreditable ingenuities. And I can testify that I have never read a reply by Bernard Shaw that did not leave me in a better and not a worse temper or frame of mind; which did not seem to come out of inexhaustible fountains of fair-mindedness and intellectual geniality. . . . It is necessary to disagree with him as much as I do, in order to admire him as much as I do; and I am proud of him as a foe even more than as a friend.[38]

A LEGEND HAS run round the newspapers that Bernard Shaw offered himself as a better writer than Shakespeare. This is false and quite unjust; Bernard Shaw never said anything of the kind.

The writer whom he did say was better than Shakespeare was not himself, but Bunyan. And he justified it by attributing to Bunyan a virile acceptance of life as a high and harsh adventure, while in Shakespeare he saw nothing but profligate pessimism, the *vanitas vanitatum* of a disappointed voluptuary. According to this view Shakespeare was always saying, "Out, out, brief candle," because his was only a ballroom candle; while Bunyan was seeking to light such a candle as by God's grace should never be put out.[39]

THE TEMPORARY DECLINE of theology had involved the neglect of philosophy and all fine thinking; and Bernard Shaw had to find shaky justifications in Schopenhauer for the sons of God shouting for joy. He called it the Will to Live—a phrase invented by Prussian professors who would like to exist, but can't. Afterwards he asked people to worship the Life-Force; as if one could worship a hyphen.[40]

MR. SHAW HAS found himself, led by the same mad imp of modernity, on the side of the people who want to have phonetic spelling. The people who want phonetic spelling generally depress the world with tireless and tasteless explanations of how much easier it would be for children or foreign bagmen if "height" were spelt "hite." Now children would curse spelling whatever it was, and we are not going to permit foreign bagmen to improve Shakespeare. Bernard Shaw charged along quite a different line; he urged that Shakespeare himself believed in phonetic spelling, since he spelt his own name in six different ways. According to Shaw, phonetic spelling is merely a return to the freedom and flexibility of Elizabethan literature. . . . [But] because Shakespeare could sing better than he could spell, it does not follow that his spelling and ours ought to be abruptly altered by a race that has lost all instinct for singing.[41]

NIETZSCHE MIGHT REALLY have done some good if he had taught Bernard Shaw to draw the sword, to drink wine, or even to dance.

But he only succeeded in putting into his head a new superstition, which bids fair to be the chief superstition of the dark ages which are possibly in front of us—I mean the superstition of what is called the Superman.[42]

PEOPLE HAVE TALKED far too much about the paradoxes of Bernard Shaw. Perhaps his only pure paradox is this almost unconscious one; that he has tended to think that because something has satisfied generations of men it must be untrue.[43]

HE DOES NOT understand Christianity because he will not understand the paradox of Christianity; that we can only really understand all myths when we know that one of them is true.[44]

THE GREAT DEFECT of that fine intelligence is a failure to grasp and enjoy the things commonly called convention and tradition; which are foods upon which all human creatures must feed frequently if they are to live.[45]

THE PHRASES OF the street are not only forcible but subtle: for a figure of speech can often get into a crack too small for a definition. Phrases like "put out" or "off colour" might have been coined by Mr. Henry James in an agony of verbal precision. And there is no more subtle truth than that of the everyday phrase about a man having "his heart in the right place." It involves the idea of normal proportion; not only does a certain function exist, but it is rightly related to other functions. Indeed, the negation of this phrase would describe with peculiar accuracy the somewhat morbid mercy and perverse tenderness of the most representative moderns. If, for instance, I had to describe with fairness the character of Mr. Bernard Shaw, I could not express myself more exactly than by saying that he has a heroically large and generous heart; but not a heart in the right place. And this is so of the typical society of our time.[46]

Signs

FOR IN THE last resort all men talk by signs. To talk by statues is to talk by signs; to talk by cities is to talk by signs. Pillars, palaces, cathedrals, temples, pyramids, are an enormous dumb alphabet: as if some giant held up his fingers of stone. The most important things at the last are always said by signs, even if, like the Cross on St. Paul's, they are signs in heaven. If men do not understand signs, they will never understand words.[47]

Silence

SILENCE IS THE unbearable repartee.[48]

Simplicity and unity

THE SIMPLICITY TOWARDS which the world is driving is the necessary outcome of all our systems and speculations and of our deep and continuous contemplation of things. For the universe is like everything in it; we have to look at it repeatedly and habitually before we see it. It is only when we have seen it for the hundredth time that we see it for the first time. The more consistently things are contemplated, the more they tend to unify themselves and therefore to simplify themselves. The simplification of anything is always sensational. Thus monotheism is the most sensational of things: it is as if we gazed long at a design full of disconnected objects, and, suddenly, with a stunning thrill, they came together into a huge and staring face.[49]

Sin

NOTHING CAN BE, in the strictest sense of the word, more comic than to set so shadowy a thing as the conjectures made by the vaguer anthropologists about primitive man against so solid a thing as the human sense of sin. By its nature the evidence of Eden is something that one cannot find. By its nature the evidence of sin is something that one cannot help finding.[50]

THE FOLLOWING WORDS are written over the signature of a man whose intelligence I respect, and I cannot make head or tail of them—

> When modern science declared that the cosmic process knew nothing of a historical event corresponding to a Fall, but told, on the contrary, the story of an incessant rise in the scale of being, it was quite plain that the Pauline scheme—I mean the argumentative processes of Paul's scheme of salvation—had lost its very foundation; for was not that foundation the total depravity of the human race inherited from their first parents? . . . But now there was no Fall; there was no total depravity, or imminent danger of endless doom; and, the basis gone, the superstructure followed.

It is written with earnestness and in excellent English; it must mean something. But what can it mean? How could physical science prove that man is not depraved? You do not cut a man open to find his sins. You do not boil him until he gives forth the unmistakable green fumes of depravity. How could physical science find any traces of a moral fall? What traces did the writer expect to find? Did he expect to find a fossil Eve with a fossil apple inside her? Did he suppose that the ages would have spared for him a complete skeleton of Adam attached to a slightly faded fig-leaf? The whole paragraph which I have quoted is simply a series of inconsequent sentences, all quite untrue in themselves and all quite irrelevant to each other.[51]

Small spaces

IN THE NARROW streets of Florence Dante felt that there was room for Purgatory and Heaven and Hell. He would have been stifled by the British Empire. Great empires are necessarily prosaic; for it is beyond human power to act a great poem upon so great a scale. You can only represent very big ideas in very small spaces. My toy theatre is as philosophical as the drama of Athens.[52]

ART DOES NOT consist in expanding things. Art consists of cutting things down, as I cut down with a pair of scissors my very ugly figures of St. George and the Dragon [for my toy theatre]. Plato, who liked definite ideas, would like my cardboard dragon; for though the creature has few other artistic merits he is at least dragonish. The modern philosopher, who likes infinity, is quite welcome to a sheet of the plain cardboard. The most artistic thing about the theatrical art is the fact that the spectator looks at the whole thing through a window. This is true even of theatres inferior to my own; even at the Court Theatre or His Majesty's you are looking through a window; an unusually large window. But the advantage of the small theatre exactly is that you are looking through a small window. Has not every one noticed how sweet and startling any landscape looks when seen through an arch? This strong, square shape, this shutting off of everything else is not only an assistance to beauty; it is the essential of beauty. The most beautiful part of every picture is the frame.[53]

Social science

BUT SOCIAL SCIENCE is by no means always content with the normal human soul; it has all sorts of fancy souls for sale. Man as a social idealist will say "I am tired of being a Puritan; I want to be a Pagan," or "Beyond this dark probation of Individualism I see the shining paradise of Collectivism." Now in bodily ills there is none of this difference about the ultimate ideal. The patient may or may not want quinine; but he certainly wants health. No one says "I am tired of this headache; I want some toothache," or "The only thing for this Russian influenza is a few German measles," or "Through this dark probation of catarrh I see the shining paradise of rheumatism." But exactly the whole difficulty in our public problems is that some men are aiming at cures which other men would regard as worse maladies; are offering ultimate conditions as states of health which others would uncompromisingly call states of disease.[54]

A BOOK OF modern social inquiry has a shape that is somewhat sharply defined. It begins as a rule with an analysis, with statistics, tables of population, decrease of crime among Congregationalists, growth of hysteria among policemen, and similar ascertained facts; it ends with a chapter that is generally called "The Remedy." It is almost wholly due to this careful, solid, and scientific method that "The Remedy" is never found. For this scheme of medical question and answer is a blunder; the first great blunder of sociology. It is always called stating the disease before we find the cure. But it is the whole definition and dignity of man that in social matters we must actually find the cure before we find the disease.[55]

SOCIALISM

CHRISTIANITY IS THE only thing left that has any real right to question the power of the well-nurtured or the well-bred. I have listened often enough to Socialists, or even to democrats, saying that the physical conditions of the poor must of necessity make them mentally and morally degraded, I have listened to scientific men (and there are still scientific men not opposed to democracy) saying that if we give the poor healthier conditions vice and wrong will disappear. I have listened to them with a horrible attention, with a hideous fascination. For it was like watching a man energetically sawing from the tree the branch he is sitting on. If these happy democrats could prove their case, they would strike democracy dead.[56]

IT FILLS ME with horrible amusement to observe the way in which the earnest Socialist industriously lays the foundation of all aristocracy, expatiating blandly upon the evident unfitness of the poor to rule.[57]

IN MODERN IDEAL conceptions of society there are some desires that are possibly not attainable: but there are some desires that are not desirable. That all men should live in equally beautiful houses is a dream that may or may not be attained. But that all men should live in the same beautiful house is not a dream at all; it is a nightmare.[58]

THE IDEA OF private property—universal but private, the idea of families free but still families, of domesticity democratic but still domestic, of one man one house—this remains the real vision and magnet of mankind. The world may accept something more official and general, less human and intimate. But the world will be like a broken-hearted woman who makes a humdrum marriage because she may not make a happy one; Socialism may be the world's deliverance, but it is not the world's desire.[59]

[NO SOCIETY CAN survive the Socialist] fallacy that there is an absolutely unlimited number of inspired officials and an absolutely unlimited amount of money to pay them.[60]

A SOCIALIST MEANS a man who thinks a walking-stick like an umbrella because they both go into the umbrella-stand.[61]

WITHIN A STONE's throw of my house they are building another house. I am glad they are building it, and I am glad it is within a stone's throw; quite well within it, with a good catapult. Nevertheless, I have not yet cast the first stone at the new house not being, strictly speaking, guiltless myself in the matter of new houses. And, indeed, in such cases there is a strong protest to be made. The whole curse of the last century has been what is called the Swing of the Pendulum; that is, the idea that Man must go alternately from one extreme to the other. It is a shameful and even shocking fancy; it is the denial of the whole dignity of mankind. When Man is alive he stands still. It is only when he is dead that he swings. But whenever one meets modern thinkers (as one often does) progressing towards a madhouse, one always finds, on inquiry, that they have just had a splendid escape from another madhouse. Thus, hundreds of people become Socialists, not because they have tried Socialism and found it nice, but because they have tried Individualism and found it particularly nasty.[62]

I WAITED IN tense eagerness for the phrase that came next. . . .

"Let me tell you, sir," he said, facing round at me with the final air of one launching a paradox. "The English people 'ave some common sense, and they'd rather be in the 'ands of gentlemen than in the claws of a lot of Socialist thieves."

I had an indescribable sense that I ought to applaud, as if I were a public meeting.[63]

THE SOUL

NOTHING IS IMPORTANT except the fate of the soul; and literature is only redeemed from an utter triviality, surpassing that of naughts and crosses, by the fact that it describes not the world around us, or the things on the retina of the eye, or the enormous irrelevancy of encyclopaedias, but some condition to which the human spirit can come.[64]

ONE CAN HARDLY think too little of one's self. One can hardly think too much of one's soul.[65]

THE TRUE ANSWER of philosophy and theology is that there is nothing the matter with the human body; the trouble is with the human soul.[66]

SPEECH

WE SHOULD PROBABLY come considerably nearer to the true conception of things if we treated all grown-up persons, of all titles and types, with precisely that dark affection and dazed respect with which we treat the infantile limitations. A child has no difficulty in achieving the miracle of speech, consequently we find his blunders almost as marvellous as his accuracy. If only we adopted the same attitude towards Premiers and Chancellors of the Exchequer, if we genially encouraged their stammering and delightful attempts at human speech, we should be in a far more wise and tolerant temper.[67]

STEVENSON, ROBERT LOUIS

THE CONCEPTION WHICH unites the whole varied work of Stevenson was that romance, or the vision of the possibilities of things, was far more important than mere occurrences: that one was the soul of our life, the other the body, and that the soul was the precious thing. The germ of all his stories lies in the idea that every landscape or scrap of scenery has a soul: and that soul is a story.[68]

NOW IF THERE was one point that Stevenson more constantly and passionately emphasised than any other it was that we must worship good for its own value and beauty, without reference whatever to victory or failure in space or time.[69]

HIS LIFE WAS really coloured out of a shilling paint-box, like his toy-theatre: such high spirits as he had are the key to him: his sufferings are not the key to him.[70]

IF THE RATHER vague Victorian public did not appreciate the deep and even tragic ethics with which Stevenson was concerned, still less were they of a sort to appreciate the French finish and fastidiousness of his style; in which he seemed to pick the right word up on the point of his pen, like a man playing spillikins. But that style also had a quality that could be felt; it had a military edge to it, an *acies*; and there was a kind of swordsmanship about it. Thus all the circumstances led, not so much to the narrowing of Stevenson to the romance of the fighting spirit; but the narrowing of his influence to that romance.[71]

HE THOUGHT IT immoral to neglect romance. The whole of his real position was expressed in that phrase of one of his letters "our civilisation is a dingy ungentlemanly business: it drops so much out of a man." On the whole he concluded that what had been dropped out of the man was the boy. He pursued pirates as Defoe would have fled from them; and summed up his simplest emotions in that touching *cri de coeur* "shall we never shed blood?" He did for the penny dreadful what Coleridge had done for the penny ballad. He proved that, because it was really human, it could really rise as near to heaven as human nature could take it. If Thackeray is our youth, Stevenson is our boyhood: and though this is not the most artistic thing in him, it is the most important thing in the history of Victorian art.[72]

HE WAS A very universal man; and talked some sense not only on every subject, but, so far as it is logically possible, in every sense.[73]

STEVENSON WAS A man who came out of a world of Puritanism into a world of Pessimism. Or, rather, the point of his story was that he escaped from the first but did not enter the second. That escape was first and last an escape in pursuit of happiness, which seemed to him to be forbidden both by the religion of his ancestors and the irreligion of his contemporaries. He had to patch up a sort of makeshift philosophy of his own, which may not have been (and indeed was not) very complete or logical, but which had very vital truths in it, of a type neglected in his time.[74]

THE THINGS THAT Stevenson liked were things like the chip of hard wood hacked out of the wooden sign of the Admiral Ben Bow by the cutlass of Billy Bones the buccaneer. They were things like the crutch of the horrible cripple, that went flashing in the tropical sun sped on its errand of death. In short, the things he loved were almost always solid and were generally self-evident in the sun. Even when they were not, as in the duel scene of "The Master of Ballantrae," the starlight seems as hard as the steel and the candle-flames as steady as the swords.[75]

THE SUPER-MAN

IF A MAN came up to us (as many will soon come up to us) to say, "I am a new kind of man. I am the super-man. I have abandoned mercy and justice;" we should answer, "Doubtless you are new, but you are not nearer to the perfect man, for he has already been in the mind of God. We have fallen with Adam and we shall rise with Christ; but we would rather fall with Satan than rise with you."[76]

SWIFT, JONATHAN

CHARACTERS IN NOVELS are often described as so amiable that they hate to be thanked. It is not an amiable quality, and it is an extremely rare one; but Swift possessed it. When Swift was buried the Dublin poor came in crowds and wept by the grave of the broadest and most free-handed of their benefactors. Swift deserved the public tribute; but he might have writhed and kicked in his grave at the thought of receiving it.[77]

THERE IS A great deal of Jonathan Swift in Bernard Shaw. Shaw is like Swift, for instance, in combining extravagant fancy with a curious sort of coldness. But he is most like Swift in that very quality which Thackeray said was impossible in an Irishman, benevolent bullying, a pity touched with contempt, and a habit of knocking men down for their own good.[78]

T

TENDERNESS

THE PRIDE OF a good mother in the beauty of her daughter is one of those adamantine tendernesses which are the touchstones of every age and race.[1]

TENNYSON, ALFRED, LORD

FOR WHATEVER ELSE Tennyson was, he was a great poet; no mind that feels itself free, that is, above the ebb and flow of fashion, can feel anything but contempt for the later effort to discredit him in that respect.[2]

IN THE IDYLLS *of the King,* and in *In Memoriam* (his two sustained and ambitious efforts), particular phrases are always flashing out the whole fire of the truth.[3]

HE WAS A Victorian in the bad as well as the good sense; he could not keep priggishness out of long poems. Or again, take the case of *In Memoriam.* I will quote one verse (probably incorrectly) which has always seemed to me splendid, and which does express what the whole poem should express but hardly does.

> "That we may lift from out the dust,
> A voice as unto him that hears
> A cry above the conquered years
> Of one that ever works, and trust."

The poem should have been a cry above the conquered years. It might well have been that if the poet could have said sharply at the end of it, as a pure piece of dogma, "I've forgotten every feature of the man's face: I know God holds him alive."[4]

THEOLOGY

THERE IS NO fact of life, from the death of a donkey to the General Post Office, which has not its place to dance and sing in, in the glorious carnival of theology.[5]

YOU CANNOT ACT for twenty-four hours without deciding either to hold people responsible or not to hold them responsible. Theology is a product far more practical than chemistry.[6]

THEORISTS

THERE IS NO great harm in the theorist who makes up a new theory to fit a new event. But the theorist who starts with a false theory and then sees everything as making it come true is the most dangerous enemy of human reason.[7]

THINGS ENTIRELY ENGLISH

THERE ARE THINGS entirely English and entirely good. Kippers, for instance, and Free Trade, and front gardens, and individual liberty, and the Elizabethan drama, and hansom cabs, and cricket, and Mr. Will Crooks. Above all, there is the happy and holy custom of eating a heavy breakfast. I cannot imagine that Shakespeare began the day with rolls and coffee, like a Frenchman or a German. Surely he began with bacon or bloaters. In fact, a light bursts upon me; for the first time I see the real meaning of Mrs. Gallup and the Great Cipher. It is merely a mistake in the matter of a capital letter.

I withdraw my objections; I accept everything; bacon did write Shakespeare.[8]

THE VAGUE ENGLISH spirit loves to have the entrance to its house softened by bushes and broken by steps. It likes to have a little anteroom of hedges half in the house and half out of it; a green room in a double sense.[9]

THINGS WORTH DOING

IN EVERYTHING ON this earth that is worth doing, there is a stage when no one would do it, except for necessity or honour.[10]

THOMPSON, FRANCIS

WITH FRANCIS THOMPSON we lose the greatest poetic energy since Browning. His energy was of somewhat the same kind. Browning was intellectually intricate because he was morally simple. He was too simple to explain himself; he was too humble to suppose that other people needed any explanation. But his real energy, and the real energy of Francis Thompson, was best expressed in the fact that both poets were at once fond of immensity and also fond of detail. Any common Imperialist can have large ideas so long as he is not called upon to have small ideas also. Any common scientific philosopher can have small ideas so long as he is not called upon to have large ideas as well. But great poets use the telescope and also the microscope. Great poets are obscure for two opposite reasons; now, because they are talking about something too large for any one to understand, and now again because they are talking about something too small for any one to see. Francis Thompson possessed both these infinities.[11]

IN FRANCIS THOMPSON'S poetry, as in the poetry of the universe, you can work infinitely out and out, but yet infinitely in and in. These two infinities are the mark of greatness; and he was a great poet.[12]

THE THREE WISE MEN

Step softly, under snow or rain,
To find the place where men can pray;
The way is all so very plain
That we may lose the way.
Oh we have learnt to peer and pore,
On tortured puzzles from our youth.
We know all labyrinthine lore,
We are the three Wise Men of yore,
And we know all things but the truth.
Go humbly . . . it has hailed and snowed . . .
With voices low and lanterns lit,
So very simple is the road,
That we may stray from it.
The world grows terrible and white,
And blinding white the breaking day,
We walk bewildered in the light,
For something that is too large for sight.
And something much too plain to say.
The Child that was ere worlds begun
(. . . We need but walk a little way . . .
We need but see a latch undone . . .)
The Child that played with moon and sun
Is playing with a little hay.
The house from which the heavens are fed,
The old strange house that is our own;
Where tricks of words are never said,
And Mercy is as plain as bread,
And Honour is as hard as stone.

Go humbly; humble are the skies,
And low and large and fierce the Star,
So very near the Manger lies
That we may travel far.
Hark! Laughter like a lion wakes
To roar to the resounding plain,
And the whole heaven shouts and shakes
For God Himself is born again,
And we are little children walking
Through the snow and rain.[13]

THROWING BOMBS

IF YOU THROW one bomb you are only a murderer; but if you keep on persistently throwing bombs, you are in awful danger of at last becoming a prig.[14]

TOM JONES (THE NOVEL BY HENRY FIELDING)

IF TOM JONES violated morality, so much the worse for Tom Jones. Fielding did not feel, as a melancholy modern would have done, that every sin of Tom Jones was in some way breaking the spell, or we may even say destroying the fiction of morality. Men spoke of the sinner breaking the law; but it was rather the law that broke him. And what modern people call the foulness and freedom of Fielding is generally the severity and moral stringency of Fielding. He would not have thought that he was serving morality at all if he had written a book all about nice people. . . . Telling the truth about the terrible struggle of the human soul is surely a very elementary part of the ethics of honesty. If the characters are not wicked, the book is.

This older and firmer conception of right as existing outside human weakness and without reference to human error can be felt in the very lightest and loosest of the works of old English literature. It is commonly unmeaning enough to call Shakespeare a great moralist; but in this particular way Shakespeare is a very typical moralist. Whenever he alludes to right and wrong it is always with this old implication. Right is right, even if nobody does it. Wrong is wrong, even if everybody is wrong about it.[15]

TOM JONES IS still alive, with all his good and all his evil; he is walking about the streets; we meet him every day. We meet with him, we drink with him, we smoke with him, we talk with him, we talk about him. The only difference is that we have no longer the intellectual courage to write about him.... We have grown to associate morality in a book with a kind of optimism and prettiness; according to us, a moral book is a book about moral people. But the old idea was almost exactly the opposite; a moral book was a book about immoral people.[16]

THERE SEEMS TO be an extraordinary idea abroad that Fielding was in some way an immoral or offensive writer. I have been astounded by the number of the leading articles, literary articles, and other articles written about him just now in which there is a curious tone of apologising for the man. One critic says that after all he couldn't help it, because he lived in the eighteenth century; another says that we must allow for the change of manners and ideas; another says that he was not altogether without generous and humane feelings; another suggests that he clung feebly, after all, to a few of the less important virtues. What on earth does all this mean? Fielding described Tom Jones as going on in a certain way, in which, most unfortunately, a very large number of young men do go on. It is unnecessary to say that Henry Fielding knew that it was an unfortunate way of going on. Even Tom Jones knew that. He said in so many words that it was a very unfortunate way of going on; he said, one may almost say, that it had ruined his life; the passage is there for the benefit of any one who may take the trouble to read the book. There is ample evidence (though even this is of a mystical and indirect kind), there is ample evidence that Fielding probably thought that it was better to be Tom Jones than to be an utter coward and sneak. There is simply not one rag or thread or speck of evidence to show that Fielding thought that it was better to be Tom Jones than to be a good man. All that he is concerned with is the description of a definite and very real type of young man; the young man whose passions and whose selfish necessities sometimes seemed to be stronger than anything else in him.[17]

Trade unions

THERE IS ONLY one thing that stands in our midst, attenuated and threatened, but enthroned in some power like a ghost of the Middle Ages: the Trade Unions.[18]

Tradition

TRADITION MEANS GIVING votes to the most obscure of all classes, our ancestors. It is the democracy of the dead. Tradition refuses to submit to the small and arrogant oligarchy of those who merely happen to be walking about.[19]

Trains

THE ONLY WAY of catching a train I have ever discovered is to be late for the one before. Do this, and you will find in a railway station much of the quietude and consolation of a cathedral. It has many of the characteristics of a great ecclesiastical building; it has vast arches, void spaces, coloured lights, and, above all, it has recurrence or ritual. It is dedicated to the celebration of water and fire—the two prime elements of all human ceremonial. Lastly, a station resembles the old religions rather than the new religions in this point, that people go there.[20]

Trees

SOME LITTLE TIME ago I stood among immemorial English trees that seemed to take hold upon the stars like a brood of Ygdrasils. As I walked among these living pillars I became gradually aware that the rustics who lived and died in their shadow adopted a very curious conversational tone. They seemed to be constantly apologizing for the trees, as if they were a very poor show. After elaborate investigation, I discovered that their gloomy and penitent tone was traceable to the fact that it was winter and all the trees were bare....

There was evidently a general feeling that I had caught the trees in a kind of disgraceful deshabille, and that they ought not to be seen until, like the first human sinners, they had covered themselves with leaves. [But] so far from the line of the tree when it is bare appearing harsh and severe, it is luxuriantly indefinable to an unusual degree; the fringe of the forest melts away like a vignette. The tops of two or three high trees when they are leafless are so soft that they seem like the gigantic brooms of that fabulous lady who was sweeping the cobwebs off the sky.[21]

The Trinity

FOR TO US Trinitarians (if I may say it with reverence)—to us God Himself is a society. It is indeed a fathomless mystery of theology.... Suffice it to say here that this triple enigma is as comforting as wine and open as an English fireside.... This thing that bewilders the intellect utterly quiets the heart.[22]

Truth

THERE IS NO end to the dissolution of ideas, the destruction of all tests of truth, that has become possible since men abandoned the attempt to keep a central and civilized Truth, to contain all truths and trace out and refute all errors. Since then, each group has taken one truth at a time and spent the time in turning it into a falsehood. We have had nothing but movements; or in other words, monomanias. But the Church is not a movement but a meeting-place; the trysting-place of all the truths in the world.[23]

WHEN A MAN really tells the truth, the truth he tells is that he himself is a liar.[24]

"TRUTH MUST OF necessity be stranger than fiction," said Basil placidly. "For fiction is the creation of the human mind, and therefore is congenial to it."[25]

THE TEST OF true religion is that . . . it is always trying to make men feel truths as facts; always trying to make abstract things as plain and solid as concrete things; always trying to make men, not merely admit the truth, but see, smell, handle, hear, and devour the truth. All great spiritual scriptures are full of the invitation not to test, but to taste; not to examine, but to eat. Their phrases are full of living water and heavenly bread, mysterious manna and dreadful wine. Worldliness, and the polite society of the world, has despised this instinct of eating; but religion has never despised it.[26]

TRUTH IS SO terrible, even in fetters, that for a moment Syme's slender and insane victory swayed like a reed. But you could not have guessed it from Syme's bleak blue eyes.[27]

TWAIN, MARK

WE ARE ALWAYS told that there is something specially sinister in the death of a great jester. I am not so sure about the point myself, seeing that so many thousand human beings—diplomatists, financiers, kings, bankers, and founders of philosophies—are engaged in functions that are more ultimately fruitless and frivolous than really making the smallest schoolboy laugh. If the death of a clown makes pantomimes for a moment tragic, it is also true that the death of a statesman makes statesmanship for a moment highly comic; the irony cuts both ways. But in the case of Mark Twain there is a particular cause which at once emphasises and complicates this contrast between the comic and the serious. The point I mean is this: that while Mark Twain's literary merits were very much of the uproarious and topsy-turvy kind, his personal merits were very much of the stoical or even puritanical kind. While irresponsibility was the energy in his writings, an almost excessive responsibility was the energy of his character. The artistic European might feel that he was, perhaps, too comic when he was comic; but such a European would also feel that he was too serious when he was serious.[28]

THE WIT OF Mark Twain was avowedly and utterly of the extravagant order. It had that quality of mad logic carried further and further into the void, a quality in which many strange civilisations are at one. It is a system of extremes, and all extremes meet in it; thus houses piled one on top of the other is the ideal of a flat in New York and of a pagoda in Peking. Mark Twain was a master of this mad lucidity. He was a wit rather than a humorist; but I do not mean by this (as so many modern people will certainly fancy) that he was something less than a humorist. Possibly, I think, he was something more than a humorist.[29]

A MAN MAY enjoy humour all by himself; he may see a joke when no one else sees it; he may see the point and avoid it. But wit is a sword; it is meant to make people feel the point as well as see it. All honest people saw the point of Mark Twain's wit. Not a few dishonest people felt it.

But though it was wit it was wild wit, as wild as the pagoda in China or the other pagodas in New York. It was progressive, and the joke went forward by arithmetical progression. In all those excruciating tales of his, which in our youth made us ill with laughing, the idea always consisted in carrying some small fact or notion to more and more frantic lengths of deduction. If a man's hat was as high as a house Mark Twain would think of some way of calling it twenty times higher than a house. If his hat was smashed flat as a pancake, Mark Twain would invent some startling and happy metaphor to prove that it was smashed twenty times flatter than a pancake. His splendid explosive little stories, such as that which describes how he edited an agricultural paper, or that which explains how he tried to decipher a letter from Horace Greeley, have one tremendous essential of great art. I mean that excitement mounts up perpetually; the stories grow more and more comic, as a tragedy should grow more and more tragic.[30]

NO WRITER OF modern English, perhaps, has had such a genius for making the cow jump over the moon; that is, for lifting the heaviest and most solemn absurdity high up into the most starry adventures. He was never at a loss for a simile or a parable, and they were never, strictly speaking, nonsense. They were rather a kind of incredible sense. They were not suddenly inconsequent, like Lewis Carroll; rather they were unbearably consequent, and seemed capable of producing new consequences for ever. Even that fantastic irreverence and fantastic ignorance which sometimes marked his dealings with elements he insufficiently understood, were never abrupt departures, but only elaborate deductions from his idea. It was quite logical that when told that a saint's heart had burst his ribs he should ask what the saint had for dinner. It was quite logical that his delightful musician, when asked to play music appropriate to the Prodigal Son, should play, "We all get blind drunk when Johnny comes marching home." These are things of real wit, like that of Voltaire; though they are not uttered with the old French restraint, but with a new American extravagance.[31]

SOMEBODY IN AN advanced Socialist paper that I saw the other day said that Mark Twain was a cynic. I suppose there never was a person so far removed from cynicism as Mark Twain. A cynic must at least mean a man who is flippant about serious things; about things that he thinks serious. Mark Twain was always serious to the verge of madness. He was not serious about St. Francis; he did not think St. Francis serious. He honestly supposed the marvels of St. Francis to be some ecclesiastical trick of Popes and Cardinals. He did not happen to know that the Franciscan movement was something much more certainly popular than the revolution that rent America from England. He derided King Arthur's Court as something barbaric. He did not happen to know that the only reason why that dim and highly dubious Court has made a half-entry into history is that it stood, if it ever stood at all, for the remnant of high civilisation against the base advance of barbarism. He did not happen to know that, in his time, St. Francis stood for the ballot-box. He did not happen to know that, in his time, King Arthur stood for the telephone. He could never quite get rid of the American idea that good sense and good government had begun quite a little while ago; and that the heavier a monumental stone was to lift the more lightly it might be thrown away. But all these limitations of his only re-emphasize the ultimate fact: he never laughed at a thing unless he thought it laughable. He was an American; that is, an unfathomably solemn man. Now all this is due to a definite thing, an historical thing, called Republican virtue. It was worth while to issue the Declaration of Independence if only that Mark Twain might declare his independence also.[32]

[TWAIN] HAMMERED CALVINISM in his youth and Christian Science in his old age. But he was not an "advanced" thinker, not a mind in revolt; rather he was a conservative and rustic grandfather older than all such follies. But this strength in him and his country truly came from a great spirit which England resisted and has forgotten; the spirit which, when all is said, made it no nonsense to compare Washington to Cincinnatus; the austere love of liberty and of the ploughshare and the sword.[33]

TYRANNY

WHEN YOU HAVE vast systems . . . you do in fact find that those who rule are the few. . . . We say there ought to be in the world a great mass of scattered powers, privileges, limits, points of resistance, so that the mass of the Commons may resist tyranny. And we say there is a permanent possibility of that central direction . . . becoming a tyranny. I do not think it would be difficult to suggest a way in which it could happen.[34]

CAN YOU IMAGINE . . . a civilisation in which no one could be praised or blamed? Above all, can you imagine it humane and democratic, after your own heart? Can you believe that men would be better off when they could not even denounce or disgrace an oppressor? Do you think tyrants would be more tender when their victims could not even curse them? Have you found the rulers of the earth so sweet and tactful that they can be trusted in a world without a whisper of blame? I can imagine such a world only wildly—men moving about with faces shining with a horrible innocence, and murdering men as children pick flowers.[35]

THE GREAT GREY masses of men still toil and tug and sway hither and thither around the great grey tower; and the tower is still motionless, as it will always be motionless. These men will be crushed before the sun is set; and new men will arise and be crushed, and new wrongs done, and tyranny will always rise again like the sun, and injustice will always be as fresh as the flowers of spring. And the stone tower will always look down on it. Matter, in its brutal beauty, will always look down on those who are mad enough to consent to die, and yet more mad, since they consent to live.[36]

U

Ugliness and beauty

IT APPEARS TO us that of all the fairy tales none contains so vital a moral truth as the old story, existing in many forms, of Beauty and the Beast. There is written, with all the authority of a human scripture, the eternal and essential truth that until we love a thing in all its ugliness we cannot make it beautiful.[1]

Uniqueness

EVERYONE ON THIS earth should believe, amid whatever madness or moral failure, that his life and temperament have some object on the earth. Everyone on the earth should believe that he has something to give to the world which cannot otherwise be given. Everyone should, for the good of men and the saving of his own soul, believe that it is possible, even if we are the enemies of the human race, to be the friends of God.[2]

Universalism

THE FANATIC IS the father of one creed; but the tolerant sceptic is the father of a thousand contradictory creeds. Universalism gives birth to myriad bigotries.[3]

The universe

THE UNIVERSE IS a single jewel, and while it is a natural cant to talk of a jewel as peerless and priceless, of this jewel it is literally true. This cosmos is indeed without peer and without price: for there cannot be another one.[4]

Unreason

WHEN THE PEOPLE have got used to unreason they can no longer be startled at injustice.[5]

Utopia

WE NEED WATCHFULNESS even in Utopia, lest we fall from Utopia as we fell from Eden.[6]

I COULD NEVER conceive or tolerate any Utopia which did not leave to me the liberty for which I chiefly care, the liberty to bind myself.[7]

ALL MY MODERN Utopian friends look at each other rather doubtfully, for their ultimate hope is the dissolution of all special ties. But again I seem to hear, like a kind of echo, an answer from beyond the world. "You will have real obligations, and therefore real adventures when you get to my Utopia. But the hardest obligation and the steepest adventure is to get there."[8]

IT DOES NOT matter (comparatively speaking) how often humanity fails to imitate its ideal; for then all its old failures are fruitful. But it does frightfully matter how often humanity changes its ideal; for then all its old failures are fruitless.[9]

BUT THE MAN we see every day—the worker in Mr. Gradgrind's factory, the little clerk in Mr. Gradgrind's office—he is too mentally worried to believe in freedom. He is kept quiet with revolutionary literature. He is calmed and kept in his place by a constant succession of wild philosophies. He is a Marxian one day, a Nietzscheite the next day, a Superman (probably) the next day; and a slave every day.[10]

I AM NOT at all fond of regimentation or repression; that is why I have never written a novel about Utopia, as is the case with almost all of the sinful human race who have written anything in our time. Utopia always seems to me to mean regimentation rather than emancipation; repression rather than expansion. It is generally called a Republic, and it always is a Monarchy. It is a Monarchy in the old and exact sense of the term; because it is really ruled by one man, the author of the book. He may tell us that all the characters in the book spontaneously delight in the beautiful social condition, but somehow we never believe him. His ideal world is always the world that he wants, and not the world that the world wants. Therefore, however democratic it may be in theory or in the book, it is always pretty despotic when it begins to be approached in practice through the law.[11]

V

Velasquez

DIEGO RODRIGUEZ DE Silva Velasquez, the living man, was court-painter, polished, stately and serene. The trouble is that three centuries after his entombment, the dead man has suddenly become a demagogue, a controversialist, a party leader. He is the captain of the Impressionists. Fortunately for himself, Velasquez lived in an age which did not call upon him to be any sort of an "ist," except an Artist. He was impressional, decorative or realistic, as he felt inclined, and had no new critic looking over his shoulder to weep when he lapsed into lucidity. One of the very few virtues we are really losing is the virtue of inconsistency.[1]

Vice

FOR YEARS AND decades past the rich have been preaching their own virtues. Now that they have begun to preach their vices too, I think it is time to kick.[2]

FOR THE WORST and most dangerous hypocrite is not he who affects unpopular virtue, but he who affects popular vice. The jolly fellow of the saloon bar and the race-course is the real deceiver of mankind; he has misled more than any false prophet, and his victims cry to him out of hell.[3]

The Victorian age in literature

IT ONLY REMAINS for me, therefore, to take the more delicate and entangled task; and deal with the great Victorians, not only by dates and names, but rather by schools and streams of thought. It is a task for which I feel myself wholly incompetent; but as that applies to every other literary enterprise I ever went in for, the sensation is not wholly novel: indeed, it is rather reassuring than otherwise to realise that I am now doing something that nobody could do properly. The chief peril of the process, however, will be an inevitable tendency to make the spiritual landscape too large for the figures. I must ask for indulgence if such criticism traces too far back into politics or ethics the roots of which great books were the blossoms; makes Utilitarianism more important than Liberty or talks more of the Oxford Movement than of *The Christian Year*. I can only answer in the very temper of the age of which I write: for I also was born a Victorian; and sympathise not a little with the serious Victorian spirit. I can only answer, I shall not make religion more important than it was to Keble, or politics more sacred than they were to Mill.[4]

ENGLAND, LIKE ALL Christian countries, absorbed valuable elements from the forests and the rude romanticism of the North; but, like all Christian countries, it drank its longest literary draughts from the classic fountains of the ancients. . . . The English tongue and talent of speech did not merely flower suddenly into the gargantuan polysyllables of the great Elizabethans; it had always been full of the popular Latin of the Middle Ages.[5]

THE SAME EIGHTEENTH-CENTURY emancipation which in France produced the pictures of David, in England produced the pictures of Blake. There never were, I think, men who gave to the imagination so much of the sense of having broken out into the very borderlands of being, as did the great English poets of the romantic or revolutionary period; than Coleridge in the secret sunlight of the Antarctic, where the waters were like witches' oils; than Keats looking out of those extreme mysterious casements upon that ultimate sea.[6]

BROADLY, THE PHASE in which the Victorian epoch closed was what can only be called the Imperialist phase. Between that and us stands a very individual artist who must nevertheless be connected with that phase. As I said at the beginning, Macaulay (or, rather, the mind Macaulay shared with most of his powerful middle class) remains as a sort of pavement or flat foundation under all the Victorians. They discussed the dogmas rather than denied them. Now one of the dogmas of Macaulay was the dogma of progress. A fair statement of the truth in it is not really so hard. Investigation of any thing naturally takes some little time. It takes some time to sort letters so as to find a letter: it takes some time to test a gas bracket so as to find the leak; it takes some time to sift evidence so as to find the truth. Now the curse that fell on the later Victorians was this: that they began to value the time more than the truth. One felt so secretarial when sorting letters that one never found the letter; one felt so scientific in explaining gas that one never found the leak; and one felt so judicial, so impartial, in weighing evidence that one had to be bribed to come to any conclusion at all. This was the last note of the Victorians: procrastination was called progress.[7]

VIRTUES AND HOBBIES

PIETY IS ONE of the popular virtues, whereas soap and Socialism are two hobbies of the upper middle class.[8]

THE VISIBLE AND INVISIBLE

LAST WEEK, IN an idle metaphor, I took the tumbling of trees and the secret energy of the wind as typical of the visible world moving under the violence of the invisible. I took this metaphor merely because I happened to be writing the article in a wood. Nevertheless, now that I return to Fleet Street (which seems to me, I confess, much better and more poetical than all the wild woods in the world), I am strangely haunted by this accidental comparison. The people's figures seem a forest and their soul a wind. All the human personalities which speak or signal to me seem to have this fantastic character of the fringe of the forest against the sky. That man that talks to me, what is he but an articulate tree? That driver of a van who waves his hands wildly at me to tell me to get out of the way, what is he but a bunch of branches stirred and swayed by a spiritual wind, a sylvan object that I can continue to contemplate with calm? That policeman who lifts his hand to warn three omnibuses of the peril that they run in encountering my person, what is he but a shrub shaken for a moment with that blast of human law which is a thing stronger than anarchy? Gradually this impression of the woods wears off. But this black-and-white contrast between the visible and invisible, this deep sense that the one essential belief is belief in the invisible as against the visible, is suddenly and sensationally brought back to my mind.[9]

Vows

THERE ARE THRILLING moments, doubtless, for the spectator, the amateur, and the aesthete; but there is one thrill that is known only to the soldier who fights for his own flag, to the ascetic who starves himself for his own illumination, to the lover who makes finally his own choice. And it is this transfiguring self-discipline that makes the vow a truly sane thing. It must have satisfied even the giant hunger of the soul of a lover or a poet to know that in consequence of some one instant of decision that strange chain would hang for centuries in the Alps among the silences of stars and snows. All around us is the city of small sins, abounding in backways and retreats, but surely, sooner or later, the towering flame will rise from the harbour announcing that the reign of the cowards is over and a man is burning his ships.[10]

THE REVOLT AGAINST vows has been carried in our day even to the extent of a revolt against the typical vow of marriage. It is most amusing to listen to the opponents of marriage on this subject. They appear to imagine that the ideal of constancy was a yoke mysteriously imposed on mankind by the devil, instead of being, as it is, a yoke consistently imposed by all lovers on themselves. They have invented a phrase, a phrase that is a black and white contradiction in two words—"free-love"—as if a lover ever had been, or ever could be, free. It is the nature of love to bind itself, and the institution of marriage merely paid the average man the compliment of taking him at his word. Modern sages offer to the lover, with an ill-flavoured grin, the largest liberties and the fullest irresponsibility; but they do not respect him as the old Church respected him; they do not write his oath upon the heavens, as the record of his highest moment.[11]

Vulgarity

THE VULGAR PEOPLE want to enjoy life just as they want to enjoy gin because they are too stupid to see that they are paying too big a price for it. That they never find happiness, that they don't even know how to look for it, is proved by the paralysing clumsiness and ugliness of everything they do.[12]

W

WATTS, G. F.

THE SALIENT AND essential characteristic of Watts and men of his school was that they regarded life as a whole. They had in their heads, as it were, a synthetic philosophy which put everything into a certain relation with God and the wheel of things.[1]

HE HAS THE one great certainty which marks off all the great Victorians from those who have come after them: he may not be certain that he is successful, or certain that he is great, or certain that he is good, or certain that he is capable: but he is certain that he is right. It is of course the very element of confidence which has in our day become least common and least possible. We know we are brilliant and distinguished, but we do not know we are right. We swagger in fantastic artistic costumes; we praise ourselves; we fling epigrams right and left; we have the courage to play the egoist and the courage to play the fool, but we have not the courage to preach.[2]

HE, MORE THAN any other modern man, more than politicians who thundered on platforms or financiers who captured continents, has sought in the midst of his quiet and hidden life to mirror his age. He was born in the white and austere dawn of that great reforming century, and he has lingered after its grey and doubtful close. He is above all things a typical figure, a survival of the nineteenth century.[3]

[THE AGE IN which Watts lived] fell in love with abstractions and became enamoured of great and desolate words.[4]

WHETHER WE HIDE in a monastery or thunder on a platform, we are still standing in the Court of Death.... This is the great pathos and the great dignity of philosophy and theology. Men talk of philosophy and theology as if they were something specialistic and arid and academic. But philosophy and theology are not only the only democratic things, they are democratic to the point of being vulgar, to the point, I was going to say, of being rowdy. They alone admit all matters; they alone lie open to all attacks. All other sciences may, while studying their own, laugh at the rag-tag and bob-tail of other sciences. An astronomer may sneer at animalculae which are very like stars; an entomologist may scorn the stars, which are very like animalculae. Physiologists may think it dirty to grub about in the grass; botanists may think it dirtier to grub about in an animal's inside. But there is nothing that is not relevant to these more ancient studies.[5]

WEAKNESS AND COWARDICE

MEN TRUST AN ordinary man, because they trust themselves. But men trust a great man because they do not trust themselves. And hence the worship of great men always appears in time of weakness and cowardice; we never hear of great men until the time when all other men are small.[6]

WEAKNESS AND STRENGTH

MANY MODERN ENGLISHMEN talk of themselves as the sturdy descendants of their sturdy Puritan fathers. As a fact they would run away from a cow. If you asked one of their Puritan fathers, if you asked Bunyan, for instance, whether he was sturdy he would have answered with tears that he was as weak as water. And because of this he would have borne tortures.[7]

Weather

I SUPPOSE THAT, taking this summer as a whole, people will not call it an appropriate time for praising the English climate. But for my part I will praise the English climate till I die even if I die of the English climate. There is no weather so good as English weather. Nay, in a real sense there is no weather at all anywhere but in England. In France you have much sun and some rain; in Italy you have hot winds and cold winds; in Scotland and Ireland you have rain, either thick or thin; in America you have hells of heat and cold, and in the Tropics you have sunstrokes varied by thunderbolts. But all these you have on a broad and brutal scale, and you settle down into contentment or despair. Only in our own romantic country do you have the strictly romantic thing called Weather; beautiful and changing as a woman. The great English landscape painters (neglected now like everything that is English) have this salient distinction: that the Weather is not the atmosphere of their pictures; it is the subject of their pictures. They paint portraits of the Weather. The Weather sat to Constable. The Weather posed for Turner; and a deuce of a pose it was. This cannot truly be said of the greatest of their continental models or rivals. Poussin and Claude painted objects, ancient cities or perfect Arcadian shepherds through a clear medium of the climate. But in the English painters Weather is the hero; with Turner an Adelphi hero, taunting, flashing and fighting, melodramatic but really magnificent. The English climate, a tall and terrible protagonist, robed in rain and thunder and snow and sunlight, fills the whole canvas and the whole foreground.[8]

Wells, H. G.

OUT OF THE same social ferment arose a man of equally unquestionable genius, Mr. H. G. Wells. His first importance was that he wrote great adventure stories in the new world the men of science had discovered. He walked on a round slippery world as boldly as Ulysses or Tom Jones had worked on a flat one. Cyrano de Bergerac or Baron Munchausen, or other typical men of science, had treated the moon as a mere flat silver mirror in which Man saw his own image—the Man in the Moon. Wells treated the moon as a globe, like our own; bringing forth monsters as moonish as we are earthy.[9]

I FIND MYSELF still sitting in front of the last book by Mr. H. G. Wells, I say stunned with admiration, my family says sleepy with fatigue. I still feel vaguely all the things in Mr. Wells's book which I agree with; and I still feel vividly the one thing that I deny. I deny that biology can destroy the sense of truth, which alone can even desire biology. No truth which I find can deny that I am seeking the truth. My mind cannot find anything which denies my mind.[10]

WILD KNIGHT, THE

So, with the wan waste grasses on my spear,
I ride for ever, seeking after God.
My hair grows whiter than my thistle plume,
And all my limbs are loose; but in my eyes
The star of an unconquerable praise:
For in my soul one hope for ever sings,
That at the next white corner of a road
My eyes may look on Him.[11]

WILDE, OSCAR

SURELY ONE MIGHT pay for extraordinary joy in ordinary morals. Oscar Wilde said that sunsets were not valued because we could not pay for sunsets. But Oscar Wilde was wrong; we can pay for sunsets. We can pay for them by not being Oscar Wilde.[12]

The winning side

THERE IS NO such thing as fighting on the winning side; one fights to find out which is the winning side.[13]

Wisdom and folly

OUR WISDOM, WHETHER expressed in private or public, belongs to the world, but our folly belongs to those we love.[14]

> MORRIS. Well, well, they didn't know everything in those old times.
>
> SMITH. No, and in those old times they knew they didn't. [*Dreamily.*] Where shall wisdom be found, and what is the place of understanding?
>
> CONJURER. Somewhere in America, I believe.
>
> SMITH. [*Still dreamily.*] Man knoweth not the price thereof; neither is it found in the land of the living. The deep sayeth it is not in me, the sea sayeth it is not with me. Death and destruction say we have heard tell of it. God understandeth the way thereof and He knoweth the place thereof. For He looketh to the ends of the earth and seeth under the whole Heaven. But to man He hath said: Behold the fear of the Lord, that is wisdom, and to depart from evil is understanding.[15]

Wit and satire

BREVITY MAY BE the soul of wit; but it would be quite as true to say in such cases that lengthiness is the soul of satire.[16]

FOR WIT IS always connected with the idea that truth is close and clear. Humour, on the other hand, is always connected with the idea that truth is tricky and mystical and easily mistaken.[17]

I WOULD ALWAYS trust the old wives' fables against the old maids' facts. As long as wit is mother wit it can be as wild as it pleases.[18]

WONDER

THE WORLD WILL never starve for want of wonders; but only for want of wonder.[19]

THERE IS ONE thing which gives radiance to everything. It is the idea of something around the corner.[20]

THE GRASS SEEMED signalling to me with all its fingers at once; the crowded stars seemed bent upon being understood.[21]

THAT THE TREES are high and the grasses short is a mere accident of our own foot-rules and our own stature. But to the spirit which has stripped off for a moment its own idle temporal standards the grass is an everlasting forest, with dragons for denizens; the stones of the road are as incredible mountains piled one upon the other; the dandelions are like gigantic bonfires illuminating the lands around; and the heath-bells on their stalks are like planets hung in heaven—each higher than the other. Between one stake of a paling and another there are new and terrible landscapes; here a desert, with nothing but one misshapen rock; here a miraculous forest, of which all the trees flower above the head with the hues of sunset; here, again, a sea full of monsters that Dante would not have dared to dream. These are the visions of him who, like the child in the fairy tales, is not afraid to become small.

Meanwhile, the sage whose faith is in magnitude and ambition is, like a giant, becoming larger and larger, which only means that the stars are becoming smaller and smaller. World after world falls from him into insignificance; the whole passionate and intricate life of common things becomes as lost to him as is the life of the infusoria to a man without a microscope. He rises always through desolate eternities. He may find new systems, and forget them; he may discover fresh universes, and learn to despise them. But the towering and tropical vision of things as they really are—the gigantic daisies, the heaven-consuming dandelions, the great Odyssey of strange-coloured oceans and strange-shaped trees, of dust like the wreck of temples, and thistledown like the ruin of stars—all this colossal vision shall perish with the last of the humble.[22]

DID YOU EVER hear a small boy complain of having to hang about a railway station and wait for a train? No; for to him to be inside a railway station is to be inside a cavern of wonder and a palace of poetical pleasures. Because to him the red light and the green light on the signal are like a new sun and a new moon. Because to him when the wooden arm of the signal falls down suddenly, it is as if a great king had thrown down his staff as a signal and started a shrieking tournament of trains. I myself am of little boys' habit in this matter. They also serve who only stand and wait for the two fifteen.[23]

THE WORLD

THE WORLD IS not a lodging house at Brighton, which we are to leave because it is miserable. It is the fortress of our family, with flag flying on the turret; and the more miserable it is the less we should leave it. The point is not that this world is too sad to love or too glad not to love; the point is that when you do love a thing its gladness is a reason for loving it, and its sadness a reason for loving it more.[24]

THIS WORLD CAN be made beautiful again by beholding it as a battlefield. When we have defined and isolated the evil thing, the colours come back into everything else. When evil things have become evil, good things, in a blazing apocalypse, become good.[25]

THE OPTIMISM WHICH talks about this as "the best of all possible worlds" misses the point altogether. The precise fact which makes the world so wonderful and valuable is the fact that you cannot compare it with anything. It is everything; it is our father and our mother. It is not the best of all possible worlds: but it is the best of all possible things that a world should exist.[26]

THE REAL TROUBLE with this world of ours is not that it is an unreasonable world, nor even that it is a reasonable one. The commonest kind of trouble is that it is nearly reasonable, but not quite. Life is not an illogicality; yet it is a trap for logicians. It looks just a little more mathematical and regular than it is; its exactitude is obvious, but its inexactitude is hidden; its wildness lies in wait.[27]

WHATEVER IS IT that we are all looking for? I fancy that it is really quite close. When I was a boy I had a fancy that Heaven or Fairyland or whatever I called it, was immediately behind my own back, and that this was why I could never manage to see it, however often I twisted and turned to take it by surprise. I had a notion of a man perpetually spinning round on one foot like a teetotum in the effort to find that world behind his back which continually fled from him. Perhaps this is why the world goes round. Perhaps the world is always trying to look over its shoulder and catch up the world which always escapes it, yet without which it cannot be itself.[28]

WORLDVIEW

A COSMIC PHILOSOPHY is not constructed to fit a man; a cosmic philosophy is constructed to fit a cosmos. A man can no more possess a private religion than he can possess a private sun and moon.[29]

BUT THERE ARE some people, nevertheless—and I am one of them—who think that the most practical and important thing about a man is still his view of the universe.[30]

THE WRONG PLACE

THE MODERN PHILOSOPHER had told me again and again that I was in the right place, and I had still felt depressed even in acquiescence. But I had heard that I was in the *wrong* place, and my soul sang for joy, like a bird in spring.[31]

Z

ZOLA, EMILE

BUT IN ZOLA even the ideals are undesirable; Zola's mercy is colder than justice—nay, Zola's mercy is more bitter in the mouth than injustice. When Zola shows us an ideal training he does not take us, like Rabelais, into the happy fields of humanist learning. He takes us into the schools of inhumanist learning, where there are neither books nor flowers, nor wine nor wisdom, but only deformities in glass bottles, and where the rule is taught from the exceptions. Zola's truth answers the exact description of the skeleton in the cupboard; that is, it is something of which a domestic custom forbids the discovery, but which is quite dead, even when it is discovered.[1]

ACKNOWLEDGMENTS

For several years, I have cherished the hope of creating a *Quotable Chesterton*—a stout compendium modeled on Tyndale's superb reference work, *The Quotable C. S. Lewis.* That this book became a reality is due entirely to the vision of Joel Miller, vice president of acquisitions and editorial at Thomas Nelson, who invited me to undertake this project before I even had the chance to craft a formal book proposal describing it.

I am deeply grateful for the privilege—and no less grateful for Thomas Nelson's sterling commitment to commend a great writer anew. I owe a great debt to Joel, editor Bryan Norman, copy editor extraordinaire Cheryl Dunlop, and all others on the Thomas Nelson team for investing such time and care in this project.

This book is dedicated to Os Guinness, a cherished friend of many years. When I was on the eve of entering college, and all during my undergraduate years, Os's writings helped me navigate the ever-widening world of ideas that I encountered. In him, my wife and I have no finer or more valued friend. Thank you, Os, for all the fond memories, wisdom, and laughter.

Lastly, and as ever, I wish to thank my wife, Kelly, and my four-year-old son, Sam. They have been generous and patient in allowing me space and time to work. The thought that there are many things for them within the covers of this book is a very pleasant thought indeed.

NOTES

Publisher's Note: Endnotes are listed for essays first, then for alphabetical quotes. Unless otherwise noted, all books are by G. K. Chesterton.

Epigraph
1. *The Man Who Was Thursday*, chapter 4, "The Tale of a Detective" (New York: Dodd, Mead and Company, 1908), 65–66.
2. *Autobiography*, chapter 4, "How to Be a Lunatic" (London: Hutchinson & Co., 1936), 94–95.

A Fixture of the Times: An Introduction to G. K. Chesterton
1. "G. K. Chesterton, 62, Noted Author Dies," obituary in the Monday, June 15, 1936, edition of the *New York Times*.
2. The unsigned article, "Three Literary Giants of Today," appeared as a 1,923-word feature in the Sunday, May 7, 1916, edition of the *New York Times Book Review*.
3. As quoted in William Oddie, *Chesterton and the Romance of Orthodoxy* (New York: Oxford Univ. Press, 2009), 13.
4. From "Review 4," a 141-word unsigned review published on Saturday, June 27, 1903, on page BR1 of the *New York Times' Saturday Review of Books and Art*. Clement King Shorter (1857–1926), the author of this quote, was a noted English journalist, editor, and avid collector of material related to the Brontës. Shorter's collection and research eventually developed into several books on this literary family. In 1891 he was made editor of the *Illustrated London News*, where he also edited *Album* and *Pick-me-up*. In addition to editing, Shorter founded three papers: *Sketch* (1893), *The Sphere* (1900), and the *Tatler* (1903).
5. F. Scott Fitzgerald, *This Side of Paradise* (New York: Charles Scribner's Sons, 1920), 36.
6. Ernest Hemingway, "The Three-Day Blow," in *In Our Time* (Paris: Three Mountains Press, 1924). See also Ernest Hemingway, *The Complete Short Stories of Ernest Hemingway* (New York: Scribner/Simon & Schuster, 2003), 88. The Walpole referred to in this passage is Chesterton's contemporary, the writer Hugh Walpole.
7. For a fine introduction to Chesterton the public debater, see "A Century of

'Thursday's," an article by Allan Barra in the December 27, 2008, issue of the *Wall Street Journal*, posted online at: http://online.wsj.com/article/SB123032986340736063.html.

8. Clifton Fadiman and André Bernard, *Bartlett's Book of Anecdotes* (Boston: Little, Brown and Company, 2000).

9. *The Victorian Age in Literature*, chapter 3, "The Great Victorian Poets" (London: Williams & Norgate, 1914), 175–76. The French phrase *"Jongleurs de Dieu"* means "jugglers of God."

10. Garry Wills, *Chesterton* (New York: Doubleday, 2001), 186.

11. André Maurois (Emile Herzog), *Poet and Prophet* (London: Cassell, 1933), 141–74.

12. *Orthodoxy* (New York: John Lane Company, 1909), 13–14.

13. C. S. Lewis, *Surprised by Joy* (New York: Harcourt, Brace Jovanovich, 1955), 213–15.

14. Ibid., 191.

15. C. S. Lewis, *The Essential C. S. Lewis*, ed. Lyle W. Dorsett (New York: Touchstone Books, 1996), 47.

16. Unsigned review, "Three Literary Giants of Today: Critical Studies of Kipling, G. K. Chesterton and G. B. Shaw Present an Interesting Picture of Contemporary Literature," a 1,923-word article from the Sunday, May 7, 1916, issue of the *New York Times Book Review*, BR189.

Reasons for His Hope: Chesterton the Apologist

1. Dorothy L. Sayers, preface to Chesterton's play *The Surprise*, London, 1952, 5.

2. *Orthodoxy* (New York: John Lane Company, 1909), 18.

3. *Tremendous Trifles*, chapter 1, "Tremendous Trifles" (New York: Dodd, Mead and Co, 1909), 7.

4. Frederick Buechner, *Speak What We Feel* (San Francisco: HarperCollins, 2001), 92–96, 119.

5. A point cogently argued by David Stewart in his review of Buechner's *Speak What We Feel*, which appears in the July 29, 2002, issue of *Books and Culture*. This article is posted online at: http://www.christianitytoday.com/bc/columns/bookculturecorner/020729.html?start=2.

6. *Orthodoxy*, 13–14.

7. C. S. Lewis, *The Essential C. S. Lewis*, ed. Lyle W. Dorsett (New York: Touchstone Books, 1996), 47.

8. C. S. Lewis to Sheldon Vanauken, 14 December 1950—a letter in the public domain and posted online at: http://www.catholiceducation.org/articles/arts/al0176.html.

9. Ibid. See chapter 14 of C. S. Lewis, *Surprised by Joy* (London: Geoffrey Bles, 1955). Lewis's comments here about the influence of George MacDonald and Chesterton on his embrace of Christianity deserve to be quoted in full: "George MacDonald had done more to me than any other writer; of course

it was a pity he had that bee in his bonnet about Christianity. He was good *in spite of it*. Chesterton had more sense than all the other moderns put together; bating, of course, his Christianity."

The Father of Father Brown: Chesterton as a Mystery Writer

1. See Martin Gardener, ed., *The Annotated Innocence of Father Brown* (Oxford Univ. Press, 1987), 279, wherein it is stated that the story "Valentin Follows a Curious Trail" was published on 7/23/1910. This story later appeared as "The Blue Cross" in the first collection of Father Brown mystery stories called *The Innocence of Father Brown* (London: Cassell, 1911/New York: John Lane, 1911). Chesterton scholar Hugh Robson has traced the initial publication of the first twelve Father Brown stories to the *Saturday Evening Post* in 1910–1911, where they appeared under different titles than those given them in *The Innocence of Father Brown*.

2. A tally confirmed by author Sinclair McKay in the 19 December 2009 issue of the *Spectator*. This article is posted online at: http://www.spectator.co.uk/essays/5635928/bring-back-father-brown.thtml.

3. Alec Guinness, *Blessings in Disguise* (1985), as quoted in the following *Christianity Today* web posting: http://www.christianitytoday.com/ch/2002/issue75/14.2.html?start=2.

4. Karen Robinson, writing in the *Sunday Times*, has said of Timson's reading of *The Innocence of Father Brown*: "David Timson is one of those audio-book readers who, rather than giving a 'signature' performance like some of the big stars of the genre, simply inhabits and projects his subjects with a delicate empathy, so it's the book and its characters that linger in the mind. Which makes him an excellent choice for G. K. Chesterton's tales of the unassuming Catholic priest." This review published on June 21, 2009, is posted online at: http://entertainment.timesonline.co.uk/tol/arts_and_entertainment/books/audio_books/article6528255.ece.

Wielder of the Facile Pen: Chesterton the Essayist

1. A tally stated by Chesterton scholar D. J. Conlon on the inside front leaf of the scholarly anthology he edited, entitled *G. K. Chesterton: The Critical Judgments, Part I, 1900–1937* (Antwerp, Belgium: Antwerp Studies in English Literature, 1976).

2. See David Roberts, "Charles Dickens and the 'Daily News': Editorials and Editorial Writers," *Victorian Periodicals Review* 22, no. 2 (Summer, 1989), 51–63. This scholarly journal is published by the Johns Hopkins University Press on behalf of the Research Society for Victorian Periodicals. For online attribution, see: http://www.jstor.org/stable/20082378.

3. T. S. Eliot, signed obituary for Chesterton, *The Tablet*, 20 June 1936, 785.

Radio Dramatization: Mr. Welles and Mr. Chesterton

1. The audio file for this program, titled OW93, is archived online at: http://relicradio.com/orsonwelles/.

2. *Poems* (London: Burns & Oates, Ltd., 1917), 69–70.

3. For more on the history of the Mercury Radio Theatre, see the website posting at: http://www.mercurytheatre.info/.

4. The story of the friendship of Chesterton and H. G. Wells is well documented. See, for example, Alzina Stone Dale's Chesterton biography *The Outline of Sanity* (Grand Rapids: Eerdmans, 1982), 116–17ff.

5. Jorge Luis Borges, review of *Citizen Kane* entitled "An Overwhelming Film," translated into English and published by MIT Press in the journal *October*, vol. 15 (Winter, 1980), 12–14. This review is posted online at: http://www.jstor.org/stable/778448.

6. Kingsley Amis, Introduction to G. K. Chesterton, *The Man Who Was Thursday* (London: Penguin Books, 1986).

7. Welles said this during his Introduction to the Mercury Theatre on the Air's presentation of *The Man Who Was Thursday*, originally broadcast throughout America by the network of affiliates comprising the Columbia Broadcasting System (CBS) and a "coast to coast network" of the CBC in Canada on Monday, September 5, 1938. Welles offered his spoken tribute during the time period lasting from 1 minute 28 seconds into the program to 1 minute 53 seconds into the program. This celebrated radio theater adaptation of Chesterton's novel was described in critic Richard Corliss's *Time* magazine article "That Old Feeling: Mercury, God of Radio," posted online at: http://www.time.com/time/sampler/article/0,8599,172672,00.html.

The Edwardian Dr. Johnson: Chesterton as a Man of Letters

1. Bruce F. Murphy, Introduction, G. K. Chesterton, *The Man Who Was Thursday* (New York: Barnes & Noble, 2004), x.

2. A quotation from Pat Rogers's essay on Samuel Johnson in *The New Oxford Dictionary of National Biography* (2004).

3. *Appreciations and Criticisms of the Works of Charles Dickens*, chapter 4, "Nicholas Nickleby" (London: J. M. Dent & Sons, 1911), 26.

4. *Manalive*, part 2, chapter 5, "How the Great Wind Went from Beacon House" (New York: John Lane Company, 1912), 309.

5. *The Everlasting Man*, part 2, chapter 6, "The Five Deaths of the Faith" (London: Hodder & Stoughton, 1947), 297.

6. Garry Wills, *Chesterton* (New York: Doubleday, 2001), 107.

7. *Orthodoxy* (New York: John Lane Company, 1909), 136.

8. Garry Wills, "A Chesterton for the Religious Right," *Christian Century*, May 16–23, 1990, 532.

9. For a complete overview of Bergman's production of Chesterton's play *Magic*, see pages 534–35 of Birgitta Steene's *Ingmar Bergman: A Reference Guide* (Amsterdam Univ. Press, 2005).

10. New Introduction to Garry Wills, *Chesterton* (New York: Doubleday/Image Books, 2001), xvi.

Always a Journalist, Always a Jester: Chesterton the Journalist

1. *Heretics* (New York: John Lane Company, 1905), 217.
2. Luke Timothy Johnson, "God's Journalist," book review of the intellectual biography by Garry Wills, entitled *Chesterton* (New York: Doubleday, 2001), 2. This review appeared in the January 25, 2002 issue of *Commonweal* magazine, and it is posted online at: http://findarticles.com/p/articles/mi_m1252/is_2_129/ai_82361782/?tag=content;col1.
3. *The G. K. C. Calendar: A Quotation from the Works of G. K. Chesterton for Every Day in the Year* (London: Cecil Palmer, 1921), 7.
4. As quoted in Archibald Henderson, *Mark Twain*, chapter 3, "The Humorist" (New York: Frederick A. Stokes Company, 1912), 110.
5. Garry Wills, *Chesterton* (New York: Doubleday, 2001), 186.

A Writer's True Calling: Chesterton the Literary Critic

1. See Jacqueline Banerjee's article "G. K. Chesterton," posted online at http://www.victorianweb.org/authors/chesterton/bio.html.
2. T. S. Eliot, *Selected Essays*, 3rd enlarged ed. (London: Faber, 1951).
3. William Oddie, *Chesterton and the Romance of Orthodoxy: The Making of GKC, 1874–1908* (New York: Oxford Univ. Press, 2009), 311.
4. Iain Finlayson, *Robert Browning: A Private Life* (London: HarperCollins, 2004), 9.
5. Oddie, *Chesterton and the Romance*, 310.
6. Bernard Bergonzi, "Chesterton, Gilbert Keith (1874–1936)," *Oxford Dictionary of National Biography*, online ed., accessed 18 August 2009.
7. *William Blake* (London: Duckworth & Co., 1910), 210.

Unconventional: Chesterton the Novelist

1. A seventh unpublished novel, once thought lost, was discovered in 1989 after the death of Dorothy Collins, Chesterton's former secretary. Given the title *Basil Howe*, it is a romantic novel that has been compared to the novels of Jane Austen. See the article written about this work, and the research of Chesterton scholar Denis Conlon, posted online at: http://www.catholiceducation.org/articles/arts/al0096.html.
2. *The Ball and the Cross* was serialized in the British publication *The Commonwealth* in 1905–1906. It was first published in America (New York: John Lane) in 1909. See the back cover matter for Martin Gardner, ed., G. K. Chesterton, *The Ball and the Cross* (Mineola, NY: Dover Publications, 1995).
3. *The Man Who Was Thursday* was originally published in a 1907 pilot edition by J. W. Arrowsmith in Bristol, England.
4. From page 273 of the essay that serves as Garry Wills's Appendix to *Chesterton* (New York: Doubleday, 2001).
5. T. S. Eliot, signed obituary for Chesterton, *The Tablet*, 20 June 1936, 785.
6. L. Wardlaw Miles's review of *The Ball and the Cross* was published in volume

18 of the *Sewanee Review*, ed. John M. McBryde, Jr. (New York: Longmans, Green & Co., 1910), 508–11.

7. Unsigned review in the *Times Literary Supplement*, 29 February 1912.

8. Unsigned review in the *Times Literary Supplement*, 12 May 1927.

9. Unsigned review in the *Sunday Times*, 15 May 1927.

10. *William Blake* (London: Duckworth & Co., 1910), 131.

A Lover of Wisdom: Chesterton the Philosopher

1. Garry Wills, *Chesterton* (New York: Doubleday, 2001), 107.

2. *Heretics* (New York: John Lane Company: 1907), 16.

3. Ibid., 17.

4. Ibid., 22–24.

5. Ibid., 305.

6. Ibid.

The Singer of the White Horse: Chesterton the Poet

1. *The Wild Knight and Other Poems* (London: J. M. Dent & Sons, Ltd., 1914), 16–17.

2. *Poems* (Burns & Oates, Ltd., 1917), 4–5.

3. This unpublished manuscript poem is taken from papers housed in the British Library, and has the following call number: BL MS Add. 73334. fo. 5. It is also reprinted in Maisie Ward, *Gilbert Keith Chesterton* (New York: Sheed & Ward, 1943), 61.

4. From Auden's essay on Chesterton in John Sullivan, ed., *G. K. Chesterton: A Centenary Appraisal* (London: Paul Elek, 1974). See also literary scholar Henry J. Donaghy's review of *G. K. Chesterton*, by Lawrence J. Clipper, and *G. K. Chesterton: A Centenary Appraisal*, edited by John Sullivan. Donaghy's review appeared in *Victorian Studies* 18, no. 4 (June 1975), 493–94. In the full text of Auden's essay, he mentions Lear, as well as Lewis Carroll.

5. Garry Wills, "A Chesterton for the Religious Right," *Christian Century*, 16–23 (May 1990): 532.

6. C. S. Lewis to George Sayer, as quoted in George Sayer, *Jack: C. S. Lewis and His Times* (London: Macmillan, 1988), xvi.

7. C. S. Lewis, *On Stories and Other Essays on Literature*, ed. Walter Hooper (New York: Harcourt Books, 1982), 116.

8. Ibid.

9. Introduction to G. K. Chesterton, *The Ballad of the White Horse* (San Francisco: Ignatius Press, 2001), xxix.

10. Auden's assessment appears in Bernadette Sheridan's introduction to G. K. Chesterton, The Ballad of the White Horse.

11. Garry Wills, *Chesterton* (New York: Doubleday, 2001), 171.

12. Graham Greene, as interviewed in the *Observer*, 12 March 1978. See Joseph Pearce, *Wisdom and Innocence: A Life of G. K. Chesterton* (San Francisco: Ignatius Press, 1996), 166.

13. Bernard Bergonzi, "Chesterton, Gilbert Keith (1874–1936)," *The Oxford Dictionary of National Biography* (2004).
14. See Wills, *Chesterton*, 171–72.

A

1. As quoted in *Nash's Pall Mall Magazine*, April 1935.
2. *Heretics*, chapter 8, "The Mildness of the Yellow Press" (New York: John Lane Company, 1907), 120–21.
3. *What's Wrong with the World*, part 3, chapter 9, "Sincerity and the Gallows" (London: Cassell and Company, Ltd., 1910), 164–65.
4. *The Everlasting Man*, part 2, chapter 5, "The Escape from Paganism" (London: Hodder & Stoughton, 1947), 285. For a discussion of the affinity of this statement with C. S. Lewis's thought, see Alan Jacob, *The Narnian: The Life and Imagination of C. S. Lewis* (New York: HarperCollins, 2005), 124.
5. *The Napoleon of Notting Hill*, book 1, chapter 2, "The Man in Green" (London: John Lane, 1912), 25.
6. *Orthodoxy*, chapter 7, "The Eternal Revolution" (New York: John Lane Company, 1909), 210.
7. "Why I Believe in Christianity," from chapter 3, part 7 of *The Religious Doubts of Democracy*, ed. George Haw (New York: The Macmillan Company, 1904), 62.
8. *Alarms and Discursions*, chapter 1, "The Fading Fireworks" (New York: Dodd, Mead and Company, 1911), 2.
9. *Orthodoxy*, chapter 9, "Authority and the Adventurer," 277.
10. *What I Saw in America*, chapter 2, "Meditation in a New York Hotel" (London: Hodder & Stoughton, 1922), 19.
11. Ibid., 31.
12. Ibid., chapter 3, "A Meditation in Broadway," 39.
13. Ibid., chapter 4, "Irish and Other Interviewers," 47–48.
14. *The Man Who Was Thursday*, chapter 1, "The Two Poets of Saffron Park" (New York: Dodd, Mead and Company, 1908), 13–14.
15. Ibid., chapter 2, "The Secret of Gabriel Syme," 23–24.
16. Ibid., chapter 4, "The Tale of a Detective," 51.
17. Ibid., chapter 12, "The Earth in Anarchy," 224–25.
18. Ibid., chapter 15, "The Accuser," 275–76.
19. *All Things Considered*, chapter 1, "The Case for the Ephemeral" (London: Methuen, 1908), 7.
20. *The Everlasting Man*, part 1, chapter 8, "The End of the World," 179.
21. *Orthodoxy*, chapter 6, "The Paradoxes of Christianity," 186.
22. As quoted in a letter appearing in Maisie Ward's biography, *Gilbert Keith Chesterton* (London: Sheed and Ward, 1944), 48.
23. *Divorce Versus Democracy* (London: The Society of SS Peter & Paul— Publishers to the Church of England, 1916), 4. The title page of this work states: "Reprinted from 'Nash's Magazine.'"

24. *George Bernard Shaw*, chapter 1, "The Irishman" (New York: John Lane Company, 1910), 20.

25. *G. F. Watts* (London: Duckworth & Co., 1904), 110.

26. From Chesterton's Introduction to *Thackeray* (London: George Bell and Sons, 1909), xxx.

27. *The Everlasting Man*, part 2, chapter 6, "The Five Deaths of the Faith," 297.

28. *Robert Browning*, chapter 5, "Browning in Later Life" (New York: The Macmillan Company, 1903), 113.

29. As quoted in *The Illustrated London News*, July 16, 1910.

30. *The Uses of Diversity*, chapter 22, "Questions of Divorce" (London: Methuen and Co., 1920), 116.

31. *William Blake* (London: Duckworth & Co., 1910), 179. Cheapside is a street in London.

32. From the Introduction to *Thackeray*, xiii.

33. *Robert Browning*, chapter 1, "Browning in Early Life," 81.

34. *All Things Considered*, chapter 25, "The Error of Impartiality," 211–12.

35. *Orthodoxy*, chapter 6, "The Paradoxes of Christianity," 155–57.

36. Ibid., 153–55.

37. Ibid., chapter 7, "The Eternal Revolution," 208–9.

38. *Tremendous Trifles*, chapter 19, "The Giant" (London, Methuen & Co., 1909), 123.

39. Ibid., chapter 17, "The Tower," 110.

40. *Heretics*, chapter 19, "Slum Novelists and the Slums," 275–76.

41. *What's Wrong with the World*, part 1, chapter 10, "Oppression by Optimism," 68–69.

42. *Orthodoxy*, chapter 7, "The Eternal Revolution," 225–26.

43. *The Victorian Age in Literature*, chapter 1, "The Victorian Compromise and its Enemies" (London: Williams & Norgate, 1914), 75.

44. *The Defendant*, chapter 12, "A Defence of Humility" (New York: Dodd, Mead & Co., 1902), 99.

45. *The G. K. C. Calendar: A Quotation from the Works of G. K. Chesterton for Every Day in the Year* (London: Cecil Palmer, 1921), 45.

46. *The Defendant*, chapter 5, "A Defence of Nonsense," 47.

47. *Tremendous Trifles*, chapter 1, "A Piece of Chalk," 4–5.

48. *All Things Considered*, chapter 9, "French and English," 78–79.

49. "On Regulating the Broadcasters," *Illustrated London News*, 7 May 1927.

50. *St. Francis of Assisi*, chapter 5, "Le Jongleur de Dieu" (London: Hodder and Stoughton, 1933), 88.

51. *Orthodoxy*, chapter 3, "The Suicide of Thought," 65–66.

52. *Victorian Age in Literature*, chapter 2, "The Great Victorian Novelists," 109.

B

1. *Alarms and Discursions*, chapter 38, "The Chorus" (London: Methuen and Co., 1910), 250–51.

2. *All Things Considered*, chapter 27, "Humanitarianism and Strength" (London: Methuen and Co., 1908), 226.

3. *Robert Browning*, chapter 6, "Browning as a Literary Artist" (New York: The Macmillan Company, 1903), 165.

4. *The Man Who Was Thursday*, chapter 1, "The Two Poets of Saffron Park" (New York: Dodd, Mead and Company, 1908), 12–13.

5. Ibid., chapter 15, "The Accuser," 280–81.

6. *All Things Considered*, chapter 28, "Wine When It Is Red," 232.

7. *The Wit and Wisdom of G. K. Chesterton* (New York: Dodd, Mead and Company, 1911), 1. From an article originally published in the *Daily News*.

8. *Magic*, Act I: The Prelude (New York: G.P. Putnam's Sons, 1913), 31.

9. From the 1920 reprinting of *William Blake* (London: Duckworth & Co., 1910), 196–97.

10. As quoted in "The Bigot," an essay in *Lunacy and Letters*, ed. Dorothy Collins (New York: Sheed and Ward, 1958).

11. *Heretics*, chapter 20, "Concluding Remarks on the Importance of Orthodoxy" (New York: John Lane Company, 1907), 295.

12. From the Introduction to *The Defendant* (New York: Dodd, Mead & Co., 1902), 2.

13. As quoted in *The Religious Doubts of Democracy*, part 7, chapter 3, "Why I Believe in Christianity," ed. George Haw (London: Macmillan & Co., Ltd., 1904), 61.

14. Ibid., part 12, chapter 2, "The Eternal Heroism of the Slums," 107.

15. "Mr. Blatchford and My Neighbour," *Daily News*, 14 November 1906.

16. "The Return of the Angels," *Daily News*, 14 March 1903.

17. *What I Saw in America*, chapter 5, "Some American Cities" (London: Hodder & Stoughton, 1922), 74.

18. *The Wit and Wisdom of G. K. Chesterton*, 124. This quote originally appeared in Chesterton's "Introduction to *American Notes*."

19. *The Victorian Age in Literature*, chapter 2, "The Great Victorian Novelists" (London: Williams & Norgate, 1914), 111.

20. Ibid., chapter 3, "The Great Victorian Poets," 177–78.

21. Ibid., 178–79.

22. Ibid., 181.

23. *Robert Browning*, chapter 8, "The Philosophy of Browning" (New York: The Macmillan Company, 1903), 178.

24. *Victorian Age in Literature*, chapter 1, "The Victorian Compromise," 40–41.

25. Ibid., chapter 3, "The Great Victorian Poets," 169.

26. Ibid., 175–76. The French phrase *"Jongleurs de Dieu"* means "jugglers of God."

27. *Robert Browning*, chapter 1, "Browning in Early Life," 2.

28. Ibid., chapter 6, "Browning as a Literary Artist," 134.

29. Ibid., chapter 1, "Browning in Early Life," 16.

30. Ibid., 26.

31. Ibid.

32. Ibid., 19.

33. Ibid., 24.

34. *Alarms and Discursions*, chapter 22, "The Wings of Stone," 168–69.

35. Ibid., 170–71.

36. Introduction to John Bunyan, *The Pilgrim's Progress* (London: Cassell and Co., 1904), 6.

37. Ibid., 11–12.

C

1. *Tremendous Trifles*, chapter 1, "A Piece of Chalk" (London: Methuen & Co., 1909), 5–6.

2. *Divorce Versus Democracy* (London: Society of SS Peter & Paul—Publishers to the Church of England, 1916), 12. The title page of this work states: "Reprinted from 'Nash's Magazine.'"

3. From the 1920 reprinting of G. K. Chesterton, *William Blake* (London: Duckworth & Co., 1910), 195.

4. Chesterton and F. G. Kitton, *Charles Dickens* (New York: James Pott and Company, 1903), 15.

5. Ibid., 12–13.

6. *Alarms and Discursions*, chapter 12, "The Philosophy of Sight-Seeing" (New York: Dodd, Mead and Company, 1911), 95–97.

7. *The Man Who Was Thursday*, chapter 7, "The Unaccountable Conduct of Professor De Worms," (New York: Dodd, Mead and Company, 1908), 109.

8. *Heretics*, chapter 12, "Paganism and Mr. Lowes Dickinson" (New York: John Lane Company, 1907), 158–59.

9. *The Victorian Age in Literature*, chapter 2, "The Great Victorian Novelists" (London: Williams & Norgate, 1914), 97–98.

10. *Alarms and Discursions*, chapter 9, "Cheese," 70.

11. Ibid., 72.

12. *Appreciations and Criticisms of the Works of Charles Dickens*, chapter 3, "The Pickwick Papers" (London: J. M. Dent & Sons, Ltd., 1911), 14.

13. *The Defendant*, chapter 14, "A Defence of Baby-Worship" (New York: Dodd, Mead & Co., 1902), 116.

14. Ibid., 113–14.

15. Ibid., 112–13.

16. The first four lines of the dedicatory poem to Hilaire Belloc that appears in Chesterton's novel *The Napoleon of Notting Hill* (London: John Lane, 1904).

17. *Alarms and Discursions*, chapter 24, "The Steward of the Chiltern Hundreds," 182–83.

18. A poem about Christ by Chesterton, as quoted in Joseph Pearce, *Wisdom and Innocence: A Life of G. K. Chesterton* (San Francisco: Ignatius, 1996), 29.

19. *St. Thomas Aquinas: The Dumb Ox*, chapter 1, "On Two Friars" (New York: Sheed & Ward, 1933).

20. *The Ball and the Cross*, chapter 14, "A Museum of Souls" (London: Wells, Gardner, Darton & Co., Ltd., 1910), 279.

21. *Orthodoxy*, chapter 5, "The Flag of the World" (New York: John Lane Company, 1909), 142.

22. *Heretics*, chapter 12, "Paganism and Mr. Lowes Dickinson," 67.

23. *Defendant*, chapter 12, "A Defence of Humility," 97.

24. *Orthodoxy*, chapter 7, "The Eternal Revolution," 218–19.

25. As quoted in *The Religious Doubts of Democracy*, part 7, chapter 3, "Why I Believe in Christianity," ed. George Haw (London: Macmillan & Co., Ltd., 1904), 61.

26. *Orthodoxy*, chapter 5, "The Flag of the World," 146–47.

27. Ibid., 146.

28. Ibid., 144–45.

29. *All Things Considered*, chapter 34, "A Dead Poet" (London: Methuen and Co., 1908), 277.

30. *Ball and Cross*, chapter 8, "An Interlude of Argument," 148.

31. *Orthodoxy*, chapter 2, "The Maniac," 49–50.

32. Ibid., chapter 6, "The Paradoxes of Christianity," 160–62.

33. *Defendant*, chapter 12, "A Defence of Humility," 98–99.

34. *Orthodoxy*, chapter 6, "The Paradoxes of Christianity," 150.

35. As quoted in the *Illustrated London News*, 11 August 1928.

36. *Poems*, "The House of Christmas" (London: Burns & Oates, Ltd., 1917), 58–59.

37. *Orthodoxy*, chapter 5, "The Flag of the World," 135–36.

38. Introduction to *The Defendant*, 6.

39. *Alarms and Discursions*, chapter 21, "The New House," 161.

40. *Orthodoxy*, chapter 7, "The Eternal Revolution," 191.

41. *Ball and Cross*, chapter 8, "An Interlude of Argument," 148.

42. *All Things Considered*, chapter 34, "A Dead Poet," 277–78.

43. *The Wit and Wisdom of G. K. Chesterton* (New York: Dodd, Mead and Company, 1911), 129. This quotation originally appeared in Chesterton's book *The Ball and the Cross*.

44. *The Napoleon of Notting Hill*, book 1, chapter 2, "The Man in Green" (London: John Lane, 1904), 42.

45. *What's Wrong with the World*, part 3, chapter 2, "The Universal Stick" (London: Cassell and Company, Ltd., 1910), 125.

46. *Napoleon of Notting Hill*, Introductory Remarks, 14–15.

47. *Orthodoxy*, chapter 7, "The Eternal Revolution," 194.

48. *What I Saw in America*, chapter 5, "Some American Cities" (London: Hodder & Stoughton, 1922), 65–66.

49. *Alarms and Discursions*, chapter 27, "The Triumph of the Donkey," 203–4.

50. *All Things Considered*, chapter 24, "Spiritualism," 203.

51. Ibid., 202–3.
52. *Manalive*, chapter 4, "The Wild Weddings; or, the Polygamy Charge" (New York: John Lane Company, 1912), 302.
53. *Alarms and Discursions*, chapter 10, "The Red Town," 76–77.
54. Ibid., chapter 5, "A Drama of Dolls," 41.
55. *Orthodoxy*, chapter 4, "The Ethics of Elfland," 82–83.
56. *Tremendous Trifles*, Preface, vi.
57. *What's Wrong with the World*, part 2, chapter 2, "Wisdom and the Weather," 86–87.
58. *All Things Considered*, chapter 12, "Woman," 99.
59. "Tennyson," an essay in *Varied Types* (New York: Dodd, Mead and Company, 1915), 252.
60. *Orthodoxy*, chapter 3, "The Suicide of Thought," 70.
61. *Alarms and Discursions*, chapter 19, "The Anarchist," 148.
62. *Heretics*, chapter 13, "Celts and Celtophiles," 171.
63. *George Bernard Shaw*, chapter 1, "The Irishman" (New York: John Lane Company, 1910), 23.
64. *Orthodoxy*, chapter 6, "The Paradoxes of Christianity," 170.
65. "Miracles and Modern Civilisation," from chapter 2, part 8 of *The Religious Doubts of Democracy*, ed. George Haw, 88.
66. *Orthodoxy*, chapter 6, "The Paradoxes of Christianity," 151–52.
67. *Alarms and Discursions*, chapter 13, "A Criminal Head," 100–101.
68. Ibid., 99–100.
69. *Autobiography*, chapter 7, "The Crime of Orthodoxy" (London: Hutchinson & Co., 1936), 178.
70. *Generally Speaking*, chapter 1, "On Detective Novels" (Freeport, New York: Books for Libraries Press, Inc.), 2. Copyright 1929. Renewed 1957 by Oliver Chesterton, reprinted 1968 by arrangement with Dorothy Edith Collins.
71. *What's Wrong with the World*, part 1, chapter 4, "The Fear of the Past," 32–33.
72. *Robert Browning*, chapter 7, "The Ring and the Book" (New York: The Macmillan Company, 1903), 162.
73. *Ball and Cross*, chapter 10, "The Swords Rejoined," 207.
74. *What's Wrong with the World*, part 4, chapter 9, "The Need for Narrowness," 220.
75. *Napoleon of Notting Hill*, book 3, chapter 2, "The Remarkable Mr. Turnbull," 160.
76. *Robert Browning*, chapter 5, "Browning in Later Life," 124.

D

1. *Charles Dickens: A Critical Study*, chapter 7, "Dickens and Christmas" (New York: Dodd, Mead and Company, 1917), 169.
2. *Orthodoxy*, chapter 7, "The Eternal Revolution" (New York: John Lane Company, 1909), 206.

3. *The Victorian Age in Literature*, chapter 4, "The Break-up or the Compromise" (New York: Henry Holt and Company, 1913), 206–7.

4. Ibid., 208–9.

5. Ibid., 209–10.

6. Ibid., 212.

7. *What's Wrong with the World*, part 1, chapter 3, "The New Hypocrite" (London: Cassell, 1910), 21.

8. *All Things Considered*, chapter 25, "The Error of Impartiality" (London: Methuen and Co., 1908), 213.

9. Ibid., 210.

10. As quoted in the *Illustrated London News*, 29 August 1931.

11. *Orthodoxy*, chapter 4, "The Ethics of Elfland," 86. The word *ruck* means "the ordinary run of persons or things."

12. Ibid., 82.

13. Ibid., 84.

14. *What's Wrong with the World*, part 1, chapter 5, "The Unfinished Temple," 41.

15. *Divorce Versus Democracy* (London: Society of SS Peter & Paul—Publishers to the Church of England, 1916), 5. The title page of this work states: "Reprinted from 'Nash's Magazine.'"

16. *Tremendous Trifles*, chapter 31, "The Travellers in State" (London, Methuen & Co., 1909), 213–14.

17. *Orthodoxy*, chapter 4, "The Ethics of Elfland," 82.

18. *The Napoleon of Notting Hill*, book 1, chapter 2, "The Man in Green" (London: John Lane, 1904), 43.

19. Ibid.

20. *Divorce Versus Democracy*, 12.

21. G. K. Chesterton, ed., *Thackeray*, Introduction (London: George Bell and Sons, 1909), xx. This book was part of the Masters of Literature series.

22. *Robert Browning*, chapter 1, "Browning in Early Life" (New York: The Macmillan Company, 1903), 31.

23. *The Defendant*, chapter 15, "A Defence of Detective Stories" (New York: Dodd, Mead & Co., 1902), 122–23.

24. "Principles of the Detective Story," *Illustrated London News*, 19 August 1922.

25. *Orthodoxy*, chapter 4, "The Ethics of Elfland," 104–6.

26. *Victorian Age in Literature*, chapter 1, "The Victorian Compromise and Its Enemies," 79–80.

27. *Dickens*, chapter 12, "A Note on the Future of Dickens," 300.

28. *Tremendous Trifles*, chapter 12, "The Dickensian," 79.

29. *Victorian Age in Literature*, chapter 1, "The Victorian Compromise and Its Enemies," 81.

30. Ibid., chapter 2, "The Great Victorian Novelists," 123.

31. Ibid., 121.

32. Ibid., 119–20.

33. Ibid., 121–22.

34. *Dickens*, chapter 1, "The Dickens Period," 2–3.

35. Chesterton and F. G. Kitton, *Charles Dickens* (New York: James Pott and Company, 1903), 3–6.

36. *What's Wrong with the World*, part 3, chapter 4, "The Romance of Thrift," 141.

37. *The G. K. C. Calendar: A Quotation from the Works of G. K. Chesterton for Every Day in the Year* (London: Cecil Palmer, 1921), 16.

38. *What I Saw in America*, chapter 1, "What Is America?" (London: Hodder & Stoughton, 1922), 1.

39. *Orthodoxy*, chapter 6, "The Paradoxes of Christianity," 186.

40. As quoted in the *Illustrated London News*, 19 April 1930.

41. *Orthodoxy*, chapter 4, "The Ethics of Elfland," 81–82.

42. *The Man Who Was Thursday*, chapter 14, "The Six Philosophers" (New York: Dodd, Mead and Company, 1908), 266.

43. Ibid., chapter 15, "The Accuser," 268–69.

44. *Heretics*, chapter 20, "Concluding Remarks on the Importance of Orthodoxy" (New York: John Lane Company, 1907), 303–4.

45. *George Bernard Shaw*, chapter 1, "The Irishman" (New York: John Lane Company, 1910), 20.

46. *What's Wrong with the World*, part 4, chapter 4, "The Truth about Education," 197.

47. *Generally Speaking*, chapter 4, "On Europe and Asia" (New York: Dodd, Mead & Company), 23.

48. *Napoleon of Notting Hill*, book 2, chapter 3, "Enter a Lunatic," 114.

49. *Divorce Versus Democracy*, 4.

50. From the Dedicatory Poem in *Napoleon of Notting Hill*.

E

1. *Twelve Types*, chapter 10, "Savonarola" (London: Arthur L. Humphreys, 1902), 168.

2. *Divorce Versus Democracy* (London: Society of SS Peter & Paul—Publishers to the Church of England, 1916), 13. The title page of this work states: "Reprinted from 'Nash's Magazine.'"

3. Ibid., 13.

4. *The Collected Works of G. K. Chesterton: Illustrated London News, 1905–1907* (San Francisco: Ignatius Press, 1986), 71.

5. *All Things Considered*, chapter 8, "An Essay on Two Cities" (London: Methuen and Co., 1908), 69.

6. *Autobiography*, chapter 3, "How to Be a Dunce" (London: Hutchinson & Co., 1936), 58.

7. *What's Wrong with the World*, part 1, chapter 2, "Wanted, An Unpractical Man" (London: Cassell and Company, Ltd., 1910), 11.

8. *Charles Dickens: A Critical Study*, chapter 4, "The Pickwick Papers" (New York: Dodd, Mead & Company, 1917), 85–86.

9. *All Things Considered*, chapter 5, "The Vote and the House," 40–41.

10. *The Victorian Age in Literature*, chapter 2, "The Great Victorian Novelists" (New York: Henry Holt and Company, 1913), 103–4.

11. Ibid., 104.

12. Ibid., 107.

13. *The Napoleon of Notting Hill*, book 5, chapter 1, "The Empire of Notting Hill" (New York: John Lane Company, 1904), 273–74.

14. *Tremendous Trifles*, chapter 30, "The Riddle of the Ivy" (London, Methuen & Co., 1909), 205.

15. *Divorce Versus Democracy*, 14.

16. *George Bernard Shaw*, chapter 5, "The Dramatist" (New York: John Lane Company, 1910), 161.

17. *The Wisdom of Father Brown*, chapter 2, "The Paradise of Thieves" (London: Cassell and Company, Ltd., 1914), 36.

18. *Napoleon of Notting Hill*, book 3, chapter 1, "The Mental Condition of Adam Wayne," 138.

19. *What I Saw in America*, chapter 1, "What Is America?" (London: Hodder & Stoughton, 1922), 17.

20. As quoted in Maisie Ward, *Return to Chesterton* (London: Sheed & Ward, 1952), 137.

21. *Dickens: A Critical Study*, chapter 4, "The Pickwick Papers," 89–90.

22. *Utopia of Usurers and Other Essays*, chapter 6, "Science and the Eugenists" (New York: Boni & Liveright, 1917), 43–44.

23. *What's Wrong with the World*, part 4, chapter 2, "The Tribal Terror," 190.

24. *The Innocence of Father Brown*, chapter 4, "The Flying Stars" (New York: John Lane Company, 1911).

25. *Dickens: A Critical Study*, chapter 1, "The Dickens Period," 21.

F

1. "A Visit to Holland," *Illustrated London News*, 29 April 1922.

2. *All Things Considered*, chapter 3, "The Fallacy of Success" (London: Methuen and Co., 1908), 27.

3. *Tremendous Trifles*, chapter 16, "The Red Angel" (London, Methuen & Co., 1909), 102–3.

4. *Orthodoxy*, chapter 4, "The Ethics of Elfland" (New York: John Lane Company, 1909), 100.

5. Ibid., 101.

6. Ibid., 104.

7. Ibid., 97–98.

8. Ibid., 88–89.

9. *Tremendous Trifles*, chapter 16, "The Red Angel" (London, Methuen & Co., 1909), 104.

10. *Orthodoxy*, chapter 4, "The Ethics of Elfland," 87.

11. *Tremendous Trifles*, chapter 15, "The Dragon's Grandmother," 97–98.

12. *Charles Dickens: A Critical Study*, chapter 4, "The Pickwick Papers" (New York: Dodd, Mead & Company, 1917), 85.

13. *Magic*, Act I: The Prelude (New York: G. P. Putnam's Sons, 1913), 10.

14. Ibid., 10–11.

15. *G. F. Watts* (London: Duckworth & Co., 1904), 101.

16. *Magic*, Act II, 62–63.

17. *Orthodoxy*, chapter 3, "The Suicide of Thought," 58.

18. *Alarms and Discursions*, chapter 29, "Five Hundred and Fifty-Five" (New York: Dodd, Mead and Company, 1911), 217.

19. *Orthodoxy*, chapter 3, "The Suicide of Thought," 55.

20. *What's Wrong with the World*, part 5, chapter 3, "The Dreadful Duty of Gudge" (New York: Dodd, Mead and Company, 1910), 347.

21. *Heretics*, chapter 14, "On Certain Modern Writers and the Institution of the Family" (New York: John Lane Company, 1907), 188.

22. Ibid., 188–89.

23. *The Defendant*, chapter 11, "A Defence of Farce" (New York: Dodd, Mead & Co., 1902), 91.

24. Ibid., 93.

25. *Generally Speaking*, chapter 20, "On Holland" (London: Methuen & Co. Ltd., 1928), 137.

26. *The Innocence of Father Brown*, chapter 1, "The Blue Cross" (New York: The Macaulay Company, 1911), 4.

27. *The Wisdom of Father Brown*, chapter 1, "The Absence of Mr Glass" (London: Cassell and Company, Ltd., 1914), 3.

28. Ibid., 19.

29. Ibid., chapter 2, "The Paradise of Thieves," 34.

30. *The Scandal of Father Brown*, chapter 7: "The Point of a Pin" (London: Cassell, 1935).

31. *The Incredulity of Father Brown*, chapter 6, "The Dagger with Wings" (London: Cassell and Company, Ltd., 1926).

32. *All Things Considered*, chapter 32, "Tom Jones and Morality," 259.

33. *The Man Who Was Thursday*, chapter 8, "The Professor Explains" (New York: Dodd, Mead and Company, 1908), 121.

34. *The G. K. C. Calendar: A Quotation from the Works of G. K. Chesterton for Every Day in the Year* (London: Cecil Palmer, 1921), 46.

35. *Alarms and Discursions*, chapter 1, "The Fading Fireworks" (New York: Dodd, Mead and Company, 1911), 1.

36. *Alarms and Discursions*, chapter 1, "Introductory: On Gargoyles" (London: Methuen & Co. Ltd., 1910), 5–6.

37. *All Things Considered*, chapter 27, 229.

38. *Alarms and Discursions*, chapter 31, "The Flat Freak," 234. (New York)

39. Ibid., 233.

40. *All Things Considered*, chapter 24, "Spiritualism," 203–4.

41. *Alarms and Discursions*, chapter 16, "The Futurists" (New York), 125.

42. *Charles Dickens*, chapter 4, "The Pickwick Papers," 98–99.

43. *Tremendous Trifles*, chapter 27, "The Lion," 185.

44. *Twelve Types*, chapter 5, "Francis" (London: Arthur L. Humphreys, 1902), 74–75.

45. *Alarms and Discursions*, chapter 38, "The Chorus," 293–94.

46. *Divorce Versus Democracy* (London: Society of SS Peter & Paul—Publishers to the Church of England, 1916), 10. The title page of this work states: "Reprinted from 'Nash's Magazine.'"

47. *Robert Browning*, chapter 7, "The Ring and the Book" (London: The Macmillan Company, 1903), 173–74.

48. Ibid., 174.

49. *The Ball and the Cross*, chapter 8, "An Interlude of Argument" (London: Wells, Gardner, Darton & Co., 1910), 146.

50. *The Victorian Age in Literature*, chapter 2, "The Great Victorian Novelists" (New York: Henry Holt and Company, 1913), 143.

51. *Orthodoxy*, chapter 8, "The Romance of Orthodoxy," 254.

52. *Defendant*, chapter 9, "A Defence of Heraldry," 80.

53. *What's Wrong*, part 1, chapter 4, "The Fear of the Past," 26–27.

54. Ibid., 24–25.

G

1. *Alarms and Discursions*, chapter 7, "The Appetite of Earth" (New York: Dodd, Mead and Company, 1911), 54.

2. *Orthodoxy*, chapter 7, "The Eternal Revolution" (New York: John Lane Company, 1909), 188–89.

3. *Alarms and Discursions*, chapter 1, "Introductory: On Gargoyles" (New York), 13–14.

4. Ibid., chapter 15, "The Gold of Glastonbury," 112.

5. Ibid., 115.

6. Ibid., 116–17.

7. Ibid., 115–16.

8. "Introduction to *The Book of Job*" (London: S. Wellwood, 1907), xxii. Garry Wills, in his introduction to *The Man Who Was Thursday* (Sheed & Ward, 1975), calls this Chesterton's "most important essay, written on the book that most profoundly influenced him all his life." This essay, writes Wills, "could almost stand as a commentary on the novel." This essay is posted online at: http://chesterton.org/gkc/theologian/job.htm.

9. *Orthodoxy*, chapter 4, "The Ethics of Elfland," 108–10.

10. *William Blake* (London: Duckworth, 1910), 142.

11. *Orthodoxy*, chapter 6, "The Paradoxes of Christianity," 175–76.

12. *The Incredulity of Father Brown*, chapter 6, "The Dagger with Wings" (London: Cassell and Company, Ltd., 1926).

13. *All Things Considered*, chapter 32, "Tom Jones and Morality" (London: Methuen and Co., 1908), 265.

14. *The Innocence of Father Brown*, chapter 8, "The Sins of Prince Saradine" (New York: The Macaulay Company, 1911), 208.

15. *Alarms and Discursions*, chapter 1, "Introductory: On Gargoyles," 7.

16. *A Short History of England* (London: Chatto & Windus, 1917), chapter 8, paragraph 1.

17. *What's Wrong with the World*, part 3, chapter 8, "The Brand of the Fleur-de-Lis" (London: Cassell and Company, Ltd., 1910), 160.

18. "The Safe Business of Governing," *Illustrated London News*, 14 January 1922.

19. *Twelve Types*, chapter 11, "Savonarola" (London: Arthur L. Humphreys, 1902), 171.

20. *Charles Dickens: A Critical Study*, chapter 1, "The Dickens Period" (New York: Dodd, Mead and Company, 1917), 8.

21. *Alarms and Discursions*, chapter 18, "The Glory of Grey," 143.

22. Ibid., 143–44.

23. Ibid., 142.

24. Ibid., 144.

25. *Poems*, "To M.E.W." (London: Burns & Oates, Ltd., 1917), 9.

26. Lines from the dedicatory poem to Edmund Clerihew Bentley in *The Man Who Was Thursday* (New York: Dodd, Mead and Company, 1908).

27. *Dickens: A Critical Study*, chapter 2, "The Boyhood of Dickens," 35.

H

1. *G. F. Watts* (London: Duckworth & Co., 1904), 18.

2. *The Victorian Age in Literature*, chapter 2, "The Great Victorian Novelists" (New York: Henry Holt and Company, 1913), 138. Owen Meredith was the pseudonym of Edward Robert Bulwer-Lytton (1831–1891), first Earl Lytton.

3. Ibid., 144.

4. *Generally Speaking*, chapter 42, "On Thomas Hardy" (New York: Dodd, Mead & Company, 1929), 290–91.

5. *Heretics*, chapter 1, "Introductory Remarks on the Importance of Orthodoxy" (London: John Lane, 1907), 12.

6. Ibid., 12–13.

7. Ibid., 14–15.

8. Ibid., 16–17.

9. Ibid., 18–19.

10. Ibid., 22.

11. *The Ball and the Cross*, chapter 8, "An Interlude of Argument" (London: Wells, Gardner, Darton and Co., Ltd., 1910), 144–45.

12. *Alarms and Discursions*, chapter 37, "The High Plains" (New York: Dodd, Mead and Company, 1911), 285.

13. *The Wit and Wisdom of G. K. Chesterton* (New York: Dodd, Mead and Company, 1911), 208–9. This quote originally appeared in Chesterton's "Introduction to *A Child's History of England*."

14. "The Romance of the Past and the Romance of the Future," *Illustrated London News*, 25 November 1922.

15. Introduction to Oliver Wendell Holmes, *The Autocrat of the Breakfast Table* (London: Blackie & Son, Ltd., 1904), iii.

16. Ibid., iii–iv.

17. Ibid., iv–v.

18. Ibid., v–vi. The verse that Chesterton cites here is from Holmes's poem entitled "Nux Postcoenatica."

19. Ibid., vi.

20. Ibid., vii.

21. Ibid., ix–x.

22. "Principles of the Detective Story," *Illustrated London News*, 19 August 1922.

23. *Alarms and Discursions*, chapter 18, "The Glory of Grey," 140.

24. Ibid., chapter 2, "The Surrender of Cockney," 16.

25. *What's Wrong with the World*, part 1, chapter 8, "The Wildness of Domesticity" (London: Cassell and Company, Ltd., 1910), 58.

26. *Charles Dickens: A Critical Study*, chapter 7, "Dickens and Christmas" (New York: Dodd, Mead and Company, 1917), 166–67.

27. Ibid., chapter 1, "The Dickens Period," 13.

28. *The Ballad of the White Horse*, book 4, "The Woman in the Forest" (London: Methuen and Co., 1911), 75.

29. *Robert Browning*, chapter 8, "The Philosophy of Browning" (London: Macmillan & Co., 1903), 202.

30. *Orthodoxy*, chapter 7, "The Eternal Revolution" (New York: John Lane Company, 1909), 213.

31. *The Napoleon of Notting Hill*, chapter 1, "Introductory Remarks on the Art of Prophecy" (London: John Lane, 1904), 13–14.

32. *Tremendous Trifles*, chapter 29, "The Little Birds Who Won't Sing" (London: Methuen & Co., 1909), 200–1.

33. *The Man Who Was Thursday*, chapter 8, "The Professor Explains" (New York: Dodd, Mead and Company, 1908), 116–17.

34. *Ballad of the White Horse*, book 8, "The Scouring of the Horse," 163.

35. *Alarms and Discursions*, chapter 37, "The High Plains," 284–85.

36. *The Defendant*, chapter 12, "A Defence of Humility" (New York: Dodd, Mead and Co., 1902), 102–3.

37. *Ballad of the White Horse*, book 4, "The Woman in the Forest," 84.

38. *Tremendous Trifles*, chapter 9, "On Lying in Bed," 61.

39. As quoted in the *Illustrated London News*, 5 May 1928.

40. *All Things Considered*, chapter 4, "On Running After One's Hat" (London: Methuen and Co., 1908), 35.

41. *The Innocence of Father Brown*, chapter 3, "The Queer Feet" (New York: John Lane Company, 1911), 77.

42. *All Things Considered*, chapter 4, "On Running After One's Hat," 34.

43. Ibid., chapter 1, "The Case for the Ephemeral," 2.

44. Ibid., chapter 2, "Cockneys and Their Jokes," 13.

45. Ibid., 10.

46. *Heretics*, chapter 9, "The Moods of Mr. George Moore," 131.

47. *What's Wrong with the World*, part 1, chapter 3, "The New Hypocrite," 17.

I

1. From the Dedication to Charles F. G. Masterman in *What's Wrong with the World* (London: Cassell and Company, 1910).

2. *Heretics*, chapter 20, "Concluding Remarks on the Importance of Orthodoxy" (New York: John Lane Company, 1907), 298.

3. *Alarms and Discursions*, chapter 8, "Simmons and the Social Tie" (New York: Dodd, Mead and Company, 1911), 61.

4. *Orthodoxy*, chapter 7, "The Eternal Revolution" (New York: John Lane Company, 1909), 190–91.

5. *What's Wrong with the World*, part 1, chapter 4, "The Fear of the Past" (London: Cassell and Company, 1910), 29–30.

6. Ibid., part 1, chapter 5, "The Unfinished Temple," 36.

7. *The G. K. C. Calendar: A Quotation from the Works of G. K. Chesterton for Every Day in the Year* (London: Cecil Palmer, 1921), 15.

8. *Tremendous Trifles*, chapter 6, "The Advantages of Having One Leg" (London, Methuen & Co., 1909), 42.

9. *All Things Considered*, chapter 5, "The Vote and the House" (London: Methuen and Co., 1908), 43.

10. *The Incredulity of Father Brown*, chapter 6, "The Dagger with Wings" (London: Cassell and Company, Ltd., 1926).

11. *Orthodoxy*, chapter 2, "The Maniac," 46–47.

12. *Twelve Types*, chapter 8, "Stevenson" (London: Arthur L. Humphreys, 1902), 110.

13. *Tremendous Trifles*, chapter 11, "The Wind and the Trees," 72.

14. *Orthodoxy*, chapter 2, "The Maniac," 50.

15. *The Man Who Was Thursday*, chapter 4, "The Tale of a Detective" (New York: Dodd, Mead and Company, 1908), 57.

J

1. *The G. K. C. Calendar: A Quotation from the Works of G. K. Chesterton for Every Day in the Year* (London: Cecil Palmer, 1921), 29.

2. *The Defendant*, chapter 16, "A Defence of Patriotism" (New York: Dodd, Mead & Co., 1902), 126.

3. Ibid., 125.

4. *Orthodoxy*, chapter 3, "The Suicide of Thought" (New York: John Lane Company, 1909), 78–79.

5. *What's Wrong with the World*, part 2, chapter 3, "The Common Vision" (London: Cassell and Company, Ltd., 1910), 96–98.

6. Ibid., part 1, chapter 3, "The New Hypocrite," 21–22.

7. *All Things Considered*, chapter 20, "On the Cryptic and the Elliptic" (London: Methuen and Co., 1908), 177.

8. Ibid., 175.

9. *Tremendous Trifles*, chapter 32, "The Prehistoric Railway Station" (London: Methuen & Co., 1909), 222.

10. *The Ball and the Cross*, chapter 4, "A Discussion at Dawn" (London: Wells, Gardner, Darton & Co., Ltd, 1910), 68–69.

11. *All Things Considered*, chapter 20, "On the Cryptic and the Elliptic," 177.

12. Ibid., chapter 17, "The Boy," 150.

13. Ibid., chapter 20, "On the Cryptic and the Elliptic," 174–75.

14. Ibid., chapter 19, "Anonymity and Further Counsels," 167–68.

15. Ibid., chapter 18, "Limericks and Counsels of Perfection," 159.

16. Chesterton and F. G. Kitton, *Charles Dickens* (New York: James Pott and Company, 1903), 6.

17. "Christianity and Rationalism," *The Clarion*, 22 July 1904.

18. *Orthodoxy*, chapter 9, "Authority and the Adventurer," 298.

19. Ibid., 296.

20. *The Man Who Was Thursday*, chapter 14, "The Six Philosophers" (New York: Dodd, Mead and Company, 1908), 249–50.

K

1. *The Defendant*, Introduction (New York: Dodd, Mead & Co., 1902), 5.

L

1. *The Napoleon of Notting Hill*, book 5, chapter 1, "The Empire of Notting Hill" (London: John Lane, 1904), 260–61.

2. *Appreciations and Criticisms of the Works of Charles Dickens*, chapter 13, "Introduction to *David Copperfield*" (London: J. M. Dent & Sons, Ltd., 1911), 135.

3. *Divorce Versus Democracy* (London: Society of SS Peter & Paul—Publishers to the Church of England, 1916), 6. The title page of this work states: "Reprinted from 'Nash's Magazine.'"

4. *All Things Considered*, chapter 16, "Thoughts Around Koepenick" (London: Methuen and Co., 1908), 142.

5. *The Defendant*, chapter 5, "A Defence of Nonsense" (New York: Dodd, Mead & Co., 1902), 46–47.

6. *The Man Who Was Thursday*, chapter 14, "The Six Philosophers" (New York: Dodd, Mead and Company, 1908), 249.

7. *Orthodoxy*, chapter 4, "The Ethics of Elfland" (New York: John Lane Company, 1909), 81–82.

8. Ibid., chapter 6, "The Paradoxes of Christianity," 176.

9. *What I Saw in America*, chapter 8, "Presidents and Problems" (London: Hodder & Stoughton, 1922), 128.

10. *Napoleon of Notting Hill*, book 3, chapter 3, "The Experiment of Mr. Buck," 181.

11. *Charles Dickens: A Critical Study*, chapter 11, "On the Alleged Optimism of Dickens" (New York: Dodd, Mead and Company, 1917), 288.

12. *Orthodoxy*, chapter 4, "The Ethics of Elfland," 115–16.

13. *The G. K. C. Calendar: A Quotation from the Works of G. K. Chesterton for Every Day in the Year* (London: Cecil Palmer, 1921), 40.

14. *Defendant*, chapter 5, "A Defence of Nonsense," 47.

15. *All Things Considered*, chapter 10, "The Zola Controversy," 87.

16. *Defendant*, chapter 8, "A Defence of Useful Information," 73.

17. As quoted in the *Daily News*, 25 February 1905.

18. *Orthodoxy*, chapter 2, "The Maniac," 29.

19. *Twelve Types*, chapter 9, "Thomas Carlyle" (London: Arthur L. Humphreys, 1902), 125.

20. Ibid., 126.

21. *Tremendous Trifles*, chapter 32, "The Prehistoric Railway Station" (London, Methuen & Co., 1909), 220–21.

22. *Alarms and Discursions*, chapter 3, "The Surrender of a Cockney" (New York: Dodd, Mead and Company, 1911), 22.

23. *Napoleon of Notting Hill*, book 1, chapter 2, "The Man in Green," 25–26.

24. *Twelve Types*, chapter 1, "Charlotte Bronte," 12.

25. *George Bernard Shaw*, chapter 6, "The Philosopher" (New York: John Lane Company, 1910), 181–82. Chesterton is referring here to George Bernard Shaw.

26. *The Flying Inn*, chapter 24, "The Enigmas of Lady Joan" (New York: John Lane Company, 1914), 314.

27. *Tremendous Trifles*, chapter 6, "The Advantages of Having One Leg," 42.

28. *Defendant*, "In Defense of a New Edition," 8.

29. *Robert Browning*, chapter 2, "Early Works" (London: Macmillan & Co., 1903), 43.

30. *All Things Considered*, chapter 16, "Thoughts Around Koepenick," 139.

31. *Orthodoxy*, chapter 2, "The Maniac," 22.

32. *Dickens: A Critical Study*, chapter 6, "Dickens and America," 153.

M

1. *The Victorian Age in Literature*, chapter 1, "The Victorian Compromise and Its Enemies" (New York: Henry Holt and Company, 1913), 33–34.

2. Ibid., 34.

3. Ibid., 39–40.

4. Ibid., chapter 2, "The Great Victorian Novelists," 152.

5. Introduction to Greville MacDonald, *George MacDonald and His Wife* (London: George Allen & Unwin, 1924), 1.

6. Ibid.

7. Ibid.

8. Ibid., 2.

9. Ibid.

10. Ibid.

11. Ibid., 3.

12. Ibid., 3–4.

13. Ibid., 4.

14. *Orthodoxy*, chapter 2, "The Maniac" (New York: John Lane Company, 1909), 32.

15. *The Napoleon of Notting Hill*, book 2, chapter 1, "The Charter of the Cities" (London: John Lane, 1904), 66.

16. Ibid., book 2, chapter 3, "Enter a Lunatic," 117–18.

17. *Magic*, Act I: The Prelude (New York: G. P. Putnam's Sons, 1913), 28–29.

18. Ibid., 33.

19. *Orthodoxy*, chapter 7, "The Eternal Revolution," 189.

20. *The G. K. C. Calendar: A Quotation from the Works of G. K. Chesterton for Every Day in the Year* (London: Cecil Palmer, 1921), 84–85.

21. *Orthodoxy*, chapter 6, "The Paradoxes of Christianity," 173.

22. Ibid., chapter 7, "The Eternal Revolution," 218.

23. *The Napoleon of Notting Hill*, introductory remarks, 13.

24. *All Things Considered*, chapter 28, "Wine When It Is Red" (London: Methuen & Co., 1908), 232–33.

25. *Orthodoxy*, chapter 4, "The Ethics of Elfland," 94–95.

26. *Victorian Age*, chapter 2, "The Great Victorian Novelists," 96–97.

27. *The Everlasting Man*, part 1, chapter 1, "The Man in the Cave" (London: Hodder & Stoughton, 1947), 36–37.

28. *What's Wrong with the World*, part 1, chapter 9, "History of Hudge and Gudge" (London: Cassell, 1910), 65–66.

29. *All Things Considered*, chapter 28, "Wine When It Is Red" (London: Methuen and Co., 1908), 233–34.

30. *Charles Dickens: A Critical Study*, chapter 7, "Dickens and Christmas" (New York: Dodd, Mead & Company, 1917), 169–70.

31. *Robert Browning*, chapter 2, "Early Works" (London: Macmillan & Co., 1903), 43.

32. *Divorce Versus Democracy* (London: Society of SS Peter & Paul—Publishers to the Church of England, 1916), 13–14. The title page of this work states: "Reprinted from 'Nash's Magazine.'"

33. *Appreciations and Criticisms of the Works of Charles Dickens*, chapter 13, "David Copperfield" (London: J. M. Dent & Sons, Ltd., 1911), 133.

34. *Tremendous Trifles*, chapter 11, "The Wind and the Trees" (London: Methuen & Co., 1909), 74.

35. *Orthodoxy*, chapter 2, "The Maniac," 42–43.

36. Ibid., 41. A. N. Wilson, who recently reembraced Christianity after a long period of atheist belief, closed an article in the *New Statesman* with words that form a powerful complement to Chesterton's in the citation above. "Turn to the Table Talk of Samuel Taylor Coleridge," Wilson wrote. "Read the first chapter of Genesis without prejudice and you will be convinced at once. . . .

'The LORD God formed man of the dust of the ground, and breathed into his nostrils the breath of life.' And then Coleridge adds: "'And man became a living soul.' Materialism will never explain those last words." From the article "Why I Believe Again," accessed on the Web site of the *New Statesman* on 17 December 2009: http://www.newstatesman.com/religion/2009/04/conversion-experience-atheism.

37. *G. K.'s Weekly*, 17 January 1931.
38. *Orthodoxy*, chapter 2, "The Maniac," 42.
39. *Tremendous Trifles*, chapter 13, "In Topsy-Turvy Land," 85–86.
40. *Alarms and Discursions*, chapter 5, "A Drama of Dolls" (New York: Dodd, Mead and Company, 1911), 38.
41. *The Defendant*, "In Defense of a New Edition" (London: J. M. Dent, 1918), 5.
42. *Orthodoxy*, chapter 9, "Authority and the Adventurer," 284.
43. *Robert Browning*, chapter 1, "Browning in Early Life," 26.
44. *What's Wrong*, part 1, chapter 5, "The Unfinished Temple," 39.
45. A partial citation of a Latin phrase from the *Satires* of Juvenal, which translated, means "The dogmas of men, their prayers, fear, wrath, pleasure, delights, and recreations, are the subject of this book."
46. *Tremendous Trifles*, chapter 29, "The Little Birds Who Won't Sing," 195–96.
47. *Charles Dickens: A Critical Study*, chapter 4, "The Pickwick Papers," 97.
48. *Orthodoxy*, chapter 9, "Authority and the Adventurer," 261.
49. Ibid., chapter 8, "The Romance of Orthodoxy," 235–36.
50. Ibid., 237–38.
51. As quoted in *The Religious Doubts of Democracy*, ed. George Haw (New York: The Macmillan Company, 1904), 89.
52. *The Innocence of Father Brown*, chapter 1, "The Blue Cross" (New York: The Macaulay Company, 1911), 6.
53. *Alarms and Discursions*, chapter 38, "The Chorus," 290–91.
54. *Orthodoxy*, chapter 3, "The Suicide of Thought," 76–77.
55. *George Bernard Shaw*, chapter 7, "The Philosopher" (New York: John Lane Company, 1910), 174.
56. *Orthodoxy*, chapter 8, "The Romance of Orthodoxy," 232.
57. Ibid., chapter 7, "The Eternal Revolution," 205–6.
58. *Appreciations and Criticisms*, chapter 17, "Hard Times," 169.
59. *The Napoleon of Notting Hill*, book 2, chapter 3, "Enter a Lunatic," 119.
60. *Orthodoxy*, chapter 7, "The Eternal Revolution," 214.
61. *What's Wrong*, part 1, chapter 4, "The Fear of the Past" (London: Cassell and Company, Ltd., 1910), 28.
62. *Shaw*, chapter 7, "The Philosopher," 250.
63. *Alarms and Discursions*, chapter 19, "The Anarchist," 153.
64. *Tremendous Trifles*, chapter 32, "The Prehistoric Railway Station," 224.
65. *What's Wrong*, part 1, chapter 4, "The Fear of the Past," 32.
66. *All Things Considered*, chapter 18, "The Worship of the Wealthy," 179–80.

67. *What's Wrong*, part 1, chapter 4, "The Fear of the Past," 32.

68. *All Things Considered*, chapter 13, "The Modern Martyr," 107–8.

69. *Dickens: A Critical Study*, chapter 10, "The Great Dickens Characters," 254.

70. *All Things Considered*, chapter 23, "The Methuselahite," 197.

71. Ibid., 196.

72. *G. K. C. Calendar*, 61.

73. *What's Wrong*, part 1, chapter 3, "The New Hypocrite," 16.

74. As quoted in the *Illustrated London News*, 2 May 1931.

75. *What's Wrong*, part 1, chapter 6, "Enemies of Property," 56.

76. *Heretics*, chapter 20, "Concluding Remarks on the Importance of Orthodoxy" (New York: John Lane Company, 1907), 302.

77. *All Things Considered*, chapter 17, "The Boy," 149–50.

78. Ibid., 147–48.

79. *Orthodoxy*, chapter 3, "The Suicide of Thought," 52–53.

80. *All Things Considered*, chapter 1, "The Case for the Ephemeral," 3.

81. Ibid., 4. This might well be the origin of C. S. Lewis's statement (if indeed he coined the phrase) about "chronological snobbery."

82. *Orthodoxy*, chapter 8, "The Romance of Orthodoxy," 233.

83. *Napoleon of Notting Hill*, Book 3, chapter 2, "The Remarkable Mr. Turnbull," 149.

84. Ibid., 148.

85. *Orthodoxy*, chapter 8, "The Romance of Orthodoxy" (New York: John Lane Company, 1909), 230.

86. *Shaw*, chapter 7, "The Philosopher," 244.

87. As quoted in the *Illustrated London News*, 27 December 1919.

88. *William Blake* (London: Duckworth & Co., 1910), 177.

89. *Shaw*, chapter 6, "The Philosopher," 184–85.

90. *Alarms and Discursions*, chapter 2, "The Nightmare," 27–28.

91. *Orthodoxy*, chapter 5, "The Flag of the World," 123.

92. Ibid., chapter 3, "The Suicide of Thought," 62.

93. *Alarms and Discursions*, chapter 26, "The Strangeness of Luxury," 199–200.

94. *The Wit and Wisdom of G. K. Chesterton* (New York: Dodd, Mead and Company, 1911), 200. This quote originally appeared in an article written by Chesterton for the *Daily News*.

95. *The Man Who Was Thursday*, chapter 4 (New York: Dodd, Mead and Company, 1908), 60.

96. *Shaw*, chapter 5, "The Critic," 95–96.

97. *Browning*, chapter 5, "Browning in Later Life," 111.

98. *What's Wrong*, part 2, chapter 2, "Wisdom and the Weather," 87.

99. *Tremendous Trifles*, chapter 28, "Humanity: An Interlude," 194.

100. Ibid., 192–93.

101. *Man Who Was Thursday*, chapter 13, "The Pursuit of the President," 241–42.

102. Ibid., chapter 14, "The Six Philosophers," 257.

103. Ibid., chapter 13, "The Pursuit of the President," 233.

104. *Orthodoxy*, chapter 5, "The Flag of the World," 129–30.

105. "The Mystery of Mystics," *The Daily News*, 30 August 1901, 6.

N

1. *Alarms and Discursions*, chapter 2, "The Nightmare" (New York: Dodd, Mead and Company, 1911), 23.

2. *Tremendous Trifles*, chapter 24, "A Cab Ride Across Country" (London: Methuen & Co., 1909), 164–65.

3. *Alarms and Discursions*, chapter 11, "The Furrows," 84.

4. *The Man Who Was Thursday*, chapter 1, "The Two Poets of Saffron Park" (New York: Dodd, Mead and Company, 1908), 4.

5. Ibid., chapter 14, "The Six Philosophers," 262–63.

6. Ibid., chapter 15, "The Accuser," 272–73.

7. *The Flying Inn*, chapter 6, "The Hole in Heaven" (London: Methuen and Co., 1914), 58–59.

8. *Orthodoxy*, chapter 7, "The Eternal Revolution" (New York: John Lane Company, 1909), 207.

9. Ibid., 204–5. The word *chiaroscuro* means "the interplay of light and shadow."

10. *Man Who Was Thursday*, chapter 11, "The Criminals Chase the Police," 188.

11. *The Napoleon of Notting Hill*, book 3, chapter 1, "The Mental Condition of Adam Wayne" (London: John Lane, 1904), 135.

12. *Orthodoxy*, chapter 2, "The Maniac," 24.

13. Ibid., chapter 8, "The Romance of Orthodoxy," 233–35.

14. *The Victorian Age in Literature*, chapter 1 (New York: Henry Holt and Company, 1913), 47–48.

15. Ibid., 48.

16. *Orthodoxy*, chapter 7, "The Eternal Revolution," 213–14.

17. *The Defendant*, 2nd ed., chapter 12 (London: R. Brimley Johnson, 1902).

18. *Orthodoxy*, chapter 7, "The Eternal Revolution," 192–93.

19. Ibid., chapter 3, "The Suicide of Thought," 76.

20. *Alarms and Discursions*, chapter 3, "The Nightmare," 28–29.

21. *Robert Browning*, chapter 3, "Browning and His Marriage" (London: Macmillan & Co., 1903), 65.

22. As quoted in the *Illustrated London News*, 15 October 1921.

23. *Heretics*, chapter 15, "On Smart Novelists and the Smart Set" (New York: John Lane Company, 1907), 196.

24. *The Victorian Age in Literature*, chapter 2, "The Great Victorian Novelists" (New York: Henry Holt and Company, 1913), 99.

25. Ibid., 90.

26. Ibid., 93.

O

1. *Orthodoxy*, chapter 7, "The Eternal Revolution" (New York: John Lane Company, 1909), 221–22.

2. Ibid., chapter 2, "The Maniac," 26.

3. "Introduction to *The Book of Job*" (London: S. Wellwood, 1907), x.

4. Ibid., xii.

5. Ibid., xiii.

6. Ibid., xxi.

7. Ibid., xxiii.

8. *The Defendant*, chapter 6, "A Defence of Planets" (London: R. Brimley Johnson, 1902), 64–65.

9. *The Napoleon of Notting Hill*, book 5, chapter 3, "Two Voices" (New York: John Lane Company, 1904), 291–92.

10. *What's Wrong with the World*, part 1, chapter 6, "The Enemies of Property" (London: Cassell and Company, Ltd., 1910), 44.

11. Unpublished letter, written in early 1904, housed at the G. K. Chesterton Study Centre, Bedford, England.

12. *Napoleon of Notting Hill*, book 4, chapter 2, "The Correspondent of the 'Court Journal,'" 220.

13. *Orthodoxy*, chapter 5, "The Flag of the World," 119–20.

14. *Charles Dickens: A Critical Study*, chapter 2, "The Boyhood of Dickens" (New York: Dodd, Mead and Co., 1917), 40–41.

15. *Heretics*, chapter 12, "Paganism and Mr. Lowes Dickinson" (New York: John Lane Company, 1907), 167.

16. *Orthodoxy*, chapter 1, "Introduction: In Defense of Everything Else," 18.

17. Ibid., *Orthodoxy*, Preface vii–viii.

18. Ibid., chapter 1, "Introduction: In Defence of Everything Else," 20.

19. Ibid., chapter 6, "The Paradoxes of Christianity," 185–87.

P

1. *Orthodoxy*, chapter 8, "The Romance of Orthodoxy" (New York: John Lane Company, 1909), 247–48.

2. *The Man Who Was Thursday*, chapter 1, "The Two Poets of Saffron Park" (New York: Dodd, Mead and Company, 1908), 15.

3. Ibid., chapter 4, "The Tale of a Detective," 58–59.

4. Ibid., chapter 14, "The Six Philosophers," 255–56.

5. Chesterton and F. G. Kitton, *Charles Dickens* (New York: James Pott and Company, 1903), 6.

6. *Orthodoxy*, chapter 9, "Authority and the Adventurer," 298.

7. *The Napoleon of Notting Hill*, book 3, chapter 1, "The Mental Condition of Adam Wayne" (London: John Lane, 1904), 133.

8. As quoted in the *Illustrated London News*, 3 March 1906.

9. "Overdoing It in the Movies," the *Illustrated London News*, 27 August 1927.

10. *The Man Who Was Thursday*, chapter 15, "The Accuser," 273–74.

11. *The Wit and Wisdom of G. K. Chesterton* (New York: Dodd, Mead and Company, 1911), 188. This quote originally appeared in an article written by Chesterton for the *Daily News*.

12. *Heretics*, chapter 3, "On Mr. Rudyard Kipling and Making the World Small" (New York: John Lane Company, 1907), 51.

13. *Tremendous Trifles*, chapter 34, "A Glimpse of My Country" (London, Methuen & Co., 1909), 233–34.

14. *Charles Dickens: A Critical Study*, chapter 10, "The Great Dickens Characters" (New York: Dodd, Mead and Co., 1917), 244.

15. *The G. K. C. Calendar: A Quotation from the Works of G. K. Chesterton for Every Day in the Year* (London: Cecil Palmer, 1921), 36.

16. *G. F. Watts* (London: Duckworth & Co., 1904), 114.

17. *The Napoleon of Notting Hill*, book 4, chapter 1, "The Battle of the Lamps" (London: John Lane, 1904), 193.

18. Introduction to John Bunyan, *The Pilgrim's Progress* (London: Cassell and Company, 1904), 11–12.

19. Ibid., 13–14.

20. Ibid., 11.

21. Ibid., 12–13.

22. *The Defendant*, chapter 12, "A Defence of Humility" (New York: Dodd, Mead & Co., 1902), 100.

23. *Magic*, Act III (New York: G. P. Putnam's Sons, 1913), 78.

24. *Utopia of Usurers and Other Essays*, chapter 6, "Science and the Eugenists" (New York: Boni & Liveright, 1917), 38.

25. *The Victorian Age in Literature*, chapter 1, "The Victorian Compromise and Its Enemies" (New York: Henry Holt and Company, 1913), 51.

26. Lines 13–15 of Chesterton's poem "The Great Minimum," posted online by the University of Toronto at: http://rpo.library.utoronto.ca/poem/3868.html.

27. Ibid., lines 17–21.

28. Ibid., lines 1–6.

29. *Tremendous Trifles*, chapter 25, "The Two Noises," 170.

30. "The Praise of Dust," *The Wild Knight, with Additional Poems* (London: J. M. Dent & Sons, Ltd., 1914), 95.

31. *Robert Browning*, chapter 7, "The Philosophy of Browning" (London: Macmillan & Co., 1903), 185–86.

32. Ibid., 186.

33. "The Blue Cross," *The Innocence of Father Brown* (London, Cassell and Company, Ltd., 1911), 6–7.

34. *Orthodoxy*, chapter 2, "The Maniac," 27.

35. *Alarms and Discursions*, chapter 23, "The Three Kings of Men" (New York: Dodd, Mead and Company, 1911), 177.

36. Ibid., 175–76.

37. Ibid., 174.

38. Ibid., chapter 33, "The Sentimentalist," 249.

39. As quoted in the *Cleveland Press*, 1 March 1921.

40. *All Things Considered*, chapter 1, "The Case for the Ephemeral" (London: Methuen and Co., 1908), 2.

41. Ibid., chapter 20, "On the Cryptic and the Elliptic," 174.

42. As quoted in the *Illustrated London News*, 4 April 1924.

43. *George Bernard Shaw*, chapter 4, "The Progressive" (New York: John Lane Company, 1910), 60–61.

44. *The Club of Queer Trades*, chapter 6, "The Eccentric Seclusion of the Old Lady" (New York: Harper & Brothers, 1905), 241.

45. *Orthodoxy*, chapter 7, "The Eternal Revolution," 214–15.

46. From a review of a book on Poussin Chesterton published without attribution in *The Bookman* in 1898. See Michael Coren, *Gilbert: The Man Who Was G. K. Chesterton* (New York: Paragon House, 1990), 108; and also Michael Ffinch, *G. K. Chesterton: A Biography* (San Francisco: Harper & Row, 1986), 67–69.

47. *G. F. Watts* (London: Duckworth & Co., 1904), 110.

48. *Heretics*, chapter 9, "The Moods of Mr. George Moore," 131.

49. *Orthodoxy*, chapter 7, "The Eternal Revolution," 224.

50. *Appreciations and Criticisms of the Works of Charles Dickens*, chapter 15, "Bleak House" (London: J. M. Dent & Sons, Ltd., 1911), 154.

51. *Shaw*, chapter 7, "The Philosopher," 233–34.

52. "The Three Tools of Death," *The Innocence of Father Brown*, (New York: John Lane Company, 1911), 331.

53. *Orthodoxy*, chapter 7, "The Eternal Revolution," 211.

54. Ibid., 200.

55. Introduction to Greville MacDonald, *George MacDonald and His Wife* (London: George Allen & Unwin, 1924), 1.

56. *Orthodoxy*, chapter 7, "The Eternal Revolution," 195.

57. Ibid.

58. Introduction, *The Defendant* (London: J. M. Dent & Sons, Ltd., 1918), 16.

59. *What's Wrong with the World*, part 1, chapter 10, "Oppression by Optimism" (London: Cassell and Company, Ltd., 1910), 69.

60. *What I Saw in America*, chapter 10, "Fads and Public Opinion" (London: Hodder & Stoughton, 1922), 171.

61. *What's Wrong with the World*, part 1, chapter 6, "The Enemies of Property," 47.

62. *Dickens: A Critical Study*, chapter 1, "The Dickens Period," 4.

63. "A Ballade of an Anti-Puritan," *Poems* (New York: Dodd, Mead and Company, 1922), 149.

64. *What I Saw in America*, chapter 10, "Fads and Public Opinion," 162.

65. *Divorce Versus Democracy*, (London: Society of SS Peter & Paul—Publishers to the Church of England, 1916) 13.

66. *Dickens: A Critical Study*, chapter 10, "The Great Dickens Characters," 265.

67. *All Things Considered*, chapter 17, "The Boy," 153.

R

1. *Orthodoxy*, chapter 8, "The Romance of Orthodoxy" (New York: John Lane Company, 1909), 245–46.

2. *Tremendous Trifles*, chapter 29, "Humanity: An Interlude" (New York: Dodd, Mead and Company, 1909), 227.

3. "The Blue Cross," *The Innocence of Father Brown* (London: Cassell and Company, Ltd., 1911), 25.

4. *All Things Considered*, chapter 1, "The Case for the Ephemeral" (London: Methuen and Co., 1908), 8.

5. *Orthodoxy*, chapter 4, "The Ethics of Elfland," 116.

6. *Alarms and Discursions*, chapter 10, "The Red Town" (New York: Dodd, Mead and Company, 1911), 81–82.

7. Ibid., 82–83.

8. *Orthodoxy*, chapter 7, "The Eternal Revolution," 194–95.

9. Ibid., chapter 6, "The Paradoxes of Christianity," 157–58.

10. *Charles Dickens: A Critical Study*, chapter 1, "The Dickens Period" (New York: Dodd, Mead & Co., 1917), 10.

11. *Heretics*, chapter 20, "Concluding Remarks on the Importance of Orthodoxy" (New York: John Lane Company, 1907), 299.

12. *What's Wrong with the World*, part 3, chapter 2, "The Universal Stick" (London: Cassell and Company, Ltd., 1910), 121.

13. "Thought Versus Slogans," *Illustrated London News*, 18 February 1928.

14. *Autobiography*, chapter 11, "The Shadow of the Sword" (London: Hutchinson & Co., 1936), 238.

15. *All Things Considered*, chapter 1, "The Case for the Ephemeral," 5.

16. *Alarms and Discursions*, chapter 5, "A Drama of Dolls," 40.

17. *The G. K. C. Calendar: A Quotation from the Works of G. K. Chesterton for Every Day in the Year* (London: Cecil Palmer, 1921), 35.

18. *What's Wrong with the World*, part 4, chapter 6, "Authority and the Unavoidable," 203.

19. *The Flying Inn*, chapter 18, "The Republic of Peaceways" (New York: John Lane Company, 1914), 234.

20. *The Man Who Was Thursday*, chapter 4, "The Tale of a Detective" (New York: Dodd, Mead and Company, 1908), 52.

21. *The Napoleon of Notting Hill*, book 2, chapter 3, "Enter a Lunatic" (New York: John Lane Company, 1904), 106.

22. "The Return of the Angels," *Daily News*, 14 March 1903.

23. *Alarms and Discursions*, chapter 38, "The Chorus," 291–92.

24. *Twelve Types*, chapter 12, "The Position of Walter Scott" (London: Arthur L. Humphreys, 1902), 189–90.

25. Ibid., 183.

26. *The Victorian Age in Literature*, chapter 1, "The Victorian Compromise and Its Enemies" (New York: Henry Holt and Company, 1913), 65.

S

1. *Tremendous Trifles*, chapter 31, "The Travellers in State" (London: Methuen & Co., 1909), 215.

2. *The Wild Knight and Other Poems* (London: J. M. Dent & Sons, Ltd., 1914), 132.

3. *Twelve Types*, chapter 11, "Savonarola" (London: Arthur L. Humphreys, 1902), 172–73.

4. *Orthodoxy*, chapter 2, "The Maniac" (New York: John Lane Company, 1909), 45.

5. Ibid., chapter 3, "The Suicide of Thought," 58.

6. Ibid., 56.

7. Ibid., 58.

8. *Alarms and Discursions*, chapter 13, "A Criminal Head" (New York: Dodd, Mead and Company, 1911), 98.

9. *All Things Considered*, chapter 22, "Science and Religion" (London: Methuen and Co., 1908), 192–93.

10. Ibid., 191.

11. Ibid., 187.

12. Ibid., 190–91.

13. Introduction to Greville MacDonald, *George MacDonald and His Wife* (London: George Allen & Unwin, 1924), 3.

14. *Twelve Types*, chapter 12, "The Position of Walter Scott," 202–3.

15. Ibid., 180–81.

16. *Alarms and Discursions*, chapter 32, "The Garden of the Sea," 244.

17. Ibid., 240.

18. *Tremendous Trifles*, chapter 25, "The Two Noises," 167–68.

19. As quoted in the *Illustrated London News*, 24 September 1927.

20. *Christendom in Dublin* (London: Sheed & Ward, 1932).

21. *Orthodoxy*, chapter 8, "The Romance of Orthodoxy," 260.

22. *All Things Considered*, chapter 13, "The Modern Martyr," 110.

23. *The G. K. C. Calendar: A Quotation from the Works of G. K. Chesterton for Every Day in the Year* (London: Cecil Palmer, 1921), 77.

24. *The Napoleon of Notting Hill*, book 1, chapter 2, "The Man in Green" (London: John Lane, 1904), 23–24.

25. *All Things Considered*, chapter 1, "The Case for the Ephemeral," 1.

26. *Tremendous Trifles*, chapter 31, "The Travellers in State," 214.

27. *Alarms and Discursions*, chapter 33, "The Sentimentalist," 247.

28. *Orthodoxy*, chapter 7, "The Eternal Revolution," 224.

29. As quoted in *The Religious Doubts of Democracy*, ed. George Haw (New York: The Macmillan Company, 1904), 18.

30. *Magic*, Act II (New York: G. P. Putnam's Sons, 1913), 52–53.

31. *All Things Considered*, chapter 10, "The Zola Controversy," 82.

32. Ibid., 82.

33. Ibid., 85.

34. *Orthodoxy*, chapter 2, "The Maniac," 28–29.

35. *The Innocence of Father Brown*, chapter 2, "The Secret Garden" (New York: The Macaulay Company, 1911), 36.

36. *George Bernard Shaw*, "Introduction to the First Edition" (New York: John Lane Company, 1910), 5.

37. Ibid., chapter 1, "The Irishman" (New York: John Lane Company, 1910), 23.

38. *Autobiography* (London: Hutchinson & Co., 1936), 227–28. Shaw warmly returned Chesterton's friendship, saying after his death: "I enjoyed him, and nothing could have been more generous than his treatment of me." See Michael Holroyd, *Bernard Shaw: The One-Volume Definitive Edition* (London, 1997), 373.

39. *Shaw*, chapter 4, "The Critic" (New York: John Lane Company, 1910), 101–2. *Vanitas vanitatum* means "vanity of vanities."

40. Ibid., 102–3.

41. Ibid., chapter 3, "The Progressive," 64–65.

42. Ibid., chapter 6, "The Philosopher," 199. Chesterton wrote this in 1909, eight years before Lenin led the Communists to power in Russia, thirteen years before Mussolini became Italy's Fascist leader, and fully twenty-four years before Hitler led the Nazi Party to power in Germany.

43. *Shaw*, chapter 6, "The Philosopher," 179–80.

44. Ibid., 176.

45. Ibid., 177.

46. *Orthodoxy*, chapter 3, "The Suicide of Thought," 52.

47. *All Things Considered*, chapter 8, "An Essay on Two Cities," 68–69.

48. *Charles Dickens: A Critical Study*, chapter 8, "The Time of Transition" (New York: Dodd, Mead & Co., 1917), 204.

49. *The G. K. C. Calendar*, 5.

50. *All Things Considered*, chapter 22, "Science and Religion," 191–92.

51. Ibid., 189–90.

52. *Tremendous Trifles*, chapter 23, "The Toy Theatre," 151.

53. Ibid., 150–51.

54. *What's Wrong with the World*, part 1, chapter 1, "The Medical Mistake" (London: Cassell and Company, Ltd., 1910), 5–6.

55. Ibid., 3.

56. *Orthodoxy*, chapter 7, "The Eternal Revolution," 215–16.

57. Ibid., 216–17.

58. Ibid., 227.

59. *What's Wrong with the World*, chapter 11, "The Homelessness of Jones," 97.

60. As quoted in "Debate with Bertrand Russell," *BBC Magazine*, 27 November 1935.

61. *What's Wrong with the World*, part 5, chapter 2, "The Fallacy of the Umbrella Stand," 338.

62. *Alarms and Discursions*, chapter 21, "The New House," 161–62.

63. Ibid., chapter 6, "The Man and His Newspaper," 52–53.

64. *Appreciations and Criticisms of the Works of Charles Dickens*, chapter 6, "The Old Curiosity Shop" (London: J. M. Dent & Sons, Ltd., 1911), 50.

65. *The G. K. C. Calendar*, 49.

66. "Thought Versus Slogans," *Illustrated London News*, 18 February 1928.

67. *The Defendant*, chapter 14, "A Defence of Baby-Worship" (London: R. Brimley Johnson, 1902), 115.

68. *Twelve Types*, chapter 8, "Stevenson," 117.

69. *Varied Types*, chapter 8, "Stevenson" (New York: Dodd, Mead and Company, 1903), 98–99.

70. *The Victorian Age in Literature*, chapter 4, "The Break-Up, or the Compromise" (New York: Henry Holt and Company, 1913), 248.

71. Ibid., 246–47. The word *acies* refers to the ability to direct the full attention of one's sight, hearing, or other senses, toward a particular object.

72. Ibid., 244–45. The phrase *cri de coeur* is a French phrase meaning "cry from the heart."

73. Ibid., 243.

74. "The Spite Against Stevenson," *Illustrated London News*, 8 October 1927.

75. "Stevenson vs. Poe," *Illustrated London News*, 22 September 1923.

76. As quoted in *The Religious Doubts of Democracy*, ed. George Haw (New York: The Macmillan Company, 1904), 64.

77. *Shaw*, chapter 2, "The Puritan," 40.

78. Ibid., 39–40.

T

1. *What's Wrong with the World*, part 1, chapter 2 (London: Cassell and Company, Ltd., 1910), 283.

2. *The Victorian Age in Literature*, chapter 3 (New York: Henry Holt and Company, 1913), 165.

3. Ibid., 166–67.

4. Ibid., 167–68.

5. *G. F. Watts* (London: Duckworth & Co., 1904), 167–68.

6. As quoted in *The Religious Doubts of Democracy*, ed. George Haw (New York: The Macmillan Company, 1904), 62.

7. *The G. K. C. Calendar: A Quotation from the Works of G. K. Chesterton for Every Day in the Year* (London: Cecil Palmer, 1921), 16.

8. *Tremendous Trifles*, chapter 30, "The Riddle of the Ivy" (London: Methuen and Co., 1909), 206.

9. Ibid., chapter 27, "The Lion," 181–82.

10. *What's Wrong*, part 1, chapter 7, "The Free Family," 66.

11. *All Things Considered*, chapter 34, "A Dead Poet" (London: Methuen and Co., 1908), 275–76.

12. Ibid., 277.

13. *The Wit and Wisdom of G. K. Chesterton* (New York: Dodd, Mead and Company, 1911), 4–6. This poem, originally printed in the *Daily News*, also appears in G. K. Chesterton, *Poems* (London: Burns & Oates, Ltd., 1917), 55–57.

14. *William Blake* (London: Duckworth & Co., 1910), 168.

15. *All Things Considered*, chapter 32, "Tom Jones and Morality," 265–66.

16. Ibid., 263–64.

17. Ibid., 261–62.

18. *A Short History of England*, chapter 8, "The Meaning of Merry England" (New York: John Lane Company, 1917), 107.

19. *Orthodoxy*, chapter 4, "The Ethics of Elfland" (New York: John Lane Company, 1909), 85.

20. *Tremendous Trifles*, chapter 33, "The Prehistoric Railway Station," 219–20.

21. *The Defendant*, chapter 3, "A Defence of Skeletons" (London: R. Brimley Johnson, 1902), 28.

22. *Orthodoxy*, chapter 8, "The Romance of Orthodoxy," 251.

23. "Why I Am a Catholic," *Twelve Modern Apostles and Their Creeds* (New York: Duffield & Co., 1926). Cross reference "A Symposium of Creeds," a 734-word review of this book in the Sunday, 19 December 1926 edition of the *New York Times Book Review*, page BR24.

24. *What's Wrong*, 234.

25. *The Club of Queer Trades*, chapter 5, "The Noticeable Conduct of Professor Chadd" (London: Harper & Brothers, 1905), 136.

26. *Alarms and Discursions*, chapter 7, "The Appetite of Earth" (New York: Dodd, Mead and Company, 1911), 59.

27. *The Man Who Was Thursday*, chapter 3, "The Man Who Was Thursday" (New York: Dodd, Mead and Company, 1908), 47.

28. "Mark Twain," *T.P.'s Weekly* 15, no. 390, 29 April 1910.

29. Ibid.

30. Ibid.

31. Ibid.

32. Ibid.

33. Ibid.

34. G. B. Shaw and G. K. Chesterton, *Do We Agree?* (London: 1928), 22–25.

35. "Mr. Blatchford and Free Will," *The Clarion*, 7 August 1903.

36. *The Napoleon of Notting Hill*, book 4, chapter 3, "The Great Army of South Kensington" (London: John Lane, 1904), 246–47.

U

1. *Twelve Types*, chapter 2, "William Morris and His School" (London: Arthur L. Humphreys, 1902), 25–26.

2. *Robert Browning*, chapter 8, "The Philosophy of Browning" (London: Macmillan & Co., 1903), 202.

3. *The G. K. C. Calendar: A Quotation from the Works of G. K. Chesterton for Every Day in the Year* (London: Cecil Palmer, 1921), 28.

4. *Orthodoxy*, chapter 4, "The Ethics of Elfland" (New York: John Lane Company, 1909), 116–17.

5. *All Things Considered*, chapter 5, "The Vote and the House" (London: Methuen and Co., 1908), 45.

6. *Orthodoxy*, chapter 7, "The Eternal Revolution," 212.

7. Ibid., 227.

8. Ibid., 228–29.

9. Ibid., 199.

10. Ibid., 198.

11. "On Regulating the Broadcasters," *Illustrated London News*, 7 May 1927.

V

1. From a review (of a book on Velasquez) Chesterton had published without attribution in "Velasquez and Poussin," *The Bookman*, Dec. 1899. See Michael Ffinch, *G. K. Chesterton: A Biography* (San Francisco: Harper & Row, 1986), 68.

2. *Divorce Versus Democracy* (London: Society of SS Peter & Paul, 1916), 6. The title page of this work states: "Reprinted from 'Nash's Magazine.'"

3. *The G. K. C. Calendar: A Quotation from the Works of G. K. Chesterton for Every Day in the Year* (London: Cecil Palmer, 1921), 13.

4. *The Victorian Age in Literature*, Introduction (New York: Henry Holt and Company, 1913), 10–11.

5. Ibid., chapter 1, "The Victorian Compromise and Its Enemies," 13–14.

6. Ibid., 20.

7. Ibid., chapter 4, "The Break-Up, or the Compromise," 240–41.

8. *What's Wrong with the World*, part 4, chapter 12, "The Staleness of the New Schools" (New York: Dodd, Mead and Company, 1910), 305.

9. *Tremendous Trifles*, chapter 13, "In Topsy-Turvy Land" (London: Methuen & Co., 1909), 81–82.

10. *The Defendant*, chapter 2, "A Defence of Rash Vows" (London: R. Brimley Johnson, 1902), 26.

11. Ibid., 23.

12. *Manalive*, part 2, chapter 1, "The Eye of Death, or the Murder Charge" (New York: John Lane Company, 1912), 168.

W

1. *G. F. Watts* (London: Duckworth & Co., 1904), 18.

2. Ibid., 14.

3. Ibid., 10.

4. Ibid., 13.

5. Ibid., 167–68.

6. *Heretics*, chapter 19, "Slum Novelists and the Slums" (New York: John Lane Company, 1907), 269.

7. Ibid., chapter 12, "Paganism and Mr. Lowes Dickinson," 168.

8. *Alarms and Discursions*, chapter 18, "The Glory of Grey" (New York: Dodd, Mead and Company, 1911), 138–39.

9. *The Victorian Age in Literature*, chapter 4, "The Break-Up, or the Compromise" (New York: Henry Holt and Company, 1913), 238–39.

10. *Alarms and Discursions*, chapter 35, "The Long Bow," 260.

11. *The Wild Knight* (London: J. M. Dent & Sons, Ltd., 1914), 116–17.

12. *Orthodoxy*, chapter 4, "The Ethics of Elfland" (New York: John Lane Company, 1909), 104.

13. *What's Wrong with the World* (London: Cassell and Company, Ltd., 1910), 12.

14. *Robert Browning*, chapter 3, "Browning and His Marriage" (London: Macmillan & Co., 1903), 65.

15. *Magic*, Act II (New York: G. P. Putnam's Sons, 1913), 48–49. Final sentence is Job 28:28 (KJV).

16. Introductory essay to G. K. Chesterton, ed., *Thackeray* (London: George Bell and Sons, 1909), xix–xx.

17. *The G. K. C. Calendar: A Quotation from the Works of G. K. Chesterton for Every Day in the Year* (London: Cecil Palmer, 1921), 53.

18. Ibid., 52.

19. *Tremendous Trifles*, chapter 1, "Tremendous Trifles" (New York: Dodd, Mead and Co, 1909), 7.

20. As quoted in William Oddie, *Chesterton and the Romance of Orthodoxy: The Making of GKC, 1874–1908* (New York: Oxford Univ. Press, 2009).

21. *Orthodoxy*, chapter 4, "The Ethics of Elfland," 107.

22. *The Defendant*, chapter 12, "A Defence of Humility" (London: R. Brimley Johnson, 1902), 104.

23. *All Things Considered*, chapter 4, "On Running After One's Hat" (London: Methuen and Co., 1908), 32–33.

24. *Orthodoxy*, chapter 5, "The Flag of the World," 121.

25. *G. K. C. Calendar*, 6.

26. "From the Notebooks of G. K. C.," *The Tablet* (April 4, 1953).

27. *Orthodoxy*, chapter 6, "The Paradoxes of Christianity," 148.

28. *Tremendous Trifles*, chapter 34, "A Glimpse of My Country," 233.

29. *G. K. C. Calendar*, 74.

30. *Heretics*, chapter 1, "Introductory Remarks on the Importance of Orthodoxy," 15.

31. *Orthodoxy*, chapter 5, "The Flag of the World," 147.

Y

1. *The G. K. C. Calendar: A Quotation from the Works of G. K. Chesterton for Every Day in the Year* (London: Cecil Palmer, 1921), 49.

Z

1. *All Things Considered*, chapter 10, "The Zola Controversy" (London: Methuen and Co., 1908), 87–88.